THE FRENCH ARMY
1750–1820

MANCHESTER
UNIVERSITY PRESS

The French army 1750–1820

Careers, talent, merit

RAFE BLAUFARB

Manchester University Press

Copyright © Rafe Blaufarb 2002

The right of Rafe Blaufarb to be identified as the author of this work has been asserted by her in accordance with the Copyright, Designs and Patents Act 1988.

Published by Manchester University Press
Altrincham Street, Manchester M1 7JA, UK
www.manchesteruniversitypress.co.uk

British Library Cataloguing-in-Publication Data is available

ISBN 978 1 7849 9391 7 paperback

First published by Manchester University Press in hardback 2002

This edition first published 2017

The publisher has no responsibility for the persistence or accuracy of URLs for any external or third-party internet websites referred to in this book, and does not guarantee that any content on such websites is, or will remain, accurate or appropriate.

Printed by Lightning Source

Contents

List of tables	*page* vi
List of plates	vii
Acknowledgements	viii
Glossary	x
Introduction	1
1 The merits of birth: lineage and professionalism in the Old Regime	12
2 The meanings of merit in 1789	46
3 The death and rebirth of the officer corps, 1790–93	75
4 Republican meritocracy in the nexus of war, civil strife, and factionalism	106
5 The politics of professionalism during Thermidor and the Directory, 1794–99	133
6 Napoleon's improbable synthesis: monarchy and meritocracy in the reconstruction of the officer corps, 1799–1815	164
Conclusion	194
Bibliography	202
Index	222

Tables

1.1	Reductions planned by Guibert, autumn 1787	*page* 38
1.2	Reductions actually approved by the War Council	39
6.1	Sources of recruitment of directly commissioned officers, year VIII–1812	180

Plates

1 Printed application form for the Ecole royale militaire, 1786–89. (Archives nationales, M 254. Reproduced with the permission of the Centre historique des Archives nationales in Paris.) *page* 13

2 Address of the officers of the Forez Regiment to the National Assembly, October 1789. (Archives de la guerre, Mémoires et reconaissances 1718. Reproduced with the permission of the Ministère de la défense, Service historique de l'armée de terre.) 47

3 Ministerial nomination slip proposing "sons of active citizens" as replacement officers in the 13th Infantry Regiment, July 1791. (Archives de la guerre, $X^b 166$. Reproduced with the permission of the Ministère de la défense, Service historique de l'armée de terre.) 76

4 Official record of the election of an officer in the 39th Infantry Regiment, 28 Pluviôse II. (Archives de la guerre, $X^b 176$. Reproduced with the permission of the Ministère de la défense, Service historique de l'armée de terre.) 107

5 The original ministerial estimate of the number of officers who would lose their places as a result of the Directory's military downsizing, the second amalgame, Brumaire IV. (Archives de la guerre, $B^{13} 41$. Reproduced with the permission of the Ministère de la défense, Service historique de l'armée de terre.) 134

6 Presentation sheet proposing students from the Lycée of Cahors for admission to the Ecole militaire de Saint-Cyr, May 1811. (Archives nationales, $F^{17} 1740$. Reproduced with the permission of the Centre historique des Archives nationales in Paris.) 165

Acknowledgements

Without the assistance of the University of Michigan, French Ministry of Culture, Andrew W. Mellon Foundation, American Society for Eighteenth Century Studies, Stephen F. Austin State University, Auburn University, and Camargo Foundation, this book could not have been written. I would like to acknowledge their generous aid and thank them for it. I would also like to express my appreciation to the archives and libraries in France that facilitated my research: the Archives de la guerre, Archives nationales, Bibliothèque nationale, Archives départementales des Bouches-du-Rhone, Archives départementales du Cher, Archives départementales du Bas-Rhin, Archives municipales de Strasbourg, and Bibliothèque de l'Université de Strasbourg. Without the guidance and frequent *augmentations de quota* they granted to me, it would have been impossible to conduct research on the scale necessitated by the chronological span and institutional scope of my subject.

This project has taken nearly ten years to come to fruition. Along the way, many people have offered advice, encouragement, and ideas. I would like to express my gratitude to them all. In particular, I have always enjoyed the unfailing support of mentors who have cheerfully invested daunting amounts of their precious time and energy in my work-in-progress. The debt I owe to David Bien should be evident throughout the pages of this book. A continuation of his own work on the Old Regime French officer corps across the great divide of 1789, it is intended as a tribute to his incisive and inspirational scholarship. He has seen me through my first steps in the profession of history, showing me the way by his own example and giving unstintingly of himself even after his retirement from teaching. His detective's instinct, editorial rigor, and personal generosity make him a true model of *émulation*.

Many others have contributed to this project. At the University of Michigan, John Shy, Raymond Grew, and Marie-Hélène Huet read the final draft of my dissertation and commented extensively on it. Those comments, preserved on tape, have guided me through many long nights of revision. At Michigan, I also had the good fortune to count Samuel Scott as a neighbor. It was during a long summer afternoon in his back yard that Sam shared with me his unparalleled knowledge of the Archives de la guerre. His faith in my ability to carry out such a large research agenda has never flagged.

During my two years of research in France, many individuals welcomed me and supported my endeavor. Jacques Revel sponsored my application for a Bourse

Châteaubriand and gave me an institutional home at the Ecole des hautes études. The seminars of the Ecole provided an incredible degree of intellectual stimulation and introduced me to scholars who contributed in various ways to my thinking. They include Simona Cerutti, Robert Descimon, Patrice Gueniffey, Alain Guery, and Edna Lemay. The French university system was equally hospitable. At Paris I, Jean-Paul Bertaud was always ready to share his profound knowledge of the revolutionary armies. At Paris IV, Jean Chagniot and André Corvisier welcomed me to their military history seminar, where the spirit of the old French officer corps still soldiered on. And the workshop on revolutionary elections guided by Serge Aberdam and Bernard Gainot still remains a stopping-point on my trips to Paris.

Many people played midwife as my dissertation gave birth to a book. Among those who read all or part of it were Gail Bossenga, Howard Brown, Alan Forrest, Al Hamscher, Nira Kaplan, Meyer Kestnbaum, Michael Kwass, Sarah Maza, Judith Miller, John Lynn, Guy Rowlands, Sam Scott, Jay Smith, Cécile Vidal, and Isser Woloch. And it goes without saying that thanks are due to the editorial staff at the University of Manchester Press for their care in producing the present book.

This book is dedicated to my mother, father, and sister, whose unflagging, unconditional love provided a foundation from which I could venture into a world which is no more. They have given up much, especially physical proximity and all that entails, so that I could pursue my professional calling. I hope that my book lives up to the sacrifices they have made for it.

Note on translation

All translations are the work of the author unless otherwise indicated.

Glossary

académie: school designed to teach chivalric behavior to young nobles.
amalgame: successive republican efforts to consolidate military formations into new units known as *demi-brigades*.
anobli: someone who had recently entered the nobility by purchasing an ennobling office.
cadet-gentilhomme: entry-level position designed to provide a hands-on apprenticeship at soldiering for noble officers.
cahiers de doléances: grievance lists drafted in early 1789 in anticipation of the Estates-General.
Carabiniers: one of the more prestigious cavalry regiments in the royal army.
carmagnole: a popular dance, associated with the *sans-culottes*, that was fashionable during the Terror.
chasseurs: a type of light infantry.
collège: the standard Old Regime institution of secondary education, usually church-run.
commissaires: deputies of the Assembly invested with substantial powers and charged with carrying out urgent missions of national security.
commissaires des guerres: military administrators who, during the Old Regime, purchased their offices and often passed them down to their sons.
concordat: an unofficial regimental retirement fund formed from contributions levied on the younger officers.
concours: competitive examination.
Conseil des anciens: the upper chamber of the Directorial legislature.
Conseil des cinq-cents: the lower of the two legislative chambers during the Directorial period.
Cour des aides: the principal court concerned with tax matters.
demi-brigades: literally "half-brigades," military units consisting of three battalions, formed during the Republic to replace the regiments.
Du roi, régiment: the "King's Own" infantry regiment, the largest in the line army.
Ecole royale militaire: the royal military school, established in 1751 in Paris and later expanded through the creation of twelve provincial schools.
Ecole spéciale militaire: the military school created by Napoleon in 1802. Originally located in Fontainebleau, it was later transferred to Saint-Cyr.
égorgeurs: a Thermidorean term for those associated with the most violent excesses of the Terror.

émulation: the spirit of meritocratic striving.
enfants de la patrie: children of the nation, true patriots.
enfants du corps: children of soldiers who were placed on the regimental payroll at a very young age, raised in the regiment, and expected to become soldiers.
état: a term combining the ideas of profession and social status.
fédérés: battalions of patriotic volunteers who offered to march to the front in 1792.
fermiers-généraux: the tax-farmers who collected most of the kingdom's indirect taxes.
Gendarmerie: a prestigious mounted unit whose soldiers all enjoyed officer rank in the line army. It was suppressed in 1788. In 1790, the Old Regime mounted rural police (the *maréchaussée*) was renamed the Gendarmerie. This revolutionary Gendarmerie had no connection to its Old Regime namesake.
gendarmes: personnel of either the Old Regime or revolutionary Gendarmerie.
Gendarmes d'ordonnance: modeled after the Old Regime Gendarmerie, Napoleon created this unit in 1806 to attract nobles to his service.
gentilhomme: a nobleman counting at least four generations of patrilineal noble ancestry.
grande muette: literally the "big mute," a term for the politically silent army of nineteenth-century France.
honnête: socially and morally upstanding.
levée en masse: the levy in mass, theoretically subjecting all physically fit French males to military service.
livre: the French pound, worth much less than its English counterpart.
loi martiale: martial law permitting the use of force against civil disturbances.
lycées: militarized institutions of secondary education created by Napoleon to replace the *collèges* of the Old Regime.
Maison militaire du roi: the royal household troops.
Maréchaussée: the rural mounted police of the Old Regime.
mœurs: habits, morals, and social comportment.
noblesse militaire: noble status granted to non-noble families in recognition of their traditions of military service.
notabilité: the general Napoleonic elite drawn broadly from those who commanded respect in their local communities.
officiers de fortune: non-noble soldiers promoted to officer rank after many years of service.
parlements: provincial supreme courts, subordinate in their jurisdiction only to the king.
particule: the "de" that often signaled nobility, or at least pretension to nobility.
patrie: homeland, fatherland.

présentés: those permitted direct access to the royal family, a privilege theoretically limited to those descended from an unbroken chain of noble ancestors stretching back to 1400, without a known source of ennoblement.

Prytanée français: schools established by Napoleon to provide free basic education and vocational training to orphans, the sons of soldiers, and other children of modest social background.

receveurs de finances: financiers who collected taxes and lent the king money against the anticipated revenues.

recherches de noblesse: royal investigations intended to discover those who had usurped noble status.

rentiers: those who lived from investment income.

roturier: a non-noble.

vélites: special units attached to the Imperial Guard which allowed young men from good families a quick way into the officer corps.

Introduction

The revolution that broke out in France in 1789 did not bode well for Louis-Nicolas-Hyacinthe Cherin. Son of the former royal genealogist, Cherin had inherited this position upon his father's death in 1785. His principal responsibility was to ensure that candidates for the officer corps satisfied the genealogical conditions mandated by the regulation of 21 May 1781: four generations of patrilineal noble descent. Perhaps it was this constant contact with the lineage-proud military nobility that led the *roturier* (non-noble) Cherin to seek noble status for himself and his posterity. Accordingly, on 8 February 1788, he purchased an ennobling office in the *Cour des aides* (the principal tax court) of Paris. Ordinarily, this acquisition would have signaled the beginning of a slow family ascent into the ranks of the Second Estate; only in the generation of Cherin's great-grandson would the family have accumulated enough generations of nobility to secure that ultimate symbol of aristocratic identity, a commission in the royal officer corps. This was not to be. Abolishing venal offices, genealogical admissions barriers, and the nobility itself, the French Revolution destroyed Cherin's livelihood, thwarted his ambition, and shattered his world.

But in a remarkable recovery from adverse fortune, Cherin managed to achieve even more in the new meritocratic order than he had under the regime of privilege that had been so kind to his family. The Revolution would accelerate Cherin's social ascent and allow him to accomplish goals in his own lifetime that, under the Old Regime, would have taken his descendants decades to achieve. Mobilizing his Old Regime army contacts, Cherin profited from the emigration of thousands of noble officers to secure a replacement commission for himself in early 1792. Once in the service, Cherin discovered that he possessed both a pronounced military vocation and a strong sense of loyalty to the revolutionary state. In only his first year in the army, he won the admiration of his fellow soldiers for bravery at the attack on Tirlemont, the bombardment of Maestricht, and the battle of Neerwindeen. In the same year, he gained further recognition for his role in arresting General Lafayette and resisting the treasonous blandishments of General Dumouriez. The Convention rewarded his political loyalty with rapid advancement. Within three years of his entry into the service, he had risen through the ranks from second lieutenant to general. Had he not been killed in 1799, charging valiantly at the head of a mounted squadron, Cherin would surely have been rewarded by Napoleon with a title of nobility, the object of his ambition before the Revolution. The name of Cherin, the last man to oversee the operations of the Old Regime's system of noble military privilege, can be seen today on the Arc de triomphe. There, it is flanked by the names of many of his brothers-in-arms, other revolutionary generals who had been barred from the officer corps before 1789 by the very same genealogical regulations Cherin had taken such care to enforce.[1]

The example of General Cherin suggests some of the unexpected continuities embedded in the French Revolution's attempt to transform a society of birth-based noble privilege into one of equal individuals distinguished only by merit. The imbrication of old and new characteristic of Cherin's career invites us to reassess the extent to which revolutionary meritocracy represented a radical break with France's aristocratic past.

Although one of the most enduring legacies of 1789, the ideal of the career open to talent has never been the subject of historical investigation. This is surprising, especially given the centrality of meritocracy to the revolutionaries' aims and self-understanding. According to the story the Revolution told about itself, French society before 1789 was dominated by a hereditary nobility which monopolized prestigious positions in the church, army, magistracy, and government. The Revolution moved swiftly to dismantle this social order. Declaring careers open to talent, the revolutionaries abolished noble privilege and sought to build on its ruins a society in which men of all classes could rise to the level of their abilities. Napoleon's promise of "a marshal's baton in every soldier's backpack" suggests the extent to which meritocracy, particularly of the military sort, became the embodiment of the revolutionary achievement. Even Alexis de Tocqueville, whose contention that the Revolution was a primarily political phenomenon has inspired much recent research into French political culture before and after 1789, recognized that the revolutionary impulse initially arose from a desire for social transformation. The original aspiration of 1789, he held, was the creation of a society "where only merit, not wealth or birth, would classify men."[2] Yet, despite the importance of meritocracy to the revolutionary endeavor, historians have given it scant attention.

Our historiographical discussion of French Revolutionary meritocracy, therefore, does not have the luxury of engaging with an existing body of literature, but rather must confront a vexing question. Why has so fundamental an aspect of the revolutionary experience never been studied? In part, the trajectory of French Revolutionary historiography during the twentieth century – dominated

---

[1] This biographical sketch is based on the entry for Cherin in Georges Six, *Dictionnaire biographique des généraux et amiraux français de la Révolution et de l'Empire (1792–1814)*, (Paris, 1934), vol. 1, 234.

[2] Alexis de Tocqueville, *Œuvres complètes*, vol. 2, ed. J. P. Mayer, *L'Ancien Régime et la Révolution: fragments et notes inédites sur la Révolution*, ed. André Jardin (Paris, 1953), 109.

by the extended debate over the Marxist interpretation – has discouraged critical approaches to the question of merit. For the predominantly French scholars associated with this school of thought, the meritocratic transformation of society in 1789 was axiomatic.[3] As the moment when the rising bourgeoisie overthrew the old nobility and replaced feudal social relations with capitalist ones, the French Revolution naturally secured the triumph of the individualistic ideology of merit over the hereditary system of privilege. Everything that needed to be known about merit was already known.

In the 1960s, however, the findings of a new generation of researchers began to challenge this approach. Uncovering patterns of social mobility and cultural exchange between the bourgeoisie and nobility, historians such as David Bien, Roger Chartier, Guy Chaussinand-Nogaret, Colin Lucas, and Denis Richet not only initiated a revisionist movement that would ultimately bring down the Marxist interpretation, but also began to lay the foundations for a more probing, historicized examination of the idea and practice of merit.[4]

But François Furet's sweeping attack on what was left of the beleaguered Marxist orthodoxy cut short this nascent revisionist reexamination of the social origins of the Revolution.[5] With his uncompromising argument that the French Revolution had momentarily replaced the struggle of class interests with discursive competition for symbolic power, Furet drew the field's attention away from the social altogether and refocused it on the political, ideological, and cultural. This reorientation spawned a range of innovative approaches, but the question of merit in the French Revolution receded from view once again.[6] Although the

---

[3] The works of the various authors associated with the Marxist interpretation, notably Georges Lefebvre and Alfred Soboul, are too numerous to mention here. For a good overview, see Geoffrey Ellis, "The 'Marxist Interpretation' of the French Revolution," *English Historical Review*, 90 (1978), 353–76. For a more recent account, see William Doyle, *Origins of the French Revolution* (Oxford, 1999), 5–9.

[4] It is significant that many of the most influential revisionist works emphasized the related problems of merit and social mobility as the keys to a new, non-Marxist social interpretation of the French Revolution. See David D. Bien, "La Réaction aristocratique avant 1789: l'exemple de l'armée," *Annales E.S.C.*, 29 (1974), 23–48 and 505–34; Roger Chartier, "Un recrutement scolaire au XVIIIème siècle: l'Ecole royale du génie de Mézières," *Revue d'histoire moderne et contemporaine*, 20 (1973), 353–75; Guy Chaussinand-Nogaret, *The French Nobility in the Eighteenth Century: From Feudalism to Enlightenment*, trans. William Doyle (New York, 1985); Colin Lucas, "Nobles, Bourgeois, and the Origins of the French Revolution," *Past and Present*, 60 (1973), 84–126; and Denis Richet, "Autour des origines idéologiques lointaines de la Révolution française: élites et despotisme," *Annales E.S.C.*, 24 (1969), 1–23.

[5] François Furet, *Interpreting the French Revolution*, trans. Elborg Forster, (Cambridge and Paris, 1977).

[6] Examples of important trends in post-Furetian scholarship include: David Bell, *Lawyers and Citizens: The Making of a Political Elite in Old Regime France* (New York, 1994); Roger Chartier, *The Cultural Origins of the French Revolution*, trans. Lydia G. Cochrane, (Durham, NC, 1991); Suzanne Desan, *Reclaiming the Sacred: Lay Religion and Popular Politics in Revolutionary*

1990s have seen a revival of interest in social approaches, a development to which the present work seeks to contribute, the question of merit in the French Revolution remains unexamined.[7]

Perhaps a more fundamental reason for the lack of attention to the problem of meritocratic social transformation in the French Revolution is that we are the inheritors of that process, participants in a culture where equality of opportunity is taken as a self-evident good.[8] The idea of hereditary privilege appears so absurd today that it seems unnecessary to ask the fundamental question of why the revolutionaries sought to abolish this system and replace it with a new mode of social distinction based on the principle of careers open to talent. To examine critically the historical origins of the French Revolution's meritocratic program requires us to step outside our normative framework and try to understand the Old Regime's culture of privilege on its own terms. Only by dropping the blinkers of self-evidence can we begin to dispel the illusion – nurtured by the rhetoric of the revolutionaries themselves – that the opening of careers to talent was inevitable, a self-explanatory step toward social justice and professional amelioration. Only by "playing the stranger" to our own assumptions can we see that the revolutionary decision for meritocracy was neither a necessary remedy for the inequities of social privilege, nor an obvious strategy of military professionalization. Rather it was a contingent and contested choice that emerged out of, rather than in opposition to, the social and professional culture of the Old Regime.

Scholars of the Old Regime have been more attuned to the prerevolutionary culture of merit than have historians of the Revolution itself. In an important article published in 1956, Marcel Reinhard showed that, in the second half of the eighteenth century, the French monarchy instituted programs for encouraging merit in both military and civilian domains.[9] Several years later, Denis Richet

---

France, (Ithaca, 1990); Dena Goodman, *The Republic of Letters: A Cultural History of the French Enlightenment*, (Ithaca, 1994); and Sarah Maza, *Private Lives and Public Affairs: The Causes Célèbres of Prerevolutionary France*, (Berkeley, 1993).

7 Examples of the revived interest in the social include: Colin Jones, "Bourgeois Revolution Revivified: 1789 and Social Change," in *Rewriting the French Revolution: The Andrew Browning Lectures, 1989*, ed. Colin Lucas (Oxford, 1991), 69–118; Jones, "The Great Chain of Buying: Medical Advertisement, the Bourgeois Public Sphere, and the Origins of the French Revolution," *American Historical Review*, 101 (1996), 13–40; William H. Sewell, *A Rhetoric of Bourgeois Revolution: The Abbé Sieyès and* What is the Third Estate?, (Durham, NC, 1994); and Timothy Tackett, *Becoming a Revolutionary: The Deputies of the French National Assembly and the Emergence of a Revolutionary Culture (1789–1790)*, (Princeton, 1996).

8 This critique of the self-evidential approach to the question of merit in the French Revolution is inspired by the interpretive strategy articulated by Steven Shapin and Simon Schaffer in relation to the preeminent status of the experiment in modern science. See their *Leviathan and the Air-Pump: Hobbes, Boyle, and the Experimental Life* (Princeton, 1985), 4–7.

9 Marcel Reinhard, "Elite et noblesse dans la seconde moitié du XVIIIème siècle," *Revue d'histoire moderne et contemporaine*, 3 (1956), 5–37.

argued that, during the last decades of the Old Regime, the nobility and bourgeoisie began to place less emphasis on the distinctions of birth that divided them than on their shared attributes of "property, fortune, and talent."[10] Examining the royal school of military engineering, Roger Chartier found that policies reserving admission for noble applicants were seen as essential to, not incompatible with, the school's aim of encouraging technical proficiency. In the thinking of the school's directors, nobility and merit were not antithetical values.[11] Several years later, Guy Chaussinand-Nogaret went even further than Chartier in questioning the nobility's attachment to the ideology of birth-based social superiority. He argued that, far from clinging to this archaic concept, the nobility gradually absorbed liberal ideals through intermarriage and social contact with the upper strata of the bourgeoisie. By 1789 the nobility had fully assimilated its core values, "merit and equality of opportunity," and was ready to play a leading role in the events of 1789.[12] Taken together, this body of research revealed the existence of a thriving meritocratic culture in the Old Regime, raising the question of continuity between that culture and the Revolution's meritocratic project.

By demonstrating that the idea of merit had a long, prerevolutionary history, Reinhard, Richet, Chartier, and Chaussinand-Nogaret opened the way for a contextualized account of the making of French Revolutionary meritocracy. Yet this opportunity was overlooked at first because of a lack of attention to the range of meanings meritocratic language bore before 1789. Instead of asking if meritocractic terms familiar to us then carried their current meanings, they took it for granted that the meritocratic discourse of the Old Regime meant what it means today: personal rather than hereditary social distinctions, democratic rather than corporate social organization, and equal opportunity for all. This assumption undermined the import of their work. While important for showing that meritocracy had Old Regime origins, these accounts ultimately dehistoricize the idea of merit by treating it as an unchanging, monolithic concept.

Only two researchers have succeeded in stepping outside their contemporary cultural framework and asking how Old Regime France actually understood merit. The first, David D. Bien, began his sustained study of merit in the Old Regime with a pathbreaking article about the infamous Ségur regulation of 1781 which effectively closed the officer corps to all but fourth-generation nobles.[13] Questioning the then-prevailing interpretation of this measure as a manifestation of aristocratic reaction against non-nobles, Bien demonstrated that it was actually directed against non-military nobles of recent vintage. By showing that the Ségur

---

10 Richet, "Autour des origines idéologiques," 13.
11 Chartier, "Un recrutement scolaire," 353–75.
12 Chaussinand-Nogaret, *The French Nobility in the Eighteenth Century*, 22.
13 Bien, "La Réaction aristocratique avant 1789," 23–48 and 505–34.

regulation reflected tensions within the nobility, rather than between the nobility and Third Estate, Bien's article was a major contribution to the revisionist attack on the Marxist orthodoxy. But he did not rest there. In a second article Bien explained the rationale behind the nobility's exclusive professional prerogatives, especially as implemented in the recruitment of military officers.[14] He showed that these privileges were not justified in terms of blood, race, or even noble superiority, as one might expect, but rather based on interlocking assumptions about breeding, honor, and personal development. Believing that family upbringing produced values, inclinations, will, and habits, the leaders of the French army thought that the best officers of the future were likely to be from families that had provided officers in the past. Bien's research shows that, far from attacking the idea of merit, the nobility's professional privileges actually expressed a distinctive conception of merit, one far different from our own.

The second historian to interrogate the meritocratic culture of the Old Regime on its own terms is Jay M. Smith. A student of Bien, Smith went even further than his mentor in demonstrating the extent to which a meritocratic ideology informed noble identity. From at least 1600, he has argued, the French nobility had justified its elevated status in terms of merit.[15] According to this view, the nobility was honor-bound to provide the king with meritorious service generation after generation in order to justify its hereditary privileges. The king, in turn, was obliged to reward the nobility's sacrifices by granting it further opportunities to distinguish itself, particularly on the battlefield. From this perspective, the nobility's social superiority and its historic ties to the Crown were both aspects of a distinctive Old Regime culture of merit. His work suggests that merit was a sweeping discourse, a way of talking about not only talent, education, and hierarchy, but also service, honor, and justice. Signifying far more than personal qualities worthy of recompense, the noble concept of merit posited a reciprocal relationship between the state and its servitors and implied a certain moral order underpinning the polity.

Although neither Bien nor Smith extended their research chronologically, to see how Old Regime ways of thinking about merit might have influenced revolutionary actions after 1789, their work has important implications for the study of French Revolutionary meritocracy. If they are correct, the opening of careers to talent represented neither the explosive triumph of long-thwarted bourgeois ambition, nor the triumph of an Enlightenment ideal. Rather, the work of Bien and Smith suggests that the making of meritocracy in revolutionary France was less a radical break than a fundamental redefinition, a redefinition that entailed

---

14 David D. Bien, "The Army in the French Enlightenment: Reform, Reaction, and Revolution," *Past and Present*, 85 (1979), 68–98.

15 Jay M. Smith, *The Culture of Merit: Nobility, Royal Service, and the Making of Absolute Monarchy in France, 1600–1789* (Ann Arbor, 1996).

the transformation of a long-established culture of service, the restructuring of social hierarchy, and the reconfiguration of relations between state and society. These complex transformations can be best understood by setting aside traditional chronological boundaries to ask how the Old Regime culture of merit informed the revolutionaries' attempt to transform the French polity.

Assessing change and continuity in meritocratic culture before and after the French Revolution is thus a vast undertaking. I have attempted to reduce it to manageable proportions by focusing on a single institution, the French army.[16] While all the professions had to grapple with the revolutionary redefinition of merit, nowhere were its complex ramifications brought into sharper relief than in the French military. The army was not only the largest employer in eighteenth-century France (and thus the organization where meritocratic reform had the greatest human impact), but also one of the few institutions to survive the entire period intact. Although it was radically transformed in the course of the Revolution, the army – unlike the trade guilds, lawyers' associations, law courts, medical colleges, and learned societies – remained in continuous existence, thus preserving an unbroken fossil record of how merit was understood and institutionalized from the Old Regime into the nineteenth century.

The prerevolutionary composition of the officer corps, moreover, ensured that the opening of careers to talent there would be particularly difficult and therefore exceptionally revealing of the broader problems of the transition from birth to merit. Before the Revolution the officer corps was the aristocratic preserve *par excellence* – a symbol of noble identity and one of the few professions considered suitable for young men of pedigree. To ensure that it remained so, kings had formally reserved commissions for gentlemen of established ancestry. But, in the space of a few months in 1789, the Revolution ended this state of affairs. By the close of the revolutionary decade, the formerly aristocratic profession of arms had come to represent the triumph of a new meritocratic order. The army thus encapsulates both the Revolution's transformative impact and the continuities which link the histories of the Old Regime, Revolution, Empire, and Restoration.

---

16 As a subject for our study, the French army also has the advantage of having been examined in great depth by social historians over the past several decades. The most important of these works include Jean-Paul Bertaud, *La Révolution armée: les soldats-citoyens et la Révolution française* (Paris, 1979); Gilbert Bodinier, *Les Officiers de l'armée royale combattants de la Guerre d'indépendance des Etats-Unis* (Paris, 1983); Jean Chagniot, *Paris et l'armée au XVIIIème siècle: étude politique et sociale* (Paris, 1985); André Corvisier, *L'Armée française de la fin du XVIIème siècle au ministère de Choiseul*, 2 vols. (Paris, 1964); Alan Forrest, *Conscripts and Deserters: The Army and French Society during the Revolution and Empire* (New York, 1989); John A. Lynn, *The Bayonets of the Republic: Motivation and Tactics in the Army of Revolutionary France* (Chicago and Urbana, 1984); Samuel F. Scott, *The Response of the Royal Army to the French Revolution: The Role and Development of the Line Army, 1787–93* (Oxford, 1978); and Isser Woloch, *The French Veteran from the Revolution to the Restoration* (Chapel Hill, 1979).

This book examines the shifting ideas and practices of these regimes as they attempted to implement meritocracy in the military profession. The first chapter treats the Old Regime concept of merit and the efforts undertaken from 1750 to 1789 to realize it in the royal officer corps. According to this traditional understanding, merit tended to be concentrated in certain noble lineages which were bound by reciprocal ties to the monarchy. Based on the exchange of military service generation after generation for places and honors distributed by a thankful king, merit implied a socio-political order grounded in sentiments of fidelity and justice. But by the mid-eighteenth century, this ideal began to be subverted by new, alien values. The growing importance of money, venal ennoblement, and the play of influence in a factionalized Court, were increasingly seen by the military nobility as destroying the traditional relations of reciprocity which were supposed to govern its relationship to the Crown. In 1750 military reformers began to institute measures designed to insulate the military nobility from these trends and preserve its traditional service ethos. Making sharp distinctions between nobles and non-nobles, new nobles and old nobles, courtiers and provincials, these reforms divided elite society into antagonistic groups and split the officer corps into hostile factions. Seeing themselves as the victims, rather than the beneficiaries, of the Old Regime's changing social order, military nobles had become pronounced (though nostalgic) revolutionaries by 1789.

The following chapter reinterprets the meritocratic revolution of 1789 in the light of the bitter conflicts over hereditary merit (and its violations) that had polarized the officer corps during the last decades of the Old Regime. It argues that the abolition of privilege and the opening of careers to talent in 1789 were designed to address not only the frustrations of the bourgeoisie, but also those of the military nobility. Although its solemn commitment to open careers to talent broke forever the noble monopoly of officer posts, the Assembly's other military reforms – ending the sale of military commissions, abolishing the professional privileges of Court favorites, and reserving places at the military school for the sons of serving officers – sought to assuage the military nobility. Powerfully informed by the longstanding grievances of the military nobility, the meritocratic reforms of 1789 amounted to less of a historical break than has generally been assumed.

Chapter 3 examines how the carefully crafted revolutionary military reforms discussed in the previous chapter collapsed under the weight of successive revolutionary crises. Faced with unpalatable domestic policing duties, violent insubordination among the rank-and-file, Jacobin hostility, and the attempted flight of the King, the officer corps grew disenchanted with the Revolution. By the end of 1792, almost all of the officers had resigned or emigrated. The disintegration of the officer corps could not have come at a worse time, for France now found itself at war with a formidable coalition of European monarchies. To fill the vacant cadres, the Revolution resorted to extraordinary measures. It approved the unprecedented promotion of long-serving soldiers of the royal army, but, to counterbalance the influx of these plebeian personnel, it began to recruit patriotic young men of good family (like Cherin), both noble and non-noble, directly into the officer corps. It also undertook the formation of a parallel army of provincial National Guardsmen, whose battalions were officered by elected local elites. By the end of 1792, these measures had radically altered the composition of the officer corps. But far from being the result of deliberate revolutionary reforms, these changes were the result of domestic and international crises beyond the control of the legislators, not of intentional attempts at democratization.

Exploring the ideological, political, and military factors that transformed the officer corps after the overthrow of the monarchy in August 1792, the fourth chapter argues that republican rule marked a sharp, but transitory, break in the history of revolutionary meritocracy. Believing that the Revolution's earlier reforms were incompatible with egalitarian and virtuous republicanism because they appealed to egotistical ambition, implied hierarchy, and required a monarchical-type authority to select and promote, the Convention abolished all existing institutions of officer education, recruitment, and promotion. Relinquishing their own authority over military careers, republican legislators created a democratic system of advancement in which the soldiers would elect their own officers. But this renunciation of government power was short-lived. The pressures of war, civil strife, and bitter factionalism within the Convention itself pushed Montagnard legislators to abandon their initial experiment in democratic meritocracy and reassert direct control over the military. Employing political surveillance, purges, and newly restored authority over promotion, they rebuilt the power of the central government over the army to an unprecedented degree. Yet, elements from this period of republican egalitarianism – distrust of honorific awards, military education, and direct officer recruitment – survived until Napoleon's seizure of power. Hence, the entire republican period (1792–99) should be seen as a distinct interlude in which the meritocracy of 1789 was, albeit briefly, supplanted by a more egalitarian conception of state service.

The fifth chapter discusses the rise of a new sense of military professionalism during the Thermidorean and Directorial years. Although these regimes respected many of the egalitarian reforms instituted by the Convention, they made other changes which laid the foundations for the Napoleonic military establishment. The Thermidorean purge of "terrorists" and other officers too closely linked to Robespierre's regime, coupled with the largest wartime downsizing of cadres ever carried out in any army, eliminated all but committed professionals from the officer corps. The incessant campaigning, now carried on outside of France itself, reinforced the growing isolation of the army from civilian society and engendered a distinctive sense of military identity. And even the political instability of the time, which forced beleaguered governments to resort to military intervention to overcome political opposition, tended to increase military professionalism. The experience of revolutionary political precariousness taught the officers that the best strategy of professional survival lay in strict political neutrality and obedience. It was this attitude of subordinate detachment, rather than active support for a military takeover, that explains the success of General Bonaparte's coup of 18 Brumaire VIII (8 November 1799). Apolitical professionalism had become the officers' antidote to the unpredictable shifts in power that had hitherto characterized the Revolution.

The penultimate chapter examines how Napoleon's search to reconstruct monarchy and found a dynasty recombined and transformed the notions of merit his regime had inherited from the revolutionary governments of the past decade. Although Napoleon was careful not to give direct offense to revolutionary sentiment by restoring exclusive professional privileges, he took decisive steps to elevate the social composition of the officer corps and establish it as a pillar of his regime. A purge of plebeian officers, the reinstitution of military education, attempts to attract young nobles back to the service, and the imposition of *de facto* limits on the advancement of socially undistinguished officers all contributed to this end. As he consolidated his power, Napoleon also created new institutions specifically designed to renew the old meritocratic ethos of reciprocity and rebuild a hereditary elite of service bound to the fortunes of his dynasty. The creation of the Legion of Honor in 1802 and the imperial nobility in 1808 marked the return of formal systems of social distinction designed to stimulate merit and attach worthy citizens to the regime. Merit, as displayed in service to the monarch, was restored as the basis of the socio-political order. Belatedly realizing the aspirations voiced by the military nobility in 1789, Napoleon brought the revolution in merit back to its starting point.

The conclusion briefly surveys the meritocratic legacy of the Old Regime, Revolution, and Empire during the nineteenth century and beyond. Despite efforts to favor the old nobility, the restored Bourbon monarchy was forced to respect the meritocratic ideals of 1789, as refracted by Napoleonic policies. Bourbon attempts to reintroduce aristocratic privilege met opposition not only from liberal deputies alert to any attempt to extend royal power, but also from military officers determined to protect their careers and safeguard military professionalism. Mobilizing meritocratic arguments strikingly similar to those aimed by the military nobility at plutocratic and courtly intruders on the eve of the Revolution, the post-Napoleonic officer corps sought to protect its traditional conception of meritocratic service by insulating itself from these debilitating extraneous influences. But by replacing the morally inflected reciprocity that had previously structured the officers' relationship to the state with the impersonal authority of promotion boards chosen from the military's own ranks, this isolationist reflex disrupted the traditional ideal of meritocratic service it had sought to preserve. By the late nineteenth century, a new notion of bureaucratic professionalism was pushing aside the older notion of service inherited from the Old Regime.

1 The merits of birth: lineage and professionalism in the Old Regime

The inglorious performance of French arms in the wars of the mid-eighteenth century – particularly in the disastrous Seven Years' War – sent shockwaves through French society. Nowhere was the humiliation of defeat felt more sharply than in the army. There, the perception of military decline prompted reformers to enact a series of professionalizing measures which transformed the French army. Between 1750 and 1789 a network of military schools was established, logistical administration was centralized, the purchase system was abolished, and costly parade-ground units were scaled back. But in the area of officer recruitment, this reforming drive took on a reactionary coloration as increasingly stringent genealogical conditions were imposed on those who sought commissions. By 1781 only men who could prove four generations of patrilineal noble descent were admitted to the officer corps. This chapter attempts to make sense out of these seemingly contradictory impulses. It will show that, taken together, these measures were designed to enhance the effectiveness of the army by reinforcing the traditional relationship between the nobility and royal military service, a relationship grounded in a certain conception of equality, merit, and distributive justice.

Birth as merit: traditional noble conceptions of military service

The officer corps of absolutist France was dominated by the nobility. This was apparent in both its social composition, estimated at 95 percent noble in 1788, and the distinctive understanding of service that infused the military and justified the nobility's privileged position within it.[1] According to this conception, the nobility was bound to provide the king with selfless military service in order to prove itself worthy of the honors and prerogatives bestowed upon it by the Throne. The king, in turn, was obliged to reward the nobility's fidelity and sacrifices by providing it with places in the most honorable of professions, that of arms. Viewed in this way, the Second Estate's effective monopolization of officer commissions appeared as the fruit of merit – a legitimate reward for services rendered. It was this understanding that allowed one cavalry officer to describe the "distinctions" accorded to nobility as "a system of equity."[2] From his perspective, privilege was an act of justice, payment for services rendered.

---

1 The fundamental work on this subject is Smith, *The Culture of Merit*.
2 Bibliothèque du génie (hereafter B.G.), in-4 33, Thieffries Beauvoir, "Plan et principes élémentaires de constitution d'armée, d'institution militaire, et d'économie politique" (1787).

1 Printed application form for the Ecole royale militaire, 1786–89, showing the imbrication of bureaucratic and genealogical concerns.

While these conclusions may shock modern democratic sensibilities, the assumptions on which they rest are not completely alien to current understandings of meritocracy. The concept of merit still evokes notions of deservedness; those who perform exemplary actions are generally thought of as entitled to special recompense. But in contrast to the present-day notion that the rights of merit should extend no further than the meritorious individual, they were seen by the nobility of Old Regime France as transmissible from one generation of a family to the next. Since society as a whole continued to benefit from signal services rendered in the distant past, it was only fair that the descendants of long-departed benefactors continue to receive recompense for their forebears' deeds.

> The first to have been ennobled served the state; his labors and services were not limited to winning glory for his *patrie* [homeland or fatherland] and sovereign ... The following generations also reaped more or less fruit, and they cannot without injustice refuse to recognize in the descendants of a benefactor, services rendered to the *patrie*.[3]

In noble thinking, there was no more fitting way to repay young noblemen "for the blood their ancestors have spilled" than by providing them with opportunities to perpetuate their family's tradition of service.[4] Understood as hereditary deservedness, merit furnished the sons of the nobility – unproven young men with no personal accomplishments – with legitimate titles to preferential admission into the officer corps.

A second conception of merit also reinforced the nobility's special status in the military. In addition to deserving commissions as recompense for the actions of their illustrious ancestors, nobles were also recruited preferentially because they were considered to possess greater aptitude for the military profession than *roturiers*. The presumption of the nobility's hereditary predisposition to military service was rarely articulated in terms of blood, race, or innate characteristics. Rather, it was based on the widely held eighteenth-century belief that a person's character was not fixed at birth, but acquired its distinctive traits only gradually, through pervasive "environmental" impressions. And like the Enlightenment philosophers whom they read, the high-ranking noble officers responsible for designing recruitment policies believed that it was principally in the family that children received the environmental conditioning that would shape their habits, inclinations, and talents. Since boys from military families were thought to absorb martial values from an early age, it followed, in the thinking of Old Regime military reformers,

---

3 Ibid.
4 Archives de la guerre (hereafter A.G.), MR 1781, Blangermont, "Mémoires sur l'éducation des jeunes militaires et la composition des officiers des régiments d'infanterie française, à Monseigneur le prince de Montbarey" (1777).

that "the best officers of the future were likely to be from families that had given officers in the past."⁵ Although based on an ostensibly egalitarian model of character formation, this understanding of how individual dispositions and talents arose served as a powerful justification for noble exclusivism.

Officers from military backgrounds were also thought to possess special sources of motivation which guaranteed their commitment to the military profession. The deeds of past generations were understood as having established a hereditary reputation, a capital of honor passed down to the sons, which they would feel obligated to merit personally by emulating the illustrious examples of their ancestors. In a typical formulation of this idea, Captain Guynet de Montverd urged officers to "walk in the footsteps" of their ancestors "in order to immortalize [their] name by glorious actions and enhance [it] by their own distinguished merit."⁶ Birth into a noble family certainly brought with it privileges and distinctions, but, ideally, these had to be justified by the services of each new generation. In the unpublished memoirs he left for his children, the marquis de Bouthillier, a general who had the unique distinction of serving on military reform committees of the Old Regime, Revolution, and Emigration, described his family's "hereditary titles" as imparting "an obligation to make ourselves worthy."⁷ Self-disciplined and self-motivated because they felt that their personal honor, as well as that of their family, depended on their performance, nobles were thought to be more inclined to work hard and persevere than their non-noble counterparts. While the only guarantee of the would-be *roturier* officer's commitment to the military profession was "his desire to do well," that of the noble rested on the additional foundation of "the memory that his fathers have left."⁸ Seeking to make himself worthy of this weighty inheritance, the noble would endeavor to uphold his position by exemplary comportment. Impelled by the obligation and challenge of his birth, he would attach his honor to his professional functions and work all the harder to succeed at even the most tedious tasks.

It follows from this discussion that anything which altered the privileged relationship between the nobility and the military profession could be taken as a violation of the meritocratic order on which military effectiveness, social hierarchy, and even monarchy were thought to depend. If men without traditions of service were able to enter the officer corps, they would displace the military nobility from its rightful place, lower the quality of the cadres, and subvert the

---

5 Bien, "The Army in the French Enlightenment," 91.
6 A. Guynet de Montverd, *Projet, ou nouveau système militaire, pour donner des moyens sûrs de tirer parti des gens de guerre dans les différents âges de la vie humaine* (1771), 16.
7 Archives départementales (hereafter A.D.) Cher, J 2192, marquis de Bouthillier, "Mémoires particulières de M. de Bouthillier" (1810). On the growing importance during the seventeenth and eighteenth centuries of family histories to the nobility, see Smith, *The Culture of Merit*, 57–91.
8 *De la destruction de la noblesse en France* (1790).

ethos of reciprocity on which the monarchical polity rested. By the same token, if nobles ceased to merit their hereditary distinctions by real services, their privileges would come to seem like acts of usurpation. This would not only breed demoralization within the military, but also discredit the entire socio-political order. From about 1750, army reformers began to identify abuses of these sorts as an important source of French military decline, social crisis, and political breakdown. It is to their efforts against them that we now turn our attention.

The meaning of military reform after the Seven Years' War

Stung by the French army's mediocre performance in the War of Austrian Succession and outright humiliation in the Seven Years' War, military reformers began to look critically at the social composition and institutional structure of the officer corps for the source of the trouble. They believed that the grave deficiencies they perceived in these areas not only explained French military dysfunction, but also portended more far-reaching national decline. In the opinion of the marquis de Caraman, a general destined to serve on several reform committees, the defeats signaled nothing less than "the approaching destruction of our monarchy."[9] For the comte de Guibert, whose widely read *Essai général de tactique* (1772) earned him a European reputation as a far-sighted military thinker, the wars had revealed profound social malaise. In his view, France had become a country where

> almost all great rewards are usurped by intrigue; where most become hereditary; where merit languishes without powerful backers; where influence advances without talent; where making one's fortune no longer means acquiring a good reputation, but rather amassing riches; in a word, where one can simultaneously be covered with dignities and infamy, with grades and ignorance; [where one can] serve the state poorly and still possess its principal charges; [where one can] suffer public scorn and still enjoy the favor of the sovereign.[10]

Although similar denunciations of favoritism, venality, and usurpation echoed throughout the writings of all the other military reformers of the time, they did not see the nobility's privileged relationship to the military profession as the problem. On the contrary, they believed that the progressive weakening of the traditional link between nobility and military service was to blame for both social discontent and the decline of French arms. For the next twenty-five years, until the Revolution halted their efforts, they would attempt to restore national vitality

---

9 A.G. MR 1708, marquis de Caraman, "Réflexions sur l'état présent du militaire de France" (1758).

10 Jacques-Antoine-Hippolyte, comte de Guibert, *Essai général de tactique*, in *Ecrits militaires, 1772–1790*, ed. General Menard (Paris, 1977), 80.

by reforging what they saw as this constitutionally sound and militarily indispensable link.

Of particular concern to critics like Caraman and Guibert was the growing influence of money over military careers, a development many blamed for the poor composition of the officer corps. One of the first to warn that increasing emphasis on wealth was resulting in the displacement of military nobles by monied outsiders was the chevalier d'Arcq, whose impassioned defense of the nobility's military vocation defined the spirit of the nascent reform movement. In his book, *La Noblesse militaire* (1756), this illegitimate grandson of Louis XIV bemoaned the practice of awarding commissions which "should have been given to the nobility" to the sons of wealthy "financier[s], businessm[en], or merchant[s]."[11] Many observers believed that the infiltration of such outsiders had grown more common during the Seven Years' War, as the financial burden of campaign service forced poorer nobles into retirement and prompted their replacement by opulent outsiders. The comte de Saint-Germain, a career officer who would become minister of war, believed that, because of the increased cost to officers of wartime service, "all the poor nobility, destined by birth to serve and form the backbone of the army, is absolutely excluded."[12] They were being replaced by "the sons of big merchants ... of *fermiers-généraux* [tax farmers who collected many of the kingdom's indirect taxes], and of *receveurs de finances* [financiers who collected taxes and lent the King money against the anticipated revenues]," unworthy parvenus who "dared to place themselves on the same line [as] young men of quality" and "claim their rights."[13] Given the incomplete state of the records, it is impossible to measure the extent to which these critiques were founded. But ultimately, whether these perceptions were accurate or not is less important than their impact on military reform policy.

Another source of disquiet was the preferences enjoyed by courtier officers whose superior birth, wealth, and connections set them apart from their more modest noble comrades. Among the disgruntled were not only the middling, "provincial" nobility, blocked in its advancement and humiliated at being leapfrogged on the career path by young scions of France's illustrious families, but also high-ranking generals, often Court nobles themselves, who nonetheless feared the detrimental effect of favoritism on the quality of army leadership and officer morale. One of the few successful French generals of the mid-century wars, the comte de Saxe, warned that the monopolization of high

---

11 Philippe-Auguste de Sainte-Foix, chevalier d'Arcq, *La Noblesse militaire, ou le patriote françois* (n.p., 1756), 161–2.
12 A.G. A^{1}3510, "Mémoire par Saint-Germain au ministre de la guerre, le marquis de Paulmy" (8 January 1758).
13 Claude-Louis, comte de Saint-Germain, *Mémoires* (Switzerland, 1779), 67.

rank by "young men of birth," the so-called *colonels à la bavette* (colonels in bibs), was "destroying the *émulation* [spirit of meritocratic striving] of the rest of the officers."[14] Saxe spoke for many officers when he described the young courtier soldiers as

> people without experience and often without application who, having barely left an academy and having served two or three years at the head of a cavalry company, feel mistreated if they are not given command of an infantry regiment. They quickly obtain this and hurry to have themselves received. But no sooner is the ceremony completed than they begin to get bored in their garrison and proclaim their boredom in all the neighboring towns .... It is true that they return each week to drill their regiments, but they soon realize that they understand nothing about it. Nevertheless, they still want to command and, to hide their ignorance, find it more expedient to stop exercising their regiments.[15]

The comte de Rochambeau, who would later command the French at Yorktown, went so far as to propose cloistering the courtiers in a distinct career track in order to spare the middling nobles who formed the majority of the officer corps from the frustration of unequal competition.[16] The chevalier de Fleurans, a noble serving as a simple soldier, had a blunter remedy: get rid of the "marquises" and "everything else that attracts luxury."[17] From these and other examples, an important conclusion emerges: the first great outcry against the privileges of birth originated in the traditional bastion of noble identity, the officer corps.

The discontent stemmed from the divisive social distinctions drawn between different types of nobles, distinctions which flaunted the cherished ideal of intra-noble equality. The painstaking research of Gilbert Bodinier has shown that only those presented at Court had realistic prospects of advancing to regimental colonelcies, the stepping stone to army command, high posts in the Maison militaire du roi (the royal household troops), and lucrative provincial governorships. In 1763, 92 percent of infantry colonels had received the "honors of the Court."[18] The careers of these favorites – known as *présentés* – followed an irregular course characterized by venality, rapid advancement, and a marked distaste for the more rigorous branches of the service: the infantry, artillery, and engineers. Of a sample of fifty-eight colonels serving in 1789, we find no less than eighteen distinct career paths which had led them to colonelcies by the age of 36, on average. Most (83 percent) had served in at least one venal unit: the Maison militaire (34 percent), the Carabiniers (one of the most prestigious

---

14 Maurice, comte de Saxe, *Les Rêveries, ou mémoires sur l'art de la guerre* (The Hague, 1756), 22.
15 A.G. MR 1708, maréchal de Saxe, "Mémoire sur l'infanterie" (1756).
16 A.G. MR 1709, comte de Rochambeau, "Mémoire sur l'infanterie" (1761).
17 A.G. A^{1}3720, chevalier de Fleurans, "Observations militaires pour Monseigneur le prince de Montbarey, ministre de la guerre" (1780).
18 Bodinier, *Les Officiers de l'armée royale*, 59.

cavalry regiments in the royal army) or Du roi (the triple-sized "King's Own") infantry regiment (16 percent), and the cavalry (71 percent). The majority (62 percent) had never served in the hard-slogging infantry, although it testifies to a growing spirit of professionalism that the sons of certain prominent military figures had chosen to begin their careers with a rigorous apprenticeship in the studious artillery.

In contrast to the rapid promotion enjoyed by the courtier colonels, other noble officers (even those of ancient lineage) advanced slowly, rising successively through all the ranks until the grade of captain or, exceptionally, lieutenant-colonel. Of a sample of forty-three lieutenant-colonels serving in 1789, 91 percent had achieved their rank in this manner, at the age of 51, on average.[19] Consequently, the most experienced regimental officers typically found themselves subordinated to colonels many years their junior. As one noble recalled in 1807, "one was born, so to speak, either captain or colonel."[20] Like the nobility from which it was largely composed, the military profession was fractured along social lines.

To shelter the officer corps from these debilitating trends, the reformers sought to delimit a distinct military society within which the traditional meritocratic ethos of the nobility could be restored.[21] To diminish the role of money, they would nationalize unit administration, abolish the purchase system, and reduce privileged Court units. To shore up the nobility's service vocation, they would create a system of military education for the sons of officers and impose genealogical barriers to the recruitment of opulent parvenus. But, as Saint-Germain was forced to recognize soon after becoming war minister in 1775, the salutary potential of these changes continued to be undermined by persistent divisions within the military nobility itself, by the "habit of distinguishing between the great nobility and that of the provinces, between the rich and the poor."

> The first class instantly obtains the highest grades as if by right, while the second class, by the sole misfortune of its birth or poverty, is condemned to waste its life in the subaltern grades. This custom is doubly pernicious. The first class does not need to work to succeed; it obtains as if by right. And the second does not work because its efforts would be useless. Thus, all striving is destroyed.[22]

---

19 The figures in this and the previous paragraph are derived from a sample of French infantry colonels (58) and lieutenant-colonels (43) for whom sufficient information was given in F. V. S. Churchill, *Réimpression de l'état militaire de France pour l'année 1789 avec notes généalogiques et historiques* (Carnac, 1913), vols. 2–8.
20 Archives nationales (hereafter A.N.) AF IV 1306, Huguet de Semonville, "Projet pour l'institution d'un livre d'or dans lequel seraient inscrits tous les membres de la légion d'honneur" (1807).
21 In an undated, untitled manuscript, probably written during his ministry, the comte de Saint-Germain wrote that the only way to restore the moral health of the army was "to separate it as much as possible from the mass of the nation." A.G. MR 1714, "Extrait de quelques manuscrits de M. le comte de Saint-Germain" (n.d.).
22 Saint-Germain, *Mémoires*, 120–1.

As the awareness dawned that divisions within the military nobility itself were becoming the principal threat to the officers' morale, a final generation of reformers undertook an ambitious program to restore equality of opportunity between different sorts of noble officers. But, misconstrued, these efforts served only to inflame tensions within the Second Estate and push many officers into the revolutionary camp. With noble officers and bourgeois civilians united in the belief that they had suffered from the privileges of birth, there is little wonder why the Old Regime collapsed so quickly.

Equality through affirmative action: the Ecole royale militaire

The first attempts to address the problem of inequality within the officer corps sought to lessen social differences by aiding the least favored echelons of the military nobility. This initial approach to reform informed two measures enacted soon after the War of Austrian Succession. The first was the 1750 decision to create a *noblesse militaire* (military nobility) by granting hereditary nobility to non-noble officers who had reached the rank of general or who represented the third generation of their family to serve as an officer. Although a potent symbolic reaffirmation of the ennobling character of military service in the face of venal ennoblement, its practical effects were limited. Barely 200 families qualified for *noblesse militaire* before 1789.[23] The second reform, the creation of the Ecole royale militaire (Royal Military School) in 1751, had more tangible effects on the composition of the officer corps. During the final decades of the Old Regime, royal military schooling gave the sons of poorer officers of proven noble ancestry the resources they needed to begin their military careers. Despite the apparent contradiction between the first measure, which recognized the martial potential of *roturiers*, and the second, which pronounced their formal exclusion, they actually sought to achieve a common goal: to reinforce the connection between nobility and military service.

The Ecole royale militaire was founded to prepare young *gentilshommes* (noblemen counting at least four generations of patrilineal noble descent) from impecunious military families for careers as officers. By providing them with free education, monetary support, and powerful institutional backing, the Ecole was intended to enable financially pressed noble families which had given officers in the past to perpetuate their hereditary service traditions. Although the Ecole never became the main source of new officers, it furnished the army with thousands of officers before its suppression in 1793. Graduates included some of the Revolution's most famous generals, like Bonaparte and Davout, as well as many

---

[23] *Edit du roi, portant création d'une noblesse militaire* (1750). Figures on the number of families ennobled by this edict are derived from A.G. Y^{a}228–9.

of its most bitter adversaries. The Ecole represented a new departure in the way officers were trained. Before its foundation, aspirant officers seeking to acquire the rudiments of their future profession were left to their own devices, usually entering the regiments directly to serve a hands-on apprenticeship, but sometimes pausing to attend a *collège* (the standard Old Regime institution of secondary education, usually church-run), *académie* (schools designed to teach chivalric behavior to young nobles), or page school.[24] In early 1750, the Ecole royale militaire was envisioned as an alternative to this hodgepodge of practices. Unlike the *collèges* whose classically oriented curriculum was considered appropriate only for "forming subjects for the church or cloister," or the *académies* whose purpose was to inculcate in young nobles the physical skills and social graces they needed to succeed in genteel company, the Ecole would provide an education tailored to the professional destination of its students.[25] With a heavy mathematical emphasis – supplemented by doses of technical drawing, history, and contemporary foreign languages – and a militarized disciplinary regime, the new school was expected to prepare up to 500 scholarship students at a time for military careers.[26] Strictly reserved for needy military noble families, paying students were not admitted.

Intended to "aid that precious [military] portion of the nobility," the Ecole sought to promote greater equality within the officer corps by easing some of the social, economic, and cultural differences dividing it into haves and have-nots. To ensure that royal aid went only to those who needed and deserved it, all prospective students first had to furnish proof of four generations of noble descent, a requirement intended to guarantee that their nobility did not derive from recent venal ennoblement.[27] But ancient pedigree alone was not enough to enter the Ecole. Applicants were also ranked on an eight-tiered scale which gave

---

24 On the history of French military education, see Jacques Fabre de Massaguel, *L'Ecole de Sorèze de 1758 au 19 Fructidor an IV* (Issoudun, 1958); Léon Hennet, *Les Compagnies des cadets-gentilshommes et les écoles militaires* (Paris, 1889); Robert Laulan, "Pourquoi et comment on entrait à l'Ecole royale militaire de Paris," *Revue d'histoire moderne et contemporaine*, 4 (1957), 141–50; and Charles de Montzey, *Institutions d'éducation militaire jusqu'en 1789* (Paris, 1866).

25 A.N. K 149, "Mémoire sur l'utilité de l'établissement d'un collège académique pour la jeune noblesse de France" (11 January 1750). On the tradition of noble disdain for the Latin-based pedagogy characteristic of the *collèges*, see Mark Motley, *Becoming a French Aristocrat: The Education of the Court Nobility, 1580–1715* (Princeton, 1990).

26 On the school's curriculum, see David D. Bien, "Military Education in Eighteenth-Century France: Technical and Non-Technical Determinants," in *Science, Technology, and Warfare. Proceedings of the Third Military History Symposium, United States Air Force Academy, 8–9 May 1969*, ed. Monte D. Wright and Lawrence J. Paszek (Washington, DC, 1971), 51–9.

27 There was some sentiment in favor of reserving admissions for the sons of officers, whether noble or not. Rejected at the time, this would become the basis of military school recruitment during the first years of the Revolution. For one such proposal, see A.N. K 149, Untitled *mémoire* (1768).

preference to the sons of officers who had sacrificed life, limb, and fortune in the king's service.[28] This classification scheme effectively limited admission to the sons of officers; even during the Seven Years' War, when the pace of officer recruitment reached new heights, applicants whose fathers had never served were rejected out of hand because of the large numbers of military children seeking places.[29] Finally, applicants had to furnish proof of financial need to ensure that only families in danger of slipping into indigence benefited from royal largess. But the requirement that applicants' fathers had served tended to exclude noble families "so poor that it is not possible to recruit officers from them."[30] Despite some grumbling about the lax enforcement of the genealogical and financial requirements, it seems that the admissions policies were respected, producing a student body recruited primarily from the middling military nobility.

A less obvious, but no less important, function of the Ecole was to find positions in the officer corps for students who otherwise might not have been able to secure places. Previously, an aspirant had to obtain a place from a colonel with a vacancy in his regiment. But colonels, who had usually purchased their regiments, tended to regard their investments as a means of obliging clients and currying favor with peers and superiors. Poor, unconnected nobles were not always welcome.[31] As a royal institution directly under the king's patronage, the Ecole was able to overcome these habits and secure employment for all of its graduates. Most students were placed in the infantry rather than the cavalry or Maison militaire, where the purchase system held sway. Those with pronounced mathematical ability, like Bonaparte, were sent to specialized artillery and engineering schools. Although its graduates rarely advanced beyond the rank of captain, the Ecole succeeded in providing poorer military nobles with an alternative route into the officer corps, a route which bypassed the system of proprietary patronage which had previously governed officer recruitment.[32] The first in a series of reforms which augmented royal control over military nominations, the Ecole was a step toward the creation of an officer corps directly dependent on the state.

---

28   See the *Edit du roy, portant création d'une Ecole royale militaire* (1751) for the admissions categories, as originally defined. These were slightly modified in a more rigorous sense after the Seven Years' War. For the revised categories, see the *Mémoire instructif sur ce que les parens doivent observer pour proposer leurs enfans pour l'Ecole royale-militaire et pour le Collège royal de La Flèche* (1764).
29   A.D. Bouches-du-Rhone, C 2845, "Lettre de M. Cremilles" (13 April 1761).
30   A.G. MR 1706, Carcado, "Sous-officiers d'élite" (20 March 1754).
31   "Lettre du comte de Saint-Germain à M. du Verney" (24 November 1753), *Correspondence particulière du comte de Saint-Germain ... avec M. Paris du Verney* (London, 1789), vol. 1, 74.
32   A few regiments connected with members of the royal family or the princes of the blood, however, were excepted from this system and instead recruited their officers from household pages and clients. See A.G. Y^{a}147, untitled note (28 May 1777).

Students continued to receive assistance from the Ecole long after graduation. To help them meet the costs of military service, graduates received annual pensions of 200 *livres* (the French pound, worth much less than its English counterpart) until reaching the rank of captain.[33] Surviving records testify to the magnitude of this aid; by 1786, the school was disbursing over 166,000 *livres* each year to 828 former students.[34] In addition, graduates facing unforeseen expenses related to their service often received extraordinary grants or loans. For example, former students participating in the invasion of Corsica in 1769 were awarded supplemental grants of 300 *livres* to provide themselves with essential campaign equipment.[35] Occasionally exceptional aid was provided to individual students. One student, Galiffet, was provided the services of a speech expert who promised to cure his stuttering.[36] Another student, Bourgoing, one of the Ecole's most successful pupils, received aid totaling thousands of *livres*. Proposed for the diplomatic corps, he was sent to study law at the University of Strasbourg where, in addition to receiving a pension, he was given private lessons from a dancing master. After several years he was placed as an aide to the French minister to the Imperial Diet where he received a one-time grant of 2,400 *livres* and an annual pension of 1,800 *livres* to support his diplomatic lifestyle.[37] While atypical, the aid received by Bourgoing illustrates the Ecole's unwavering commitment to advancing its students' careers.

Although the system of royal military education underwent several changes in the 1760s and 1770s, its underlying purpose remained the same. In 1764 a new military school was established at La Flèche to prepare younger pupils for the main Paris school. This permitted the implementation of an even more rigorous mathematical curriculum, but did not alter the core mission of the Ecole. A more important reform was undertaken in 1776 when ten (later twelve) provincial military schools were added to the existing institutions of military education. In theory, this change expanded the capacity of royal military education from 500 to 600 students, but the actual increase was even greater since the maximum levels set for the old Ecole had never been met and the new limit was soon exceeded. In the provincial schools the royal scholarship students (still recruited under the same restrictive regulations) rubbed shoulders

---

33 A.N. MM 680, "Copie d'une lettre de Monseigneur le duc de Choiseul au conseil de l'Ecole royale militaire" (17 May 1769).
34 A.G. Y^{a}148, "Etat des pensions" (1786).
35 A.N. MM 668, "Délibération du 27 février 1769."
36 A.N. MM 661, "Délibération du 3 avril 1760."
37 The different episodes of Bourgoing's early career are found in A.N. MM 659, "Délibération du 26 mars 1771"; A.N. MM 667, "Délibération du 3 novembre 1766"; idem, "Délibération du 10 juillet 1767"; idem, "Délibération du 29 août 1768"; A.N. MM 668, "Délibération du 26 juin 1769"; and idem, "Délibération du 19 novembre 1770."

with paying nobles of sufficiently ancient lineage to enter the officer corps themselves, as well as *anoblis* (those who had recently entered the nobility by purchasing ennobling offices) and bourgeois. Only the royal scholarship students, however, were assured commissions upon graduation. While the paying students of the nobility could take up military careers if they secured commissions on their own, none was ever named to the officer corps by virtue of having graduated from a military school.[38] This distinction underlines the fundamental purpose of royal military education: to give poorer nobles from military families the institutional support, financial means, and preparation necessary to pursue military careers. A system of affirmative action for disadvantaged members of the military nobility, Old Regime military education was intended to restore within the officer corps the equality of opportunity on which meritocratic competition rested.

Against luxury and lucre: Belle-Isle, Choiseul, and Saint-Germain, 1758–77

The creation of the Ecole royale militaire was intended to counteract the ill-effects that inequalities of wealth were having on the cohesion of the nobility and the composition of the officer corps. But during the course of the Seven Years' War, the army leadership became convinced that military schooling alone was not having the desired effect. The Marshal de Belle-Isle, named war minister in 1758, was determined to free the officer corps from the corrosive grip of wealth. He believed that the influence of money over recruitment and advancement was responsible for unmerited promotions, discouragement, premature retirements, and the infiltration of parvenus into the officer corps "to the prejudice of the nobility."[39] To halt these fatal trends, Belle-Isle increased the pay of subaltern officers, attempted to curtail the illegal sale of commissions by unscrupulous colonels, and sought to abolish *concordats* (unofficial regimental retirement funds formed from contributions levied on the younger officers).[40] But Belle-Isle took no action against two other venal institutions – the private administration of companies by their captains and the purchase system of the cavalry and Maison militaire – which were no less destructive of meritocracy. The Marshal was pessimistic about the prospects of insulating the military from the ambient venal ethos of society.

---

38 A.G. Y^{a}157, "Résultat des observations du chevalier de Reynaud après l'inspection des 12 Ecoles royales militaires réparties dans les différentes provinces du royaume à l'époque du premier octobre 1783."

39 A.G. A^{1}3510, "Lettre circulaire adressée à Messieurs les colonels d'infanterie par M. le maréchal de Belle-Isle" (March 1758).

40 The best description of these practices is found in Louis Tuetey, *Les Officiers sous l'ancien régime: nobles et roturiers* (Paris, 1908), 129–74.

"It is not the work of a day," he wrote in late 1758, "and I am very old."[41] When he died in January 1761, money still played a critical role in military careers; his vision of a Spartan officer corps purged of corrupting luxury and lucre had not yet been realized.

His successor, the duc de Choiseul, did not hesitate, however, to take up this challenge. Already as a colonel in the War of Austrian Succession, Choiseul had become convinced that the army needed reform. Commanding a regiment at the Battle of Dettingen in 1743, he had been shocked by the headlong flight of panicked French troops, including the prestigious household regiment of French Guards.[42] This first-hand experience of the disastrous consequences of French "indiscipline and ignorance," he recalled later, was "one of the principal motives that convinced me to propose to the King the changes in his military that I executed in 1763."[43] No mere technical adjustment, according to the Marshal de Broglie, Choiseul's reforms "changed everything."[44] Thousands of officers were demobilized, regulations were rewritten, a permanent regimental structure (France's first) was established, and a centralized system of personnel records was instituted. The most important change was the assumption by the state of the administrative responsibilities previously borne by the captains, an unprecedented extension of central control over one of the weightiest items in the military budget.[45] The cost of this particular reform, undertaken at a time when the army was already the largest object of government expenditure and warfare the principal source of its ballooning debt, indicates the lengths to which Choiseul was prepared to go to restore French military power.[46]

By transferring to the state the administrative responsibilities of the company commanders, the captains, Choiseul sought not only to improve logistics, which had often broken down during the war, but also to ameliorate the composition and spirit of the officer corps by making considerations of personal wealth irrelevant to advancement. Private administration by the captains had been a heavy burden for many, even in peacetime. Under this system, one inspector-general reported, captains "lived in fear of being ruined, [and] were forced to go into debt to maintain their company."[47] Another inspector-general charged that the expense of

---

41 A.G. A¹3487, "Lettre de Belle-Isle au comte d'Affry" (21 November 1758).
42 For a probing analysis of the rout of French troops at the Battle of Dettingen, see Jean Chagniot, "Une panique: les gardes françaises à Dettingen (27 juin 1743)," *Revue d'histoire moderne et contemporaine*, 24 (1977), 78–95.
43 *Mémoires du duc de Choiseul*, ed. Fernand Calmettes (Paris, 1904), 10.
44 A.G. MR 1907, "Mémoire par M. le maréchal de Broglie" (n.d.).
45 For a full discussion, see my article "Noble Privilege and Absolutist State Building: French Military Administration after the Seven Years' War," *French Historical Studies*, 24 (2001), 223–46.
46 On the financial impact of the Seven Years' War, see James Riley, *The Seven Years War and the Old Regime in France: The Economic and Financial Toll* (Princeton, 1986).
47 A.G. MR 1712, Puységur, "Recrues." (n.d.).

wartime administration left captains so "exhausted" that they had to resign, forcing the army to accept as replacements "whatever mediocre subjects present themselves."[48] Professional standards declined, and the resulting mix of social types accentuated demoralizing inequalities of wealth within the officer corps. By ending this situation, Choiseul's nationalization of unit administration was intended in part to revitalize the officer corps by reinforcing its noble character.

Under the old system, captains had to dip deeply into personal and family resources to meet the demands of private administration. The case of Jacques de Mercoyrol de Beaulieu, an infantry officer during the War of Austrian Succession, illustrates the dependence of captains on support from family and friends.[49] When offered a captaincy if he would raise his own company, Beaulieu hesitated. Although he yearned for advancement, his family's financial situation gave him pause.

> I reflected on the position of my father, mother, and grandmother, whose income together amounted to less than 600 *livres*. The expenses of my three previous campaigns had [already] cost them 3,000 *livres*. I saw that it would be almost impossible for them to come to my aid.

After further consideration, however, Beaulieu finally decided to accept the offer because he realized that an admission of financial incapacity would "singularly hold back" his future advancement. After receiving the paltry sum of 300 *livres*, the only advance provided him by the state, Beaulieu set off for his home in the Vivarais. His parents lost no time finding recruits for their son: three young men who, as children, had played at soldiering under Beaulieu's command. Eventually four other men who had "served" in Beaulieu's boyhood company would "realize under [him], in a very real career, the games of [their] childhood." These seven men, along with twenty-five others, had to be paid enlistment bounties, horses and mules had to be purchased, and other equipment had to be obtained. In addition, Beaulieu needed a cash reserve for the upcoming campaign. To raise this money, his parents tapped into their own resources. His mother liquidated a 2,000 *livre* investment she had placed with the seminary of Viviers, and his father prepared to sell some land. But Beaulieu could not bear to see his patrimony alienated and persuaded his father to back out of the sale. Instead, he convinced his mother to furnish an additional 1,000 *livres* from her dowry. Thanks to his family's sacrifices, Beaulieu was able to return to the army two months later, leading the thirty-two men of his company, two horses, and two mules.

---

[48] A.G. MR 1708, comte de Bombelles, "Mémoire contenant les moyens de remédier aux défauts qui se trouvent dans le corps de l'infanterie françoise et de le porter au plus haut point de perfection" (10 November 1756).

[49] This paragraph is based on Jacques de Mercoyrol de Beaulieu, *Campagnes*, ed. le marquis de Vogüé and Auguste le Sourd (Paris, 1915), 72–82.

The cost of maintaining an established company was also substantial. Captains received a stipend to equip, lodge, and recruit their companies. Under ideal circumstances – peace, no desertion, no death of men or horses, no loss of equipment, and cheap supplies – a captain might even be able to pocket a small surplus from this sum. But in wartime, battle loss, wastage, and inflated prices could spell financial ruin for impecunious captains. The baron de Castelnau, a captain in the prestigious Carabinier regiment, had to spend 3,500 *livres* of his own money to "repair saddles and arms, look after sick horses, exercise the *carabiniers*, and keep accounts in order" during the last three campaigns of the Seven Years' War.[50] Captain d'Argenlieu of the French Guards regiment had to pay a total of 10,000 *livres* in bounties to 144 recruits to keep his company up to strength during the war.[51]

To minimize costs, some captains attempted to cut corners. It was notorious that many kept their companies under strength in order to reduce the costs of recruiting and providing for their troops. They also economized by purchasing substandard horses, equipment, and provisions. Yet, this was difficult in garrison towns where high demand drove up prices. To counter this, some captains dispersed their soldiers in rural communities; closer to the sources of food and fodder, companies distributed throughout the villages of a region were less expensive to maintain. But rural quartering reduced a company's combat effectiveness by making it impossible to train as a unit.[52] Some captains were even suspected of shunning combat to avoid the cost of replacing men, horses, and equipment lost in battle.[53] Forcing captains to choose between financial disaster and the neglect of their professional duties, private administration set up a conflict between the officers' self-interest and the good of the service. Choiseul ended this situation. By transferring administrative responsibilities to the state, he made it possible for poorer military nobles to serve without fear of ruining themselves. And by giving the state a free hand in matters of officer recruitment, Choiseul's reform was the precondition for the genealogical exclusions implemented by subsequent ministries.

Choiseul's disgrace and fall from power had little effect on military reform policy. In fact, the drive to create a more Spartan officer corps gained momentum

---

50 "Lettre à M. le baron de Gaïx, fils, commissaire des guerres à Bareges" (23 October 1762), in *Lettres du baron de Castelnau, officier de carabiniers, 1728–1793*, ed. le baron de Blay de Gaïx (Paris, 1911), 211.
51 Corvisier, *L'Armée française de la fin du XVIIème siècle*, vol. 1, 305–6.
52 A.G. MR 1725, comte de Chabo, "Mémoire sur la cavalerie" (1778); A.G. A^{1}3720, duc de Castries, "Mémoire sur la propriété des compagnies au Roi ou aux capitaines de ses troupes" (1780); and A.G. MR 1727, "Mémoire pour la cavalerie" (n.d.).
53 A.G. MR 1725, marquis d'Escouloubres, "Projet sur la cavalerie" (4 December 1760).

during the 1770s, particularly with the comte de Saint-Germain's nomination as war minister in 1775. From an undistinguished noble family, Saint-Germain had spent most of his sixty-eight years as a soldier. He had many campaigns to his credit, in both French and allied armies, and had even carried out a major military reorganization during a brief stint as war minister of Denmark. As a combat-tested career soldier, the new minister reportedly enjoyed the "fanatical" support of the junior officers, but counted "very few friends" among the generals.[54] Saint-Germain did not disappoint the army's expectations (and fears) of thoroughgoing reform. Aided by a group of brilliant young reformers – including Guibert, the artillery specialist Gribeauval, the sometime philosopher Jaucourt, and several other commanders who had won their spurs in the Seven Years' War – he dedicated his ministry to the extirpation of luxury, favoritism, and social privilege from the military profession.

Saint-Germain is best remembered for launching a frontal attack against the purchase system, which still subsisted in the cavalry. In his view, nothing was "more contrary to the good of the service, discipline, and *émulation*" than the sale of rank. Purchase not only introduced a mercantile spirit into the army, but also made it impossible to give poor, deserving officers the advancement they had "merited by their distinguished services."[55] Saint-Germain's assessment was shared by numerous military reformers. According to one anonymous complaint, the high cost of cavalry captaincies (10,000 *livres*) forced poor officers "to languish in the subaltern grades" where they found themselves "subordinated to people whose sole advantage consists in their fortune." The result was to foster "jealousy, disunity, [and] misunderstanding" throughout the entire branch.[56] But despite the obvious disadvantages of the purchase system, the chronic financial distress of the monarchy made it difficult to eliminate. The state had always relied on the captains' personal credit – credit backed by the property of their military charges – to help carry the cavalry through the inevitable breakdown of logistics in wartime. The Marshal de Castries, then commander of the Gendarmerie (a prestigious mounted unit whose soldiers all enjoyed officer rank in the line army), reluctantly recognized that "to deprive [the king] of ... the credit of the captains would take from him a precious resource" that could not be replaced. He estimated that, in the course of the Seven Years' War, cavalry captains borrowed more than two million *livres* against the collateral represented by their companies.[57] Also militating against the

---

54 Pierre-Victor, baron de Besenval, *Mémoires*, ed. M. F. Barrière (Paris, 1846), 221.
55 *Ordonnance du roi, portant suppression de la finance de tous les emplois militaires* ... (25 March 1776).
56 A.G. MR 1727, "Mémoire concernant la cavalerie et les dragons" (n.d.).
57 A.G. A^{1}3720, Castries, "Mémoire sur la propriété des compagnies au Roi ou aux capitaines de ses troupes" (1780).

suppression of venality was the realization that it would require reimbursing the sums invested in the charges, a financial burden the Crown could not afford. But Saint-Germain was not a man to let financial considerations stand in the way of military regeneration. Since the charges could not be liquidated all at once, Saint-Germain ruled that their price would be reduced by one-quarter upon each change of ownership so that their value would be extinguished at the fourth transaction.[58] Although this regulation seems to have been carried out, unlike other Old Regime schemes for abolishing venality, its staged execution ensured that nearly 50,000,000 *livres* still remained tied up in various military charges in 1791.[59]

Saint-Germain also attacked another source of venality by consolidating the numerous parade-ground units which comprised the Maison militaire du roi. Numbering nearly 10,000 men, the Maison militaire was charged with guarding the royal family and providing a proper sense of grandeur at the Court. With the exception of the Gendarmerie, the Grenadiers à cheval (Horse Grenadiers), and the common soldiers of the guards regiments, the Maison militaire was composed of nobles, new as well as old, and generally wealthy. Saint-Germain had a low opinion of their military worth. Having panicked during the War of Austrian Succession, the Maison militaire had been kept out of combat altogether during the Seven Years' War. It had become a social, rather than a military, elite. But despite its lack of real service, it still received preferential treatment. In most units of the Maison militaire, the soldiers enjoyed officer rank in the regular army. Their officers, often Court nobles who had purchased their charges at prices up to 500,000 *livres*, possessed exalted rank in the line. For example, lieutenants in the Gendarmerie had to pay 120,000 *livres* for their places and, in return, were considered the equivalent of colonels in the line army.[60] Softened by easy living at Versailles, the personnel of the Maison militaire were not only believed to lack martial capacity, but also blamed for introducing luxury, intriguing, and division into the officer corps.[61] Accordingly, Saint-Germain sought to disband five units (the Gendarmes de la garde (Gendarmes of the Guard), Chevau-légers (Light Horse), Mousquetaires (Musketeers), Grenadiers à cheval, and Gendarmerie) and downsize a sixth, the Gardes du corps (Royal Bodyguard). This would have eliminated the positions of about 2,700 men of officer rank. In the end, however, a more modest plan was forced on the minister. Only the Mousquetaires and

---

[58] *Ordonnance du roi, portant suppression de la finance de tous les emplois militaires* ... (25 March 1776).
[59] Félix de Wimpfen, "Rapport du comité militaire sur le remboursement des charges, offices, et emplois militaires" (17 March 1791), *Archives parlementaires de 1787 à 1860* (hereafter *A.P.*), ed. J. Madival and E. Laurent (Paris, 1867–1913), vol. 24, 157–67.
[60] A.G. Y^{a}309, "Etat des officiers supérieurs de la Gendarmerie susceptible par leurs services d'être faits colonels à la suite des régiments" (11 March 1788).
[61] Saint-Germain, *Mémoires*, 134.

Grenadiers à cheval were disbanded, while the Gardes du corps were slightly reduced, eliminating only 750 places conferring officer rank.[62] While promising important savings, cost-cutting was not Saint-Germain's primary reason for pruning these Court units; indeed, in the short term, reimbursement of the suppressed charges cost between four and six million *livres*. The real benefit Saint-Germain expected from the cutbacks was to rid the army of its most unmilitary institutions and the opulent officers they contained.

Equality through exclusion: Saint-Germain and Ségur, 1775–87

In mounting a direct attack on the Maison militaire, Saint-Germain had crossed an important threshold. The elimination and reduction of its units had aimed not only at checking the spread of their venal ethos into the line army, but also at curbing the professional privileges of a previously sacrosanct group, the "upper" or "Court" nobility. Although of impeccable lineage, a distressing number of these noble elites were considered to lack real dedication to their military duties. Thanks to their great wealth, illustrious pedigrees, and sterling social connections, these favorites could take their advancement for granted and, consequently, did not always feel the need to work at their profession. This situation was thought to have a doubly pernicious effect on military effectiveness. The usurpations of the Court nobility not only burdened the army with poor leadership at the highest levels, but also (and perhaps more importantly) spread demoralization throughout the ranks of the junior officers who, lacking the same advantages, saw themselves condemned to stagnate in the lower grades. If military spirit were to be revived and striving rekindled, these inequalities between nobles would have to be evened out. Only then could merit be restored as the basis of advancement. This task would occupy military reformers until 1789 and, as we shall see in the following chapter, even beyond.

The centerpiece of Saint-Germain's efforts in this regard was the creation of a comprehensive system of advancement, the first in French history to subject the careers of all officers, regardless of their status within the nobility, to the same rigorous standards. At the base of the hierarchy, Saint-Germain established the position of *cadet-gentilhomme* (a gentleman cadet) in which all new officers would be required to undergo the same professional novitiate.[63] One per company,

---

62 *Ordonnance du Roi, pour la suppression des deux compagnies des mousquetaires de la garde du roi* (15 December 1775); *Ordonnance du roi, pour réformer la compagnie des grenadiers à cheval* (15 December 1775); and *Ordonnance du roi, pour la nouvelle composition des compagnies des gardes-du-corps de sa majesté* (15 December 1775). See also Albert Latreille, *L'Œuvre militaire de la Révolution: l'armée et la nation à la fin de l'ancien régime* (Paris, 1914), 74–6.

63 Unless otherwise indicated, all citations in this paragraph are from the *Ordonnance du roi, portant création des cadets-gentilshommes dans les troupes de sa majesté* (25 March 1776).

these positions were to be a "school of obedience" intended to provide a practical apprenticeship. Under the supervision of a veteran officer and the regimental chaplain, the *cadets* were to spend at least one year mastering the duties of soldiers and non-commissioned officers before receiving their officers' commissions. Living together and wearing the uniform of common soldiers, they were to imbibe the spirit of frugality Saint-Germain wanted to instill in the entire officer corps. He particularly stressed the importance of "not permitting any distinctions of wealth to raise some above the equality that should reign among them." Places of *cadet-gentilhomme* were principally destined for military nobles – scholarship students of the provincial military schools and colonels' nominees, who were required to be "born noble." There was one significant exception to this rule. Colonels could also nominate non-nobles whose fathers had been superior officers (major or above), or who had been captains decorated with the Cross of Saint-Louis (awarded for long service or heroism in battle). This exception illustrates the thrust of Saint-Germain's reforms: in the army, military should take precedence over social factors. "In all cases," he wrote, "the good of the service should come before all other considerations."[64]

This aim informed the provisions for advancement from the positions of *cadet-gentilhomme* through the officer corps.[65] Under the new system, seniority became the basis of promotion. Slowly but surely, most officers would advance in this way through the rank of captain. There, most of their careers would come to an end, but at least they would no longer be halted as lieutenants because of poverty or lack of connections. As always, a few senior captains of superior merit would be promoted to major or lieutenant-colonel, and some might even be named to higher ranks if deemed worthy. The order of seniority was to be set aside only in favor of officers who had demonstrated outstanding "activity, zeal, application, and intelligence." But to prevent this facility from being abused to award undeserved promotion to "young men of quality," he established a series of safeguards. First, he instituted minimum service requirements – fourteen years for promotion to colonel, even if they were "of the most distinguished birth" – to ensure that candidates for regimental command possessed sufficient experience. Second, to "guarantee impartiality" in the granting of extraordinary advancement, Saint-Germain reorganized the regimental administrative councils and gave them the power to veto propositions for accelerated promotion. Composed of the lieutenant-colonel, major, and senior captain (presumably veteran officers of middling nobility), the administrative council was expected to block unmerited nominations and protect the rights of seniority.

---

64 Saint-Germain, *Mémoires*, 121–2.
65 *Ordonnance du roi portant règlement sur l'administration de tous les corps* (25 March 1776). All citations in this paragraph are from this source.

To the greatest extent possible, Saint-Germain tried to impose the same Spartan standard of conduct on all officers, regardless of their wealth or social status. A military man, wrote the minister, "should be sober, harden himself to work and to pain, and accustom himself to all sorts of privations."[66] Accordingly, Saint-Germain enacted a strict code of professional behavior.[67] He required officers to remain with their units during their period of service. Those employed in diplomacy, or in other high positions which prevented them from residing with the army, would be replaced. Colonels and generals were directed to live more frugally; henceforth, their meals were to be served "militarily, ... without ostentation, without profusion" and always without "the luxury of novelties." Officers were prohibited from gambling, contracting debts, and appearing out of uniform. Wealthy officers were ordered not to spend more than their pay to avoid "humiliating their comrades." The new martial ideal was applied to the common soldier as well. Soldiers were subjected to a tough disciplinary regime, backed by the threat of a new punishment inspired by the Prussian example: blows from the flat of a sword. Saint-Germain even contemplated making soldiers enroll for life. Civil society may have been sunk in idleness and luxury, but the minister was determined to isolate the army and make it "the ornament and model of the nation."[68]

Saint-Germain soon came under fire from those who felt that his reforms had succeeded all too well in imposing a tough, uniform standard on all officers. They claimed he had created a professional framework which forced together the rich and poor, the Court and provincial nobles, to the detriment of each group. "A military system obliging all classes of the nobility ... to follow the same route and occupy the same places," wrote one critic (significantly, a supernumerary colonel), "would only disgust the group whose wealth allows it to serve the king, not less usefully, but more comfortably and agreeably." Instead of "adapting his military ideas to our national spirit," Saint-Germain had "employed every means to change it."[69] Hardly any of the minister's reforms escaped the charge of contradicting French character and custom. Saint-Germain's creation of new administrative councils was compared to Maupeou's suppression of the *parlements* (the provincial supreme courts, subordinate in their jurisdiction only to the King) in 1771; the resulting reduction in the

---

66 Saint-Germain, *Mémoires*, 122–5.
67 This was incorporated into the *Ordonnance du roi portant règlement sur l'administration* (25 March 1776). Unless otherwise indicated, citations in this paragraph are from this source.
68 A.G. MR 1714, "Extrait de quelques manuscrits de M. le comte de Saint-Germain" (n.d.).
69 A.G. MR 1714, Scallier, "Mémoire sur les changements introduits par le comte de Saint-Germain dans notre constitution militaire" (25 December 1777). The type of officer Saint-Germain would not have respected, Jean-Baptiste Petel de Scallier was a supernumerary colonel with the rank of *maréchal de camp* in 1789. Churchill, *Etat militaire*, vol. 1, 274.

colonels' authority was condemned as nothing less than an attempt by the war minister to impose his "despotic will" over the army.[70] The disbanding of units in the Maison militaire was attacked for eliminating places needed by the nobility and, consequently, for burdening the line army with a crowd of underemployed, high-ranking officers.[71] Other commentators argued that the duties of the *cadets-gentilshommes* were so onerous that wealthy nobles would avoid the army.[72] Even one of Saint-Germain's closest collaborators, the baron de Wimpfen, felt that the new residency and service requirements were inappropriate for the French nobility, which needed time to manage its estates and attend to its affairs.[73] But of all the reforms, it was the "Prussian" method of corporal punishment, blows from the flat of a sword, that elicited the greatest outcry. To men like the baron de Besenval, the courtier general commanding the Swiss Guards of the Maison militaire, Saint-Germain's introduction of a "servile discipline impossible in France" betrayed a dangerous determination to bend the French army to an alien ideal.[74] In the end, Saint-Germain's ministry succumbed. Stung by the criticism and suffering from ill-health, he resigned in September 1777. Although his brief ministry failed to accomplish all of its aims, Saint-Germain nonetheless blazed the trail for the last military reformers of the Old Regime.

While Saint-Germain's fall from power set back the cause of reform, the appointment of the marquis de Ségur to the ministry in 1780 revitalized the movement. Committed to the same Spartan ideal as Saint-Germain, Ségur had the foresight to seek subtler ways of achieving his goals. From one of the most illustrious military dynasties in France, Ségur represented the third consecutive generation of his family to hold the rank of lieutenant-general. He had naturally enjoyed brilliant advancement, beginning as his father's *aide de camp* during the War of Austrian Succession before taking command of his family's regiment at the age of nineteen. Yet Ségur was no dilettante soldier. Seriously wounded in the chest, he recovered and returned to the army only to have his arm shot off by a cannonball.[75] While no stranger to Versailles, Ségur, like Saint-Germain, was first and foremost an experienced military professional. He entered the ministry not to undo Saint-Germain's work, but to extend it by

---

70 A.N. AF IV 1115 "Mémoire sur la constitution militaire des troupes et sur les ordonances militaires en 1776" (25 September 1776).
71 A.G. MR 1714, marquis de Toulongeon, "Réflexions sur l'état actuel du militaire au mois de novembre 1777."
72 A.G. MR 1714, Scallier, "Mémoire sur les changements ..."
73 Félix-Louis, baron de Wimpfen, *Commentaires des mémoires de M. le comte de Saint-Germain* (London, 1780), 152.
74 Besenval, *Mémoires*, 220.
75 Latreille, *L'Œuvre militaire*, 171.

making "ameliorations and clarifications."[76] He began by belatedly achieving one of Saint-Germain's unrealized goals: the formation of a permanent military committee. Composed of twenty inspector-generals, four lieutenant-generals, and one marshal of France, the formation of the committee was intended to give the military profession control over its own composition and structure. Ségur directed it to draft a comprehensive "military constitution" and oversee its execution.[77] Regularly consulting Saint-Germain's papers, Ségur and the committee would pursue the old minister's vision of a trim, functional military during the next four years.

Although they addressed a wide range of issues, their work centered on improving the composition and spirit of the officer corps. To keep out aspirants presumed to lack the proper background and motivation, they enacted new admissions criteria designed to reserve commissions for the sons of officers. Unveiled on 22 May 1781, the infamous Ségur regulation, which required aspirants to prove four generations of patrilineal noble descent, was a major step toward the creation of an officer corps recruited exclusively from military families. Although it was approved without comment by the military committee and provoked no discernible public outcry at the time, it was reviled in 1789 as a symbol of aristocratic privilege.

Until recently, historians shared the revolutionaries' view of the regulation, considering it evidence of an "aristocratic reaction" against the rising bourgeoisie.[78] But by the mid-1970s, at the height of the "revisionist" reappraisal of the Revolution's social origins, this interpretation began to be questioned. Why was such a high genealogical barrier needed to exclude *roturiers* when simple proof of nobility would have sufficed? And, since non-nobles had almost never been able to secure commissions, why were formal genealogical filters necessary at all? In a landmark article published in 1974, David D. Bien answered these questions.[79] He demonstrated that the Ségur regulation was not an example of "aristocratic reaction," but rather a professionalizing measure motivated by the same logic as was driving the broader movement of postwar French military reform. Bien showed that the Ségur regulation was not directed

---

76 Bibliothèque du Ministère de la guerre (hereafter B.M.G.), Archives historiques supplémentaires, 173–6, "Procès-verbaux du code militaire" (hereafter P.V.), "Délibération du 1er mars 1781."
77 The inspectors were Murinais, Du Lau, Livron, Ray, Jaucourt, Jumilhac, Haussonville, Vibray, Autichamp, Lambert, Ayen, Guines, Esterhazy, Salis, Cely, Narbonne, Brissac, Talleyrand, Crenolles, and Arcambal. The lieutenant-generals were Puységur, Besenval, Du Châtelet, and Caraman. The *maréchal de France* was Contades.
78 André Corvisier, "Hiérarchie militaire et hiérarchie social à la veille de la Révolution," *Revue internationale d'histoire militaire*, 30 (1970), 77–91; Latreille, *L'Œuvre militaire*, 181–8; Georges Six, "Fallait-il quatre quartiers de noblesse pour être officier à la fin de l'ancien régime?," *Revue d'histoire moderne*, 4 (1929), 46–55; and Tuetey, *Les Officiers*, 181–224.
79 Bien, "La Réaction aristocratique avant 1789," 23–48, 505–34.

against the bourgeoisie, but rather against non-military members of the nobility itself, principally the recently ennobled who were thought to lack the martial predispositions associated with upbringing in a military family. In his view, the regulation expressed a "specifically military movement of reaction against other fractions of the nobility," a professionalizing movement within the army rather than a noble counteroffensive against upwardly mobile commoners. In fact, the Ségur regulation actually made it easier for non-nobles to enter the officer corps. Whereas only the sons of high-ranking *roturier* officers decorated with the Cross of Saint-Louis had been previously exempted from making proofs of nobility, the Ségur regulation extended this privilege to the sons of all *roturier* officers with the Cross, regardless of their rank. This change underlined the aim of the Ségur regulation: to recruit officers from military families.

More controversial at the time was Ségur's attempt to adopt a mode of advancement capable of reconciling the inevitable privileges of the upper nobility with the military's need to ensure equality of opportunity and promote merit. Like many reformers, Ségur felt that Saint-Germain had erred in trying to force all officers into the same career path without regard for their social differences. Military institutions had to take into account the peculiarities of French social structure, he believed, in order "to profit from all of our means."[80] According to the minister, the officers were divided into two classes. First, there was the "upper nobility," a group "destined to occupy high positions." Although it was necessary to prepare them for their future duties, their early instruction should not be too burdensome, nor should it unduly delay their advancement. The second group, more numerous, was composed of the "middling nobility." The most these officers could expect was to finish their careers as captains or, exceptionally, lieutenant-colonels. While there was no "precise line of demarcation" between these groups, they were nonetheless "very distinct." Ségur believed that each class could be made to serve more usefully if "distributed in the military in an order more analogous to the places they occupied in civil society." Rather than directly confront inequalities between nobles, Ségur proposed "to establish more methodically what already exists."[81] Rather than pursuing the doomed course of trying to legislate social inequality out of the military profession, Ségur was determined to "anticipate this eternally reborn irregularity" and harness it by "tracing for the different classes an order of advancement relative to their position and means."

Ségur presented to the committee plans for "a double system of advancement" suited to each class of officer. The upper nobility would advance in a distinct path from the new grade of supernumerary second lieutenant through

---

80 B.M.G. P.V., "Délibération du 10 avril 1782." Unless otherwise indicated, all citations from this and the following paragraph are from this source.
81 B.M.G. P.V., Ségur's undated response to the committee's objections.

those of captain-in-second, major-in-second, and colonel-in-second before arriving at the coveted position of full colonel. Officers favored by particularly "high birth" or "the distinguished services of their fathers" could be promoted directly from captain-in-second to colonel-in-second, while others "cast into this route by great wealth alone" would not be allowed to advance beyond the grade of major-in-second. These supernumerary and "in-second" personnel would perform only limited service – generally four months per year – and receive only minimal pay. Promotion would be at the king's discretion, making it possible to select the most promising officers for rapid promotion while leaving the others to stagnate in these functionless ranks. In contrast, the second track offered good pay, responsibility, and steady (but slow) advancement to the middling nobility. Officers in this track were to advance automatically by seniority through the core grades of second lieutenant, lieutenant, captain, major, and lieutenant-colonel. Described by Ségur as the only grades "essential to and inherent in the [military] constitution," his plan of advancement effectively reserved these critical positions for the presumably more professional middling nobility. Spared the frustration of unequal competition for advancement with their social betters, officers in the slow track would regain hope and *émulation* would revive. Similarly, officers in the fast track would find themselves in competition with their social equals and, realizing that they could no longer expect easy promotion, would strive harder. A system for creating equality within functionally distinct and socially segregated subgroups within the officer corps, two-track advancement would satisfy the upper nobility's desire for elevated rank, purify the composition of officers in the core positions, and stimulate *émulation* throughout the hierarchy.

Although Ségur assured the committee that his plan did not "draw an absolute line of demarcation between the two classes," the committee was unconvinced. It protested that, far from motivating the officers, two-track advancement would quench their remaining *émulation*.[82] In an officer corps already demoralized by inequalities between nobles, warned the committee, the imposition of formal distinctions could only cause further, possibly irreparable, damage. By openly abandoning the ideal of noble equality, the plan would consecrate the division between the rich and poor, the influential and obscure, and reduce the officer corps to a permanent state of internal strife.

> It will cause a violent upheaval in opinions and will most likely stifle *émulation* which is founded on the possibility of all officers to accede to the highest grades and, in a certain fashion, confuse the consideration due to merit with that due to high birth and opulence ... If the great nobility ... ought to have assured advantages, if opulence

---

82 B.M.G. P.V., "Délibération du 17 avril 1782." Unless otherwise indicated, all citations in this paragraph are from this source.

should too ... then these distinctions should be observed in secret, in the king's cabinet. With nothing announced, no one will be discouraged or prideful; but this actual project would produce a very different effect.

The officers, proclaimed the committee, should form "only one corps" with one law for all, from the "highest lord" to a "student of the military school." Despite (or perhaps because of) Ségur's protestation that his plan only "transported into the military ... the differences which exist in the civil order," the committee maintained its stubborn opposition.[83] Although two-track advancement was defeated in 1782, Ségur did not renounce his views. As one of his last acts as minister, he would set in motion a chain of events that would ultimately lead to the adoption of two-track advancement and, as the committee feared, provoke a fatal split within the French nobility on the very eve of the French Revolution.

Guibert's War Council and the formal division of the nobility, 1787–89

After the dissolution of the war committee in 1784, Ségur bided his time, awaiting an occasion to revive his stalled reform program. That moment came three years later with the revelation of the kingdom's dire financial situation. In Ségur's eyes, the monarchy's crisis was the army's opportunity. Rather than viewing budget cuts as a threat to military effectiveness, Ségur believed that they could serve as a pretext for trimming fat – the Maison militaire, supernumerary officers, and other unmilitary personnel – from the army. To find ways to make fiscal disaster serve the cause of military regeneration, Ségur turned to Saint-Germain's former aid, the military writer Guibert, who also believed it possible to "ameliorate the military constitution and make economies" at the same time.[84] During the summer of 1787, he drafted plans for a new military committee, the War Council, and wrote a series of reports to guide its work.[85] Drawing on an idea dear to military reformers since the Seven Years' War, Guibert argued that only a council could "maintain the execution of laws, put a halt to the continual fluctuation of principles, put order and economy into expenditures, block the pretensions and demands of favoritism, and give the war department a constitution and base."[86] The Council's membership reflected the underlying coherence of prerevolutionary reform in the French army. Of its nine original members – Autichamp, Esterhazy, Fourcroy, Gribeauval, Guines, Jaucourt, Lambert, Puységur, and its secretary Guibert – all but the engineer Fourcroy had been associated with

83 B.M.G. P.V., Ségur's response to the committee's objections.
84 A.G. MR 1790, Guibert, "Instruction du roi pour le Conseil de guerre" (1787).
85 See my article, "Le Conseil de la guerre: aspects sociaux de la réforme militaire après l'édit de Ségur," *Revue d'histoire moderne et contemporaine*, 43 (1993), 446–63.
86 A.G. MR 1944, Guibert, "Mémoire de M. de Guibert sur l'établissement d'un Conseil de la guerre" (1787).

previous military committees.[87] Its principal accomplishments, the further reduction of the Maison militaire and the institution of a full-fledged system of two-track advancement, also placed the Council squarely within the reformist tradition.

Although Ségur resigned on 29 August 1787 in protest at the nomination of Loménie de Brienne as "principal minister," the cost-cutting Brienne looked favorably on Guibert's preparatory work and approved the formation of the proposed War Council on 9 October 1787. Even before its first meeting at the end of the month, Guibert secured the minister's permission to disband three units of the Maison militaire: the Gendarmes de la garde du roi, Chevau-légers, and Gardes de la porte du roi. These measures were only the prelude to a much larger program of reductions which would also encompass supernumerary and militia officers. In all, Guibert sought to eliminate the posts of nearly 5,000 subaltern and 300 superior officers. Although this vast project was eventually scaled down, the Council still managed to eliminate the posts of about 3,500 subaltern and 100 superior officers. The Council's actual reductions were over four times greater than Saint-Germain's had been.

Table 1.1 **Reductions planned by Guibert, autumn 1787**

Object of suppression or reduction	Subaltern officers	Superior officers
Chevau-légers (disbanded)	46	18
Gendarmes de la garde (disbanded)	46	18
Gardes de la porte (disbanded)	88	10
Gardes du corps du roi (reduced)	420	?
Gardes du corps des princes (reduced)	280	45
French Guards Regiment (reduced)	33	31
Supernumerary officers (dismissed)	2,424	0
The militia (disbanded)	1,625	164
Total reductions	4,962	286

Source: A.G. MR 1790, "Maison du roi"; "Mémoire concernant les gardes françaises"; "Première séance du conseil de la guerre, le 28 octobre 1787"; "Troisième mémoire: troupes provinciales"; A.G. Y^{b}76, "Contrôles de la compagnie des gendarmes de la garde"; A.G. Y^{a}250, "Etat de ce que coute annuellement la compagnie des gardes de la porte du roi"; A.G. Y^{a}242-8, "Gardes du corps"; A.G. Y^{b}25, "Registre des contrôles des gardes du corps du roi"; A.G. Y^{b}76, "Contrôles: gardes du corps des princes"; A.G. Y^{b}75, "Registre des contrôles de la Gendarmerie"; Y^{a}309, "Etat des officiers supérieurs de la gendarmerie susceptibles par leurs services d'être faits colonels à la suite des régiments"; Mémoire sur les troupes provinciales (Paris, 1790); and J. de la Trollière and R. de Montmort, *Les Chevau-légers de la Garde du roy* (Paris, 1953).

---

87 Gribeauval, Guines, Jaucourt, and Puységur had been designated for Saint-Germain's projected council. In the actual event, Guibert and Jaucourt had collaborated with Saint-Germain, and Autichamp, Esterhazy, Guines, Jaucourt, Lambert, and Puységur had sat on Ségur's war committee.

Table 1.2 **Reductions actually approved by the War Council**

Object of suppression or reduction	Subaltern officers	Superior officers
Chevau-légers (disbanded)	46	18
Gendarmes de la garde (disbanded)	46	18
Gardes de la porte (disbanded)	88	10
Gardes du corps du roi (reduced)	121	?
Gendarmerie (disbanded)	842	43
Supernumerary officers (dismissed)	2,424	0
Total reductions	3,567	89

Source: A.G. MR 1790, "Maison du roi"; "Mémoire concernant les gardes françaises"; "Première séance du conseil de la guerre, le 28 octobre 1787"; "Troisième mémoire: troupes provinciales"; A.G. Y^b76, "Contrôles de la compagnie des gendarmes de la garde"; A.G. Y^a250, "Etat de ce que coute annuellement la compagnie des gardes de la porte du roi"; A.G. Y^a242-8, "Gardes du corps"; A.G. Y^b25, "Registre des contrôles des gardes du corps du roi"; A.G. Y^b76, "Contrôles: gardes du corps des princes"; A.G. Y^b75, "Registre des contrôles de la Gendarmerie"; Y^a309, "Etat des officiers supérieurs de la gendarmerie susceptibles par leurs services d'être faits colonels à la suite des régiments"; Mémoire sur les troupes provinciales (Paris, 1790); and J. de la Trollière and R. de Montmort, *Les Chevau-légers de la Garde du roy* (Paris, 1953).

Although justified in the name of reducing expenditures, these drastic cuts were primarily intended as measures of military reform. They relieved pressure on the Crown's finances less than one might expect. By 1787 the monarchy's most pressing problem was the repayment of the high-interest, short-term loans taken out to finance intervention in the War of American Independence. Since the officers in the Maison militaire, as well as over 500 of the supernumeraries, had purchased their charges, the reductions actually exacerbated the problem of debt reimbursement. By eliminating these units and personnel, the monarchy theoretically had to return the capital invested in their charges, which would have added about 16,000,000 *livres* to the burden of debt liquidation. In fact, the monarchy put off reimbursing most of these charges and continued to pay the customary 5 percent interest on the principal which they represented. Although certain powerful nobles – such as the duc d'Aiguillon, captain of the Chevau-légers, and the prince de Guemenée, captain of the Gardes de la porte (Guards of the Gate, a small unit in the royal household troops) – secured immediate repayment, most of the others kept receiving the standard interest payments. Thus, the Council's decision to disband units of the Maison militaire and cashier supernumerary officers in the regular army had a negligible effect on personnel expenditures. For example, disbanding the Gardes de la porte reduced government expenses by only 5,000 *livres* annually. The unit even offered to forgo this small sum and serve *gratis*, but the offer was refused.[88] The Council was more interested in eliminating the

---

[88] A.G. Y^a251, "Mémoire [du prince de Guemenée]."

officers in such units than in retaining their services at no cost. Fiscal crisis provided cover for undertaking professional improvements of an unprecedented scale and political sensitivity.

From its very first session, the Council revisited the controversial issue of two-track advancement. Its discussions resulted in the promulgation on 17 March 1788 of an ordinance on "the hierarchy of all military employments." Essentially the plan of advancement unsuccessfully proposed by Ségur, the law created two career paths, a rapid one for the "young men of the first nobility which [His Majesty] designates particularly for the places of colonel in his regiments," and a slower one for the other officers, which stopped short of the rank of colonel.[89] Appearing to graft social gradations onto the military hierarchy by institutionalizing the division of the nobility into upper and lower classes, the ordinance evoked from the officers "a wave of anger much more violent than anyone had foreseen."[90] Fifteen years later, General Mathieu Dumas recalled that two-track advancement had "not been one of the least causes of the Revolution of 1789."[91]

Historians have shared the army's view of two-track advancement as an "aristocratic reaction" of the Court nobility against the lower segment of their order.[92] A detailed examination of the plan, however, reveals that two-track advancement actually reserved most of the functional positions in the officer corps for the middling military nobility, expected to pursue their careers in the slow track. One entered this track either as a *cadet-gentilhomme*, at the nomination of the colonel, or as a second lieutenant, either at the nomination of the colonel or king. The colonels were directed to favor "the children, brothers, or nephews of former officers ... a precious type that [His Majesty] had in view in creating these places."[93] The king's nomination was reserved for the pages (who had to furnish proofs of nobility dating back to 1550) and scholarship students from the military schools. From these entry points one advanced by seniority to the rank of captain. Majors were chosen from veteran captains, and lieutenant-colonels from majors and the most senior captains. These superior officers were essential to the proper functioning of the regiment since the major oversaw discipline and instruction, and the lieutenant-colonel commanded in the colonel's

---

[89] *Ordonnance du roi, portant suppression de l'emploi de mestre-de-camp en second, ... et création de l'emploi du grade de major-en-second* (17 March 1788).

[90] Jean Egret, *La Pré-révolution française, 1787–1788* (Paris, 1962), 92–3.

[91] A.N. 138 AP 22, Mathieu Dumas, "Mémoire sur la formation, le service, et le môde d'avancement de l'état-major général" (11 Ventôse XIII).

[92] Louis Hartmann, *Les Officers de l'armée royale et la Révolution* (Paris, 1910), 33; Latreille, *L'Œuvre militaire*, 287; and Emile G. Léonard, *L'Armée et ses problèmes au XVIIIème siècle* (Paris, 1958), 287.

[93] *Ordonnance du roi, portant règlement sur la hiérarchie de tous les emplois militaires, ainsi que sur les promotions et nominations auxdits emplois* (17 March 1788).

absence. As colonels were frequently absent, sometimes for years on end, the lieutenant-colonels often ran the regiments. Thus, the slow track encompassed most positions of command and execution.

The Council expected some of the officers put out of work by its reduction of the Maison militaire to seek reemployment in the slow track. To keep out job-seekers who lacked real commitment to the military profession and shelter the career officers from increased competition for places, the Council built safeguards into the new system of advancement. It adopted seniority as the principle of promotion in the slow track. Seniority was an inflexible principle of promotion which neutralized the advantages of wealth and influence possessed by many of the ex-officers of the Maison militaire. Although seniority was thought to stifle meritocratic striving, the Council considered this an acceptable price to pay for the protection it would provide the line officers from the demoralizing effects of lopsided competition. The Council also raised other barriers against the gilded outsiders. Displaced officers who wanted to rebuild their careers in the line army would first have to find colonels to propose them for entry-level places. If they succeeded in this, they could not count previous service toward their seniority.[94] By reducing them to the level of beginners in the slow track, the ordinance discouraged officers from the disbanded Court units from pursuing military careers in the line. For those who attempted it, only persistence would secure their integration. The Council also tightened restrictions against other non-military types. Guibert believed that the recent exemption from genealogical proofs granted to the sons of officers with the Cross had opened a dangerous loophole. The exemption was well-meant, Guibert conceded, but "poorly understood and badly calculated" because it opened the officer corps to the wrong kind of people: "sons of *officiers de fortune* [non-noble soldiers promoted to officer rank after many years of service] who have remained mere lieutenants, *commissaires des guerres* [military administrators who, during the Old Regime, purchased their offices and often passed them down to their sons], retired *gendarmes*, *maréchaussée* [the rural mounted police of the Old Regime] officers, all people of a quite inferior *état* [a term combining the ideas of profession and social status]."[95] On Guibert's recommendation, the Council restored the narrower exemptions (for the sons of captains with the Cross) established by Saint-Germain.

If careers in the slow track were slow but sure, advancement in the fast track was rapid but uncertain. One entered the fast track by securing the king's nomination to a place of "replacement second lieutenant," reserved for "that portion of His nobility which is most particularly summoned to the command

---

94 A.G. MR 1790, Guibert, "Infanterie, première section: de l'avancement des officiers."
95 A.G. MR 1790, Guibert, "Première séance du Conseil de la guerre."

of regiments."⁹⁶ These unpaid officers were required to serve only five months each year. From there they could become "replacement captains," contingent on the king's nomination. The conditions of service for these officers were identical to those of replacement second lieutenants. As their name suggests, the "replacement" officers had no functions of their own, but were called on if needed to replace the regular officers. After five years (of which only 25 months were on active duty), a replacement captain could be named major-in-second. These officers, also held to only five months of annual service, formed the pool from which the king chose his colonels. Offering minimal activity in supernumerary grades, meager pay, rapid advancement for those fortunate enough to enjoy the king's favor, and stalled careers for the rest, a career in the fast track held out the prospect of professional privilege with minimal duties.

The lure of a brilliant career in the fast track was intended to segregate the courtiers from the rest of the officers and give the Council greater control over their advancement. Affixing the terms "upper nobility" and "first nobility" to the fast track attached to it a prestige that would irresistibly attract officers with pretensions to membership in the high aristocracy, especially the *présentés* who had always monopolized the highest ranks in the army. These included not only the most illustrious houses of France, but also favored new nobles more concerned about their social standing than military duties. Although presentation to the Court was restricted to those few families capable of meeting rigorous genealogical requirements (nobility dating back to 1400) that ought to have excluded all but the most ancient lineages, Court favorites lacking the proper pedigree were often granted this honor by royal dispensation. Of the 942 families that received the "honors of the Court" between 1760 and 1790, 462 escaped the full rigors of the regulation.⁹⁷ For the Council's purpose, the purification of the officer corps, presentation was worse than ineffective; it was a veritable conduit for wealth and influence.

The institution of presentation had created a pool of powerful parvenus who, although lacking the proper military background, nonetheless felt entitled to the highest military honors. In Guibert's estimation, it was the source of "all the prejudices and pretensions" undermining the officer corps.⁹⁸ By clustering the *présentés* in a distinct career track, the new system of advancement made it possible to make selections among them and ensure that only the right kind of aristocrats attained positions of responsibility in the army.

The crucial factors in making this determination were to be the past military services of the family and the personal capacity of the particular young man

---

96 *Ordonnance du roi, portant règlement sur la hiérarchie* ....
97 François Bluche, *Les Honneurs de la cour* (Paris, 1958).
98 A.G. MR 1790, Guibert, "Observations présentées à l'armée et au public sur les opérations du Conseil de la guerre" (1789).

under scrutiny. Majors-in-second were to be named with special attention to "their birth and above all the services of their fathers." Colonels were to be selected by the king from a list of majors-in-second ranked by the Council according to specifically military criteria.[99] The presented nobility

> not known for their distinguished service ... ought to expect that, on the one hand, their number having increased tremendously and still growing daily, and, on the other hand, His Majesty having the firm intention not to change the rules of promotion in the future, nor to augment in any manner the number of superior officer positions, may have to wait a long time in the rank of replacement captain.[100]

While any *gentilhomme* willing to accept the "risks and perils" could opt for the fast track, the Council only intended to promote those who joined solid military traditions and personal commitment to an illustrious name.

Although it reserved colonelcies for the upper nobility, the ordinance was not intended to limit the promotion of middling nobles; they had almost never been named to the rank of colonel anyway. If it kept the colonelcies for the upper nobility, it also reserved the lieutenant-colonelcies, regular majorities, and captaincies for the provincial nobility. This was the real purpose of two-track advancement. An overlooked passage in Guibert's public defense supports this hypothesis.

> Who cannot see that the charges of replacement captain and major-in-second are outside of the [military] constitution and, in a certain way, a compromise that had to be made with custom? Who cannot see that without these supplementary and, one must acknowledge, very unconstitutional positions, all the companies in the cavalry and all the charges of major and lieutenant-colonel [in the infantry] would have ended up in the hands of only five or six hundred families to the very great detriment of the army?[101]

The ordinance was intended to entrench the provincial nobility in the critical core positions in anticipation of the expected influx of outsiders from the abolished units of the Maison militaire. The Council feared that these unmilitary types would profit from their inflated equivalent ranks, wealth, and influence at Court to secure places in the line at the expense of the regular officers. This threatened to displace the dedicated officers of the middling nobility who were seen as essential to the proper functioning of the army. It would have also spread discouragement among those who remained by diminishing their career perspectives. Two-track advancement can be best understood as the Council's response

---

99 *Ordonnance du roy, portant règlement sur la hiérarchie* ....
100 A.G. MR 1790, Guibert, "Première séance du Conseil de la guerre ..."
101 A.G. MR 1790, Guibert, "Observations présentées à l'armée et au public ..."

to these eventualities. By offering the enticement of a special pathway for the upper nobility, the fast track would keep opulent nobles from competing for promotion with the provincial nobility, considered the backbone of the army.[102] And by dividing the upper nobility into a military and a non-military class, two-track advancement completed the "militarization" of the officer corps by extending the movement toward the formation of a military caste into the highest ranks of the officer corps and noble society. Although two-track advancement has been described as a capitulation to the courtiers, it was nothing of the kind. Its formulations in favor of the Court nobility were actually intended to demarcate and shield a distinctly military sub-caste within the larger nobility.

Although the Council was not a cipher for Court interests, most of the officer corps, angered at the distinctions consecrated by the new system of advancement, perceived it as such and reacted vehemently. In the face of massive opposition, the Council moved to modify the offending ordinance. From February 1789 until the suspension of its meetings on 14 July 1789, the Council spent most of its time working on "the revision of the ordinance on the hierarchy."[103] These efforts came too late. Letters of protest, pamphlets, and *cahiers de doléances* (grievance lists drafted in early 1789 in anticipation of the Estates-General) all condemned the Council for having "in violation of the constitutional laws of the kingdom, sought, by a ridiculous ordinance, to divide the ancient and respectable corps of the French nobility whose unity had always been recognized by our kings and the assembled nation."[104] The ordinance humiliated the subaltern officer, "a well-born man" who was "often worth more than his commander."[105] To officers, it revealed the extent of inequality and injustice in the kingdom.

> Only in France could aristocrats, blinded by the abuse of their credit, adopt such an unreasonable system ... [They] must attribute very passive ideas to that portion of the nobility which does not approach the Court, which is nonetheless the real base of the army, not to imagine how much it is disgusted.[106]

The officers' anger burst forth when Guibert stood for election from the Second Estate of the province of Berry in March 1789. When he rose to speak in the

---

102 The ordinance seems to have worked as intended. Of the twenty-seven officers of the Gendarmerie who asked to be placed in the regular army, all sought positions as majors-in-second or colonels. Six, with the rank of colonel or lieutenant-colonel, even accepted demotions to be named majors-in-second. None asked to be named to the slow track. A.G. Y^{a}309, "Etat des officiers supérieurs de la Gendarmerie ..."
103 A.G. A^{3}125, "Délibérations du Conseil de la guerre: procès-verbaux des séances du 5 novembre 1787 au 4 juillet 1789," "Séance du 4 juillet 1789."
104 *Vœux d'un citoyen pour le militaire françois* (n.p., n.d.).
105 *Lettre d'un citoyen à MM. du Conseil de la guerre* (1789).
106 *L'Armée française au Conseil de guerre* (1789).

assembly of his order at Bourges, Guibert was shouted down with cries of "he rendered the ordinances which humiliate the nobility," and was forced to retreat to the nearby cathedral.[107] The officers' mistaken interpretation of two-track advancement as the victory of unmerited privilege, yet another usurpation by the upper nobility, colored their perceptions of the regime and disposed them toward change on the eve of the Revolution.

107 Guibert, *Précis de ce qui s'est passé à mon égard à l'Assemblée du Berry* (1789).

2 The meanings of merit in 1789

The National Assembly's approach to the question of merit owed more to Old Regime precedents than generally assumed. While its solemn promise to admit all citizens "without distinction of birth, to all ecclesiastical, civil, and military employments" struck a fatal blow to the nobility's formal monopoly of direct officer commissions, this one declaration hardly exhausted the National Assembly's efforts to restructure the army along meritocratic lines. If we look beyond the radical decision to open careers to talent, it becomes clear that the Assembly's broader program of military reform, as well as the officers' response to it, was articulated within a conceptual framework inherited from the Old Regime. Interpreting the National Assembly's meritocratic pronouncements in the light of their own professional frustrations, noble officers embraced the Revolution. Discounting the possibility that it might imperil their own privileged access to military careers, they saw in the revolutionary promise of equality only the prospect of abolishing the upper nobility's monopoly of high rank. The National Assembly largely satisfied their expectations. Dominated by military noble deputies who had taken part in the Old Regime reform movement, the Assembly's military committee shared the officers' concerns. Neither ideological architects of revolutionary social engineering nor reactionary defenders of the military status quo, the committee believed that they could use revolutionary meritocracy to redress the officers' longstanding grievances. In many respects a prolongation of Old Regime military reform rather than a sharp break with the past, the committee's reforms were better suited to unshackling the advancement of subaltern officers than to opening military careers to non-nobles. It would be the soldiers' direct action, not official policy, that ultimately prised open the military profession and transformed the composition of the French officer corps.

Back to the future: the nobility's *cahiers de doléances*

The nobility's first opportunity to stake out a collective position on the terrain of military reform and merit came in early 1789, when the three estates assembled to draft their *cahiers de doléances* and elect delegates to the Estates-General. The French undertook these preparations with enthusiasm, confident that they stood on the verge of national regeneration. Like those of the other orders of society, the nobility's *cahiers* reflected its faith that the Estates-General would right all wrongs, whether great or small, universal or particular, and reestablish effective,

2 Address of the officers of the Forez Regiment to the National Assembly, October 1789, denouncing "aristocratic and ministerial despotism."

harmonious government. Calling for freedom of the press, trial by jury, and similar reforms, the nobility embraced – and, to a certain extent, led – the movement for a more liberal society.

Since the 1970s, most historians have recognized that the Second Estate welcomed change in 1789.[1] Many of these "revisionist" scholars have explained the nobility's progressive outlook as the result of greater contact with the upper echelons of the Third Estate and the absorption of its values.[2] Guy Chaussinand-Nogaret has advanced the strongest statements in this regard. In his book, *The French Nobility in the Eighteenth Century*, he argued that, from the 1760s, the nobility gave up its hereditary notions of social superiority and, instead, came to define itself in terms of merit. By 1789 "the collective value of the group had been abandoned." "Nobles now demanded recognition of their personal merit, put off the protective veil of ancestry, and, not without pride, offered themselves to the judgement and competition of the Third Estate."[3] Chaussinand-Nogaret explained this transformation as the result of greater contact between the upper nobility and upper bourgeoisie: in salons, at Court, in the counting house, and at the theater, these groups got to know each other and gradually became more and more alike. Intermarriage, particularly between the daughters of "plutocratic newcomers" and noble grandees, consolidated their assimilation and produced "a fused elite" (115). On the eve of the Revolution, he concluded, "the cultural unity of the elites was an established fact at the highest level" (77).

The *cahiers* on which Chaussinand-Nogaret based his argument are indeed full of meritocratic language.[4] But in attributing their authorship to the upper nobility, he misconstrues its meaning. Far from expressing the views of the cosmopolitan elite of Paris and Versailles, the *cahiers* reflect the grievances and aspirations of the group which actually dominated the assemblies of the Second Estate in most parts of France – the predominantly military nobility of the provinces. By granting full and direct participation to all French noblemen, the electoral regulation of 24 January 1789 consecrated the principle of "one man one vote" and thereby ensured that army officers would constitute the dominant

---

[1] By 1980 the notion of a liberal nobility had won such broad acceptance that William Doyle was able to describe it as a "new international consensus." Doyle, *Origins of the French Revolution* (1980 ed.), 24. This claim was dropped in later editions of the work.

[2] The first works to discuss the spread of "bourgeois" values to the nobility were Reinhard, "Elite et noblesse," 5–37; and Richet, "Autour des origines idéologiques," 1–23. The most elegant formulation of this position is found in Lucas, "Nobles, Bourgeois, and the Origins of the French Revolution," 84–126. The extent of the nobility's liberalism in 1789 has recently been questioned, however, by Tackett in *Becoming a Revolutionary*.

[3] Chaussinand-Nogaret, *The French Nobility in the Eighteenth Century*, 4. All citations in this paragraph are from this source. Page numbers are noted in parentheses.

[4] On meritocratic demands in the *cahiers*, see Gilbert Shapiro and John Markoff, *Revolutionary Demands: A Content Analysis of the Cahiers de Doléances of 1789* (Stanford, 1998).

professional group in most assemblies.⁵ I estimate that of the approximately 40,000 French adult male nobles who could have participated, roughly 25,000 (over 60 percent) were active or retired officers.⁶

By rereading the noble *cahiers* in the light of the divisive debate over merit which had been raging in the officer corps since the mid-eighteenth century, it becomes clear that, far from reflecting bourgeois ideals, the nobility's meritocratic discourse actually stemmed from conflict within the Second Estate itself. The middling nobility deployed meritocratic arguments to attack the privileges claimed by the very same elite described by Chaussinand-Nogaret, privileges underlined only one year earlier by the War Council's controversial ordinance on advancement. In their *cahiers* nobles railed against the "marked difference ... between the courtiers, or *présentés*, and the nobility which inhabits the provinces" (La Rochelle).⁷ Thinking of the places, pensions, and dignities monopolized by certain courtier dynasties, they even dared to attack distinctions based on birth. The nobles of Toul complained that "graces and honors have become the patrimony of certain families," those of Senlis attacked the advantages given "to a more ancient extraction," and those of Arras condemned "the heredity of charges ... in the same families."⁸ The Second Estate's *cahiers* also called for an end to the corrosive influence of wealth and favoritism. The nobles of Lyon implored the Estates-General "to prevent protection or money from taking precedence over merit and talents," and those of Vermandois demanded "that fortune, a great name (an effect of chance), and favoritism no longer exclude merit from honors, grades, and dignities."⁹ With their initial perception of the Revolution shaped by their ongoing socio-professional frustrations, the nobles saw the convocation of the Estates-General as an unprecedented opportunity to extirpate the inequalities undermining the unity of their corps and well-being of the military.

To combat illegitimate distinctions within their order, noble assemblies called for the restoration of internal equality on which, they believed, noble identity had once been based. According to their *cahiers*, the nobility was supposed to be "an essentially indivisible order whose members are all equal"

---

5 "Règlement général du 24 janvier 1789," *Recueil de documents relatifs à la convocation des états-généraux de 1789*, ed. Armand Brette (Paris, 1894), vol. 1, 66–87.
6 I arrived at the figure of 25,000 eligible army officers in the following way. In 1788 Guibert informed the War Council that there were 35,000 active and retired officers. Of these, 10 percent (3,500) were probably *roturier officiers de fortune*, 5 percent (1,750) *roturiers* who had somehow managed to win an officer's commission without ever having served in the ranks, and 10 percent (3,500) foreigners in the French service. Thus, 8,750 officers on the books could not have participated in the Second Estate's assemblies, while approximately 26,250 would have been eligible.
7 *A.P.*, vol. 3, 471–8.
8 *A.P.*, vol. 6, 4–8; *A.P.*, vol. 5, 734–6; and L. M. Prudhomme, *Résumé général, ou extrait des cahiers des pouvoirs, instructions, demandes et doléances* (Paris, 1789), vol. 2, 303.
9 *A.P.*, vol. 3, 602–8; and *A.P.*, vol. 6, 140–4.

(Rouen).[10] All agreed, however, that current social practices were making a mockery out of this ideal. Protected by privilege, wealth, and favoritism, the courtier was free to pursue "his criminal pretensions," while the hardworking *gentilhomme* was left in "obscurity" (Montreuil-sur-Mer).[11] The nobles of Blois blamed national decline and the degradation of their order on "the fatal influence of the grandees, principal and almost unique source of the misfortunes which afflict the kingdom," and reminded that "from the princes of the blood to the last *gentilhomme*, there should be no legal distinction."[12] Those of Cotentin denounced "the expressions of the King's ordinance on the military hierarchy which tend to divide the nobility into several classes" as a blow "to the foundations of the French constitution."[13] The assembly of Beauvais, along with many others across the country, declared simply that it would "recognize in France only a single order of nobility."[14] Nobles were indeed concerned with merit and equality, but understood these ideals in terms of what they believed to be their traditional corporate identity.

Casting themselves as the guardians of social norms, noble assemblies called upon the Estates-General to regenerate the nobility and French society as a whole by restoring the preeminence of merit and service. To uphold the "purity" of the nobility and restore its luster in the eyes of the nation, noble assemblies demanded the abolition of venal ennoblement, a purge of nobles who had purchased their status, and the creation of new mechanisms for ennobling merit (Montpellier).[15] They argued that a nobility of merit could increase national productivity by encouraging effort in all classes of society. If made "the aim of useful services, the prize of distinguished talents, and the reward of eminent virtues," claimed the nobles of Annonay, a reformed noble institution could stimulate a general movement of national resurgence.[16] To safeguard the rights of merit, noble assemblies demanded a greater role for the nation in the process of ennoblement. Some *cahiers* proposed that, henceforth, the king confer nobility only at the request of the projected provincial estates. In close touch with local realities, these representative assemblies would be able to distinguish true merit from pretension (Mirecourt).[17] Other *cahiers* asked the king to submit all propositions for ennoblement to the Estates-General, thereby giving the nation's representatives control over new recruitment to the Second

---

10 *A.P.*, vol. 5, 594–7.
11 *A.P.*, vol. 4, 64.
12 *A.P.*, vol. 2, 378–87.
13 *A.P.*, vol. 3, 51–4.
14 *A.P.*, vol. 2, 294–8.
15 *A.P.*, vol. 4, 45–9.
16 *A.P.*, vol. 2, 47–9.
17 *A.P.*, vol. 4, 4.

Estate (Bailleul).[18] To rid the nobility of venal elements, a rigorous purge had to be undertaken. To this end, noble *cahiers* called for the formation of heraldic tribunals, provincial commissions, the enforcement of existing laws against usurpation, and even the revival of the *"recherches de noblesse* [royal investigations intended to discover those who had usurped noble status] ... which took place around 1688" (Toulouse).[19] If these proposals had been enacted, the result would have been a pared-down nobility freed from the pernicious influence of the Court, cleansed of rich *anoblis*, and continually rejuvenated by the ennoblement of meritorious public servants. Although these suggestions amounted to nothing less than the reconfiguration of the nobility and a fundamental change in the mechanisms of social mobility, proponents of these measures regarded them not as irresponsible experimentation, but rather as a return to France's historic constitution.

The spirit of outrage against courtly privilege which infused the Second Estate's *cahiers* was also apparent in its electoral choices. Of the 561 noble deputies and suppliants, 499 (89 percent) had served in the military.[20] In some assemblies, local nobles organized to defeat the candidacies of courtiers who suddenly appeared, confident of easy election. The comte d'Hodicq, a retired officer named deputy by the nobility of Montreuil, explained in a letter to Necker that, while "great lords move heaven and earth" to win election and "protect their usurpations," most nobles saw through their maneuvers and mobilized against their candidacies.[21] In the noble assembly at Melun, noted its secretary, the comte de Vaublanc, the officers of the regular army formed a "coalition" and successfully defeated the electoral bid of the duc du Châtelet, commander of the Gardes du corps.[22] It is also revealing that the only members of the War Council known to have sought election, Guibert and the duc d'Ayen, both lost bitter contests.[23] While the operations of the noble assemblies reflected profound divisions within the Second Estate, it would be incorrect to view these conflicts in purely social terms, as a fight between provincials and courtiers.[24] Not an

---

18 *A.P.*, vol. 2, 171–3.
19 *A.P.*, vol. 6, 31–5.
20 Edna Hindie Lemay, *Dictionnaire des constituants, 1789–1791*, 2 vols. (Paris, 1991). As several had served only briefly or in an honorary capacity, not all of these deputies can be considered military professionals.
21 A.N. AA 51, "Lettre d'Hodicq, maréchal de camp, au garde des sceaux" (28 February 1789).
22 Vincent-Marie Vienot, comte de Vaublanc, *Mémoires sur la Révolution de France et recherches sur les causes qui ont amené la Révolution de 1789 et celles qui l'ont suivie* (Paris, 1883), vol. 1, 183.
23 On d'Ayen's failed electoral bid, see Brette, *Recueil de documents*, vol. 3, 578.
24 The Second Estate's deputation included no less than 127 *présentés*. James Murphy and Patrice Higonnet, "Les Députés de la noblesse aux états-généraux de 1789," *Revue d'histoire moderne et contemporaine*, 20 (1973), 238.

attack on the upper nobility *per se*, the Second Estate's electoral choices amounted to the rejection by military nobles of candidates whom they saw as strangers to their milieu, as unfamiliar with their concerns or hostile to their professional interests.

Nobles initially welcomed the Revolution because its promise of equality and meritocratic regeneration spoke to their frustrations and offered redress. They were not inflexible defenders of the status quo in 1789, for they saw themselves as the victims, rather than the beneficiaries, of aristocratic privilege. For nobles, the Old Regime had come to mean the usurpation by wealthy courtiers of positions, pensions, and honors which ought to have been the reward of their own meritorious service. Prominent among their hopes was the desire to restore the purity of their order by eliminating favoritism, venality, and intrigue from it ranks. Yet, while they desired change, the nobles did not think they were seeking radical innovation. In calling for merit, nobles thought that they were demanding the return to traditional values that had been lost, diluted, or warped. Although they used egalitarian language, denounced "aristocrats" and "despotism," and condemned privilege, they did so in defense of what they saw as the "constitutional" structure of their estate. When they called for opening all ranks to seniority or talent, they were opposing the upper nobility's monopoly of the highest grades. When they insisted that promotion be based on merit, they were demanding an end to the reign of influence and intrigue which had delivered all high places to the courtiers. When they invoked equality, they meant the constitutional equality of *gentilshommes*. For the nobility in 1789, the revolutionary future lay in an idealized past.

The officers have their say: the regimental *cahiers* (fall 1789)

The precocious radicalism of the Revolution did not weaken the nobility's commitment to this nostalgic vision of change. Nor did it awaken nobles to the possibility that, in the mouths of non-nobles, the rhetoric of merit and equality might conceal a far different conception of revolutionary goals. Even the dramatic events of the summer of 1789 – the conflict over voting procedure in the Estates-General, the Third Estate's seizure of sovereign power, the Great Fear, and the abolition of privilege on the Night of 4 August – did remarkably little to check the nobility's optimism. The nobility was so blind to the egalitarian potential of meritocratic argumentation that it unhesitatingly embraced the principle of careers open to talent.[25]

---

[25] Jay Smith emphasizes the persistently blinkered character of noble meritocratic discourse in *The Culture of Merit*, especially in chapter 6, "Military Reform in the Later Eighteenth Century: Birth, Merit, and the Gaze of Absolute Monarchy," 227–61.

Evidence for the continuity of noble aspirations across this turbulent period can be found in a little-known series of petitions drafted by the officers between August and October 1789. Addressed to the National Assembly by corresponding committees comprising over seventy regiments in more than fifty French garrison towns, these documents called for "the regeneration of the military constitution."[26] Although they exposed a broad range of military grievances, merit and its abuses figured as their main concern. Employing the same language as the noble *cahiers*, they bitterly condemned the practice of basing professional status "on the chance of birth and fortune."[27] As the army was currently organized, they complained, a handful of favored officers – variously denounced as the "military aristocracy," "the privileged class," "petty despots," "perverse men," and "enemies of the *patrie*" – monopolized promotion and pensions while the deserving went unrewarded. The committees urged the Assembly to restore "hope to merit and energy to talent" by implementing in the army "that precious equality which should unite the citizens of the same empire."[28] The significance of these documents lies in their timing: drafted *after* the Assembly had declared careers open to talent, they reveal how noble officers' perceptions of the Revolution remained profoundly marked by their Old Regime experience.

In their petitions, the officers' committees focused on the "odious distinction" embodied in the War Council's 1788 ordinance on advancement.[29] Urging the Assembly "to efface the line of demarcation separating the Court nobility from the rest of the French," the officers of Colonel-Général dragoons complained that "all favors, high positions, and dignities ... are exclusively reserved for the privileged class of the nobility which intrigue or luck have placed near the Throne and in the antechamber of the ministers."[30] The Chasseurs (a type of light infantry) of Franche-Comté echoed these complaints, pleading with the Assembly "to destroy the fatal distinction which creates ... two nobilities and gives to one the places merited only by the other."[31] The officers of Maine infantry did not spare the upper nobility. In their petition they attacked "that class of privileged men"

---

26 A.G. MR 1907, "Réclamations de MM. les officiers du régiment du Maine" (1789).
27 A.G. MR 1907, "Vices et abus de la constitution actuelle du militaire français: dénoncés à l'Assemblée nationale par les officiers de la Colonel-Général, la Couronne, Condé infanterie, et des Chasseurs à cheval des évechés, composant la garnison de Lille" (6 September 1789).
28 A.G. 1 K 440, "Lettre circulaire imprimée des officiers du Colonel-Général dragons" (13 August 1789).
29 A.G. MR 1907, "Réclamations des officiers des régiments Royal, Alsace, Artillerie, Hesse-Darmstadt, Corps royal du génie: Comité général de l'infanterie de la garnison de Strasbourg" (1789).
30 A.G. 1 K 440, "Lettre circulaire imprimée des officiers du Colonel-Général dragons."
31 Cited in Henry-Joseph de Buttet, "Le Comité de la brigade de cavalerie en garnison à Strasbourg (août 1789)," *Actes du 92ème congrès des sociétés savantes, histoire moderne, Strasbourg–Colmar, 1967*, 378–9.

that owed its position to "wealth and access to the ministers," a class that strove to ensure that "merit and experience will never be titles of success."[32] Although members of a privileged order, noble officers continued to see themselves as victims of the "evils which despotism and arbitrariness have made [them] bear for so long."[33] The experience of revolution had neither calmed the officers' anger, nor led to a closing of noble ranks. On the contrary, the radical turn taken by the Revolution in the summer of 1789 had only increased the military nobility's expectation of thoroughgoing reform.

Although the 4 August resolution to open careers to talent is generally assumed to have been aimed at the nobility's professional prerogatives, the officers actually understood it differently. Introduced by a noble deputy, the marquis de Beauharnais, and accompanied by other meritocratic motions prefigured in the Second Estate's *cahiers* (the suppression of unearned pensions and the abolition of venality of office), the proposal to open careers to talent was directed not against the nobility in general, but rather at the plutocratic elite of the Court.[34] As the officers' committees understood it, the Assembly's precisely-worded promise to open "*all* ecclesiastical, civil, and military employments" to merit was plainly intended to open high ranks to the lesser nobility, to abolish "the injurious demarcation ... between the opulent Court nobility and the poor, unknown nobility."[35] For them, revolutionary meritocracy meant an end to the pernicious inequalities of birth, wealth, and influence within their own order that limited their own advancement.

While applauded by officers, the principle of careers open to talent nonetheless would seem to have posed an unmistakable threat to the noble monopoly of officer commissions. Yet, the officers assumed that revolutionary meritocracy was not incompatible with their dream of an officer corps in which professionalism would be based on hereditary military vocations. Despite the National Assembly's commitment to abolishing the exclusive privileges of birth, the officers believed that opening military careers to a broader pool of applicants did not necessarily preclude special consideration for young men from military families, so long as those *preferences* did not involve the *formal exclusion* of others. The officers therefore demanded preferential admission at an early age for their sons and nephews, confident that this did not clash with revolutionary meritocracy. According to Captain Vedel of Maine infantry, it was possible to open the military profession to all citizens while still retaining for officers "the just prerogative of placing their children in the same profession, for which they have been

32 A.G. MR 1907, "Maine."
33 A.G. 1 K 440, "Lettre [du régiment] de Vivarais."
34 *A.P.*, vol. 8, 346.
35 A.G. MR 1907, "[Régiment de] Forez." My emphasis.

raised since the cradle."[36] The garrison of Lille wrote that it was "just" that "sons of officers enjoy the right to enter the corps where their father serves or served."[37] Other committees believed that, since all Frenchmen could now aspire to military careers, it was more important than ever that hereditary military vocations receive particular encouragement. The infantry committee of Strasbourg cautioned that, since "all citizens now have the right to occupy military places," it was essential that the royal military schools accept only the sons of officers. "Noble status alone," it argued, "should no longer be counted as a legitimate title to this honor."[38] As understood by noble officers in the autumn of 1789, merit did not mean allowing broader sectors of society into the officer corps. On the contrary, military nobles saw revolutionary meritocracy as an opportunity to establish even more rigorous standards of officer selection which would finally realize a long-standing military ideal: an officer corps recruited from military families.

This aim underlay the regimental committees' approach to the question of how to regulate the promotion of deserving non-commissioned officers into the officer corps. Noble officers saw these veterans as comrades-in-arms who, like themselves, had been unjustly denied advancement. They demanded that, once commissioned, *officiers de fortune* be fully assimilated into the officer corps and permitted to rise as far as their personal merit would take them. This made it all the more necessary that such nominations be exercised with care. All too often, claimed the committees, colonels had granted such promotions "thoughtlessly" or as a reward for "adulation or spying."[39] To guarantee the quality of the *officiers de fortune*, the officers demanded that the authority to make such promotions be vested in the vote of the regimental cadres. In terms echoed by other committees, Auvergne infantry claimed that the "consent of the corps" was necessary to ensure that commissions were "awarded only to true merit."[40]

The committees' concrete proposals for the *officiers de fortune*, however, were less magnanimous than their rhetoric alone indicates. Only soldiers with many years' service would be promoted from the ranks. With advancement dependent on seniority (which the committees demanded as an antidote to favoritism), most *officiers de fortune* would have had to retire before attaining superior rank. In practical terms, therefore, the officers' promise of unlimited advancement for their non-noble colleagues was an empty one. Nor did the committees propose to increase the number of *officiers de fortune*. On the contrary, the cavalry brigade of Strasbourg wanted to limit them to six per

36 A.G. MR 1718, Vedel, "Projet d'ordonnance pour la constitution de l'infanterie françoise" (27 October 1789).
37 A.G. MR 1907, "Vices et abus."
38 A.G. MR 1907, "Comité d'infanterie de Strasbourg."
39 A.G. MR 1907, "Vices et abus."
40 A.G. MR 1907, "[Régiment d'] Auvergne" (1789).

regiment because an expansion of their numbers would slow "the advancement of the sons and relatives of serving officers."[41] Had their demands for the preferential admission of officers' relatives and the selection of *officiers de fortune* by regimental vote been implemented, then provincial noble officers would have effectively controlled the recruitment of the officer corps.

The committees also sought to restrict ministerial influence, limit the power of the colonels, and give subaltern officers a greater voice in military affairs. Like those of the Second Estate, the petitions of the officers rang with denunciations of ministerial despotism and called for the abolition of "arbitrary authority, ... the germ of military aristocracy."[42] They demanded the formation of a "military court in each regiment charged with moderating abuses of arbitrary power."[43] Chosen all or in part from the rank of the accused, these tribunals of peers would alone have the authority to dismiss those who violated "the laws of honor."[44] Barrois infantry even proposed that these courts "receive all complaints, all demands for graces, and sanction them before passing them on to the minister," thus circumventing the colonels and establishing councils of subaltern officers as intermediaries between the army and the government.[45] The committees also wanted to curb the power of colonels within their regiments. Some petitions even called for the formation of a "General Committee" on the national level, to be composed of officer-delegates from each regiment.[46] This body would receive complaints, determine the "general sentiment of the army," and suggest appropriate reforms to the National Assembly.[47] Assuming that the legislators would defer to their expertise on matters of military reform, the officers viewed the National Assembly as an ally and bulwark against the Court and other civilian meddlers. As we shall see, this assumption was largely correct.

An indirect reflection upon noble identity, the officers' petitions reveal an order still preoccupied by its internal divisions. Decrying the usurpations of the well-born and well-connected, officers demanded the reconstitution of their profession according to what they claimed was its traditional basis in internal equality, service, and merit. The possibility that the Third Estate might take up these arguments and turn them against the noble monopoly of officer posts (and eventually the existence of nobility itself) seems to have gone unrecognized. Mathieu Dumas, the officer who replaced Guibert after his disgrace at Bourges,

---

41 *Doléances du comité des chefs d'escadron, capitaines, lieutenants, sous-lieutenants de la brigade de cavalerie composée des régiments Royal et Artois* (n.p., 1789).
42 *Vœu militaire: régiment de Cambrésis, infanterie françoise.*
43 *Doléances militaires: régiment de Guyenne infanterie* (Nîmes, 1789).
44 A.G. MR 1907, "Maine."
45 A.G. MR 1718, "Barrois."
46 A.G. MR 1907, "Comité d'infanterie de Strasbourg."
47 *Doléances ... Régiments Royal et Artois*, and *Vœu militaire ... Cambrésis.*

remembered 1789 as a time of "neither suspicion, nor terror of the future."[48] On the contrary, a sense of expectant optimism infused the officer corps as it awaited the Assembly's reforms. Striding confidently into the Revolution, the officers gazed indignantly upward at the courtiers, rather than downward with apprehension at their non-noble subordinates. Even after it became apparent that the Revolution was going to force them to accept equality with all French citizens, many military nobles accepted this as a reasonable price to pay for ending the humiliating privileges enjoyed by the elite of their order. As the marquis de Ferrières sniffed in October 1789, "I'd prefer that a common man think himself my equal than to have a grandee treat me as his inferior."[49] Even as the Revolution unfolded with increasingly disastrous consequences for them, the nobility never entirely put aside the internecine rancor which had shaped its initial revolutionary aspirations.

The National Assembly's military committee

At the same time as the subaltern officers were forming regimental committees and setting their grievances down on paper, military noble deputies in the National Assembly were urging their civilian colleagues to take up the question of military reform. Their initial appeals – by the vicomte de Noailles, the baron de Wimpfen, and Alexandre de Lameth – were ignored at first; the Assembly was then engrossed in debate over the Declaration of Rights. It was only on 1 October 1789 that Wimpfen persuaded the Assembly to turn its attention to the army. Claiming that the "military constitution" fell within the "exclusive competence of the nation," he convinced the Assembly to form a committee to draft the legislation required to uproot Old Regime abuses and implement revolutionary meritocracy in the military. During its two-year existence, the military committee would consistently defend the army against revolutionary disorders and civilian interference in its internal affairs, ultimately producing a military constitution that satisfied the officers' grievances. Its work was even admired by counterrevolutionaries. One royalist general reportedly told Alexandre de Lameth, the committee's guiding light, that "when we carry out the counterrevolution ... you will be hung, but I will insist that your [military] organization be conserved because it leaves nothing to be desired."[50] Long considered a model of military organization, the committee's work would serve as the basis for French military reform in 1818 and 1830.

---

48 Mathieu Dumas, *Souvenirs du lieutenant-général le comte Mathieu Dumas de 1770 à 1836* (Paris, 1839), vol. 1, 425–6.
49 "Lettre à Madame de Medel" (8 October 1789) cited in *Marquis de Ferrières, correspondence inédite (1789, 1790, 1791)*, ed. Henri Carré (Paris, 1932), 120.
50 Théodore de Lameth, *Notes et souvenirs de Théodore de Lameth, faisant suite à ses mémoires* (Paris, 1914), 406.

The committee's prudent approach to reform was hardly surprising given its composition. Of the twenty deputies who served on the committee, eighteen were active or retired officers.[51] All but two were nobles, a reflection of the social distribution of military expertise and the Assembly's deference to it.[52] Several were veterans of Old Regime military reform. Wimpfen had collaborated with Saint-Germain and had sat on Ségur's war committee. Bouthillier had served as the inspector-general of troop equipment and, in this capacity, had worked with the War Council. Noailles had also been attached to the Council to draft maneuver regulations. The Assembly's military committee was thus dominated by professional officers well versed in military reform. In the course of their work, they consulted the papers of the Old Regime committees, and even adopted the War Council's agenda as the framework for their own deliberations.[53] They also collected the officers' regimental petitions, "studied them with the greatest care," and used them "as a guide."[54] Finally, the committee regularly consulted serving officers and collaborated closely with the war ministry.[55] Even as it worked to apply the Revolution's egalitarian principles to the new military organization, the committee remained focused on its professionalizing mission.

Far from anticipating a clash between political principles and professional imperatives, the members of the military committee believed that revolutionary meritocracy was not merely compatible with, but even offered the key to, the long-sought reinvigoration of French arms. But political and professional aims did not always mesh as easily as they hoped. The potential for conflict became apparent in one of its first meetings when one of its least military members, Dubois de Crancé, offered a plan for universal conscription and advancement by election. After the committee rejected his proposal in closed session, the determined deputy took his

---

51 The original membership included one lieutenant-general (the comte d'Egmont-Pignatelli), four *maréchaux de camp* (the baron de Flaschlanden, the comte de Gomer, the marquis de Rostaing, the baron de Wimpfen), three colonels (the marquis de Bouthillier, the baron de Menou, the vicomte de Noailles), one veteran infantry officer (the marquis de Panat), one ex-*mousquetaire* (Dubois de Crancé), one noble who had served briefly as an officer in Corsica (the comte de Mirabeau), and a lawyer in the *parlement* (Emmery). Eight more deputies eventually sat on the committee. They included three *maréchaux de camp* (the marquis d'Ambly, the comte de Crillon, the marquis de Thiboutot), two colonels (the prince de Broglie, Alexandre de Lameth), one major-in second (the vicomte de Beauharnais), one military engineer (Bureaux de Pusy), and a lawyer (Chabroud).
52 On noble over-representation in the committees, see Alison Patrick, "The Second Estate in the Constituent Assembly, 1789–1791," *Journal of Modern History*, 62 (1990), 223–52.
53 A.G. A^464, "Lettre du ministre de la guerre au comte de Rostaing, président du comité militaire" (22 June 1790); and A.G. A^472, "Lettre du président du comité militaire au ministre de la guerre" (19 September 1790).
54 Noailles, "Rapport sur les objets constitutionnels de l'armée" (1 February 1790), *A.P.*, vol. 11, 410.
55 A.G. A^472, "Comité militaire: premier repértoire," no. 863 (4 July 1790); and Mathieu Dumas, *Souvenirs*, vol. 1, 478–9.

case directly to the Assembly on 12 December 1789.[56] Asserting a contradiction between revolutionary principle and the "despotic regime" of the army, he called for a mode of recruitment consistent with the new civic order. He denounced the current system of voluntary enlistment as suited only to an "army of mercenaries" and touted conscription as the sole means of creating a national army in which "every citizen [would] be a soldier, and every soldier a citizen." Brushing aside the objection that the Third Estate's *cahiers* had overwhelmingly condemned compulsory military service, he predicted that, since the nation had reclaimed its rights, the people would now flock to become "defenders of their country's constitution." To regulate advancement, Dubois de Crancé proposed that subordinates name their superiors in democratic elections. Electoral advancement, he claimed, was the "sole guarantee of public liberty."

Horrified military deputies interrupted Dubois de Crancé's discourse, accusing him of insulting the military and meddling in matters which he did not understand. The tumult continued for several days as the officers in the Assembly put aside their political differences and, with a single voice, condemned the man and his plan.[57] The liberal deputy, the duc de Liancourt, argued that conscription, far from protecting liberty, violated it to an extent unknown under the Old Regime. Conscription would require "an active inquisition into one's comings and goings" and was "incompatible with the bases of our constitution." In military terms, it would leave the army "without instruction or discipline." Urging the Assembly to heed the opinion of "those who really know the troops," Liancourt demanded the rejection of Dubois de Crancé's plan. Echoing Liancourt, the reactionary vicomte de Mirabeau branded conscription "the harshest form of slavery" and claimed that citizen levies would be helpless against professional soldiers. And more officer-deputies of all political tendencies – Ambly, Biron, Bureau de Pusy, Harambure, Noailles, Sillery, Toulongeon, and Wimpfen – joined the fray. In a jab at Dubois de Crancé's lack of military experience, the marquis de Sillery, an officer decorated for bravery in combat, regretted that "the committees are not always composed of people knowledgeable in the matters they are supposed to treat." With similar disdain, the veteran reformer Wimpfen invited Dubois de Crancé to put away his "military novels," full of "untested theories" suitable only for creating a "hypothetical army." The united front presented by military deputies from across the political spectrum convinced the Assembly to defer to the experts and reject Dubois de Crancé's plan unanimously.

The military committee was deeply troubled by the prospect of an uncontrollable discussion of military issues on the floor of the Assembly. Fearing that

---

56 Dubois de Crancé, "Observations sur la constitution militaire, ou bases de travail proposés au comité militaire," *A.P.*, vol. 10, 595–614. All citations in this paragraph are from this source.
57 *A.P.*, vol. 10, 579–88 and 615–20. All citations in this paragraph are from this source.

lawyers, clergymen, and other uninformed civilians might take over the military debate and impose inappropriate reforms on the army, the committee moved to insulate the army from the unwanted attentions of the legislators. In its decree on the bases of the military constitution, approved by the Assembly on 28 February 1790, the committee strictly limited the Assembly's jurisdiction over military affairs.[58] The first article – confirming the king as "supreme chief of the army" – was described by Alexandre de Lameth as the "principal base" of the military constitution. The other provisions of the decree, he explained, were intended only as "precautions" against abuse of the royal prerogative. These limited royal power by declaring that the army was intended primarily for external defense, forbidding the unauthorized entry of foreign troops into France, establishing legislative control over the military budget, and reiterating the principle of careers open to talent. Only in its final article did the decree grant the legislature authority over certain precisely enumerated aspects of the military: determining annual expenditures, the number of troops, pay scales, the form of recruitment, the hiring of foreign troops, and retirement pensions. Significantly, to ensure that "merit alone would have preference," the decree also granted the legislature authority to determine the mode of officer recruitment and advancement. But everything not specifically attributed to the legislature – organization, tactics, discipline, and administration – fell within the executive sphere. While the legislature was to determine the broad constitutional framework of the military, the executive was to exercise sole authority over its internal affairs. After the easy passage of this fundamental decree, the committee settled in to work out the details of a new system of advancement which would respect revolutionary political principles while at the same time enhancing military professionalism. In the meantime the army was left much as it had been before 1789. Old Regime military laws continued to be enforced, officers continued to be recruited exclusively from the nobility, and the meritocratic promise of 4 August remained unfulfilled in practice.

The abolition of nobility

Although the committee had succeeded in heading off a politicized reform debate on the floor of the National Assembly, a new threat arose unexpectedly on the night of 19 June 1790 when the National Assembly voted to abolish hereditary noble status. Shattering the nobility's assumption that its social aspirations were shared by the Third Estate, this moment of revelation showed their initial revolutionary consensus to have been an illusion perpetuated by a

---

[58] Lameth, "Rapport sur la constitution militaire" (9 February 1790), *A.P.*, vol. 11, 521–6. All citations in this paragraph are from this source.

common vocabulary of merit. It was from this point that the first junior officers began deserting their regiments and offering their swords to the counterrevolution. Yet, despite this rude awakening, not all nobles abandoned hope that something good could yet emerge from the Revolution. On the contrary, the noble officer-deputies in the Assembly still had enough faith in the good sense of their non-noble colleagues to attempt to turn them from error and lead them back to the "true" principles of 1789. Far from seeking the abolition of nobility, they recalled, the nation had called for its regeneration. Only by purging it of venal *anoblis*, instituting new mechanisms for ennobling public service, and restoring its constitutional basis in internal equality would merit triumph and the national will receive satisfaction. Needless to say, the nobility's efforts to steer the Revolution back onto its "proper" course were of no avail. But its response to the challenge of abolition – to remind the errant Third Estate of what it understood to be the true aims of the Revolution – is nonetheless significant. In the face of the direct threat of abolition, most Second Estate deputies did not attempt to defend their order as it currently existed, but rather reiterated earlier calls for the reforms that would make nobility, thus reconstituted, the keystone of the new meritocratic order. The night of 19 June did not witness a clash between revolution and counterrevolution, but rather revealed the existence of two divergent visions of social change. Only one would emerge bearing the mantle of revolutionary legitimacy. Although, as the losers of this contest, the nobility and its ideas were branded by the victors as counterrevolutionary, nobles would have rejected this characterization at the time. As they saw it, they had remained faithful to the Revolution; hijacked by a cabal of radical deputies, it was the Revolution that had veered off its true course.

Regarded by historians as the inevitable postscript to the dismantling of privilege on the Night of 4 August, the abolition of nobility has attracted little scholarly attention.[59] Yet contemporaries, both noble and non-noble, were struck by the measure, which they viewed as neither foreordained nor necessary. Formal abolition seemed unwarranted, especially given the reforms already enacted by the National Assembly. The decrees of the Night of 4 August, as well as the Declaration of Rights, had already abolished the concrete fiscal, legal, and professional privileges enjoyed by the nobility. Since civil equality had already been instituted, since the nobility's corporate existence had already been destroyed, the Assembly's action on 19 June took many observers by surprise. Prominent revolutionary propagandists, like the journalist Brissot, had neither demanded nor foreseen the abolition of nobility. As recently as January 1790, he had used the pages of his journal, the *Patriote français*, to distinguish between opulent courtiers and provincial

---

59 A noteworthy exception is Tackett in *Becoming a Revolutionary*, 292–6.

nobles, describing the latter group as hardworking victims of the "despotism ... and aristocracy of the great and rich."[60] While the barbs of revolutionary pamphleteers were often aimed at the nobles of the Court, one finds little evidence of hostility to nobles in general. On the contrary, as patriotic officer or industrious land-owner, the middling noble seems to have enjoyed favorable press during the first year of the Revolution.[61] If a Brissot could be caught off guard by the abolition of nobility, it is understandable that ordinary Frenchmen were also mystified. In search of an explanation, one local official from a small village gingerly suggested in a letter to the Assembly that "perhaps it might not be useless to let the people know the reasons why the National Assembly issued this decree."[62] Even Edmund Burke, hardly one to underestimate the radicalism of the Revolution, was baffled by the abolition of nobility. Finding no rational reason for the measure, he concluded that it must have been the result of some shadowy cabal, "a mere work of art" foisted on an unwary Assembly.[63]

Although conspiracy theory is often a poor way of explaining revolutionary events, in this case Burke may have been right. The circumstances of the sparsely attended evening session of 19 June suggest a premeditated effort by a small group of deputies to sneak a doubtful measure past their colleagues.[64] Although the session opened in the accustomed fashion, with the usual procession of patriotic deputations, it soon took on a bizarre carnival air. As a group of National Guardsmen from Tours filed away, a costumed deputation of "foreigners" – supposedly including Chaldeans, Indians, and Syrians, as well as the more familiar Dutch, Swiss, and Italians – made its way to the bar of the Assembly. Speaking on their behalf, Anarchasis Cloots, the flamboyant Prussian "orator of the human race," praised the Revolution for showing the oppressed peoples of the world the path to freedom and asked that their representatives be allowed to participate in the upcoming Festival of Federation. This pageantry was just the prelude for an even sharper departure from the announced agenda of the session. Alexandre de Lameth, a leading figure in the Jacobin Club as well as the military committee, rose to call for the removal of four "enchained figures" on the statue of Louis XIV in the Place des victoires, figures that represented the subjection of the peripheral provinces to the king of France. At this, an obscure deputy named Lambel abruptly moved to

---

60 Cited in Henri Carré, *La Noblesse de France et l'opinion publique au XVIIIème siècle* (Paris, 1920), 123.
61 Jack Censer, *Prelude to Power: The Parisian Radical Press, 1789–1791* (Baltimore, 1976), 43, 49, and 93. Although Censer stresses the antinoble thrust of early radical journalism, the examples he cites are from the last quarter of 1790.
62 A.N. D IV 47, "Lettre du sieur Faguet, secrétaire municipal de Ribecourt près Noyon, formée d'observations sur le décret qui abolit la noblesse" (15 August 1790).
63 Edmund Burke, *Reflections on the Revolution in France* (Oxford, 1993), 139.
64 The following description of the evening session of 19 June 1790 is based on the account given in *A.P.*, vol. 16, 372–89.

suppress the use of noble titles. This new proposal was supported and extended by a succession of radical speakers: Charles de Lameth, Goupil de Prefeln, Lafayette, Noailles, Le Pelletier de Saint-Fargeau, Montmorency, Barnave, Le Chapelier, and others.[65] In a burst of choreographed spontaneity apparently designed to recall the emotional crescendo of patriotic sacrifice witnessed on the Night of 4 August, these deputies progressively added hereditary nobility, coats of arms, liveries, and the use of seigneurial last names to the conflagration. But 19 June was no 4 August. Horrified at what was happening, the handful of noble deputies in attendance rushed to denounce the proceedings, but were shouted down and prevented from speaking. Unable to block passage of the decree, they resorted to written protests, but even these had to be deposited with notaries since the president of the Assembly refused to accept their delivery.

A few of the protests – couched in terms of historical and legal precedent, absolutist order, and divine will – betrayed a startling incomprehension of how the Revolution had changed the nature of political legitimacy. For example, the vicomte du Hautoy objected that the abolition of nobility violated the 1736 compact attaching the duchies of Lorraine and Bar to France by destroying privileges the French monarchy had promised to uphold. Abolition was a flagrant contravention of a solemn treaty between sovereign powers, a foolhardy act that not only "attacked the basis of public law" in Lorraine and Bar, but also threatened similar "constitutional" arrangements regulating relations between the French monarchy and other provinces.[66] Other deputies warned of dire consequences for the monarchy if abolition were allowed to stand. Drawing on Montesquieu, the marquis de Laqueuille predicted that, without a nobility, the last buffer between the people and government would fall, liberty would succumb to "the most dangerous of aristocracies" (the radical deputies of the National Assembly), and France would "cease to be a monarchy."[67] The marquis de Vrigny charged that the true aim of those seeking to abolish nobility was to force a "republican regime" on France.[68] One deputy, the comte d'Escars, even defended nobility as an irrevocable gift of God.[69] Arguments of this sort were not likely to carry much weight in an Assembly which had already shown itself prepared to disregard precedent in its quest to remake French society.

---

65 Given the deputies who played an active role in pushing through the abolition of nobility – liberal nobles who had belonged to the Society of Thirty – it is possible to consider the orchestrated events of the night of 19 June 1790 as the last act of that "conspiracy of well-intentioned men." On the Society of Thirty, see Daniel L. Wick, *A Conspiracy of Well-Intentioned Men: The Society of Thirty and the French Revolution* (New York, 1987).
66 A.P., vol. 16, "Déclaration de M. le vicomte du Hautoy," 379–80.
67 A.P., vol. 16, "Déclaration du marquis de Laqueuille" (27 June 1790), 386.
68 *Protestation motivée de M. de Vauquelin, né marquis de Vrigny, député de la noblesse du bailliage d'Alençon* (Paris, 1790), 3–4.
69 A.P., vol. 16, "Protestation du comte François d'Escars," 380.

Significantly, however, most of the protesters invoked more modern principles and even specific revolutionary legislation to defend the existence of nobility. Many made rights-based arguments against the abolition of nobility. Assimilating nobility to property, they condemned abolition as a violation both of natural law and the fundamental rights guaranteed by the National Assembly itself. The marquis de Foucault-Lardimalie was one of many deputies who defended nobility as "an indestructible, imprescriptible, and inalienable property."[70] As "the most inviolable of properties," claimed the vicomte de Beaumont, nobility was protected by article 6 of the Declaration of Rights.[71] The protestors even found support for their arguments in the decree of 4 August, the very decree that had abolished noble privilege. In a joint statement, the comte de Lévis-Mirepoix, the abbé Perrotin de Barmond, and the marquis de Beauharnais (the very same deputy who had called for the opening of careers to talent on the Night of 4 August!) asserted that article 14 of the decree, providing that "no useful profession will entail derogation," implicitly recognized "the legitimacy of distinctions of birth."[72] The dispositions concerning derogation, another deputy elaborated, "necessarily supposed the existence of nobility in the kingdom because otherwise they would be without application and devoid of meaning."[73] Still others, like the marquis d'Argenteuil, claimed that article 11 of the 4 August decree had, in opening careers to talent "without distinction of birth," implicitly recognized the existence of such distinctions even while ending the privileges they had formerly enjoyed.[74] The nobles' use of key revolutionary legislation to support their arguments shows that they continued to identify themselves with the Revolution. But at the same time, their distinctive reading of these laws also reveals that they understood the Revolution far differently from some of their more radical colleagues. Nothing could illustrate more dramatically the extent to which the meaning of Revolution had fragmented and become an object of contestation.

Although 19 June marked a parting of ways, revealing to many nobles that the Revolution was moving in directions they had neither foreseen nor approved, they clung to the original vision of social reform expressed in the *cahiers* and still hoped to see it implemented. In combating abolition, they did not assume a blindly reactionary posture, but rather reiterated their belief that only the regeneration of nobility could achieve the creation of a truly meritocratic order.

---

70 *A.P.*, vol. 16, "Protestation du marquis de Foucault-Lardimalie" (22 June 1790), 381.
71 A.G. $A^4$65c, "Protestation d'Antoine-François, vicomte de Beaumont, chef de division des armées navales, commandeur des ordres de Saint-Louis et de Saint-Lazare."
72 Comte de Lévis-Mirepoix, marquis de Beauharnais, and abbé Perrotin de Barmond, *Noblesse* (Paris, 1790), 2.
73 *A.P.*, vol. 16, "Protestation de M. de Pleurre" (20 June 1790), 382.
74 Edmé le Bascle, marquis d'Argenteuil, *Protestation* (1790), 2.

Abolition, far from securing the triumph of meritocracy, would consummate the decline of France. By depriving the government of the power of ennoblement, its most potent means of encouraging selfless public service, abolition would leave enrichment as the sole perspective capable of exciting ambition and stimulating effort. If nobility were destroyed, warned the comte de Faucigny, the despicable aristocracy of "the bankers and usurers" would reign unchallenged.[75] By leaving wealth the sole marker of social distinction, the abolition of nobility would usher in a new regime of naked greed and thereby consecrate the triumph of egoism over the patriotic spirit of service. Rather than "destroying nobility," concluded one protestor, the proper course "would have been to purify it and restore its force."[76]

Even after the passage of the abolition decree, nobles believed that it was still not too late to reverse this mistaken policy and return to the vision of merit expressed in their *cahiers*. The protestors instructed the Third Estate how this might be accomplished. It was first necessary to rid the nobility of its unworthy elements, those "putrefied members" who had dishonored and devalued it. To this end, the protesters called for a new *recherche de noblesse*.[77] While no one submitted a fully developed plan for how a revolutionary *recherche* might be conducted, the abbé Maury urged the pursuit of "usurpers" of nobility, and the comte de Tracy insisted that "those who have appropriated the titles of ancient families be forced to return to their original names."[78] As in the Second Estate's *cahiers*, proposals for a purge were accompanied by calls for the more vigorous ennoblement of merit. While the nobility had always shunned those who had purchased their entry into the second order, assured the marquis de Laqueuille, it would always "be eager to admit to its ranks those who, by all manner of services performed for the *patrie*, have merited becoming the defenders of the king and people."[79] Only a purge accompanied by the institution of new mechanisms of ennoblement, the protesters vainly repeated, could consolidate the new meritocratic order and operate the moral regeneration of France.

If there was ever a time for noble unity, that time came on 19 June 1790. But even in the face of an open attack on what remained of their distinct social existence, French nobles remained preoccupied by the internal rivalries that had fractured their order before the Revolution. Even in their written protests against the decree, noble deputies could not refrain from attacking the groups they held responsible for their current dilemma. *Anoblis* were denounced as one of the

---

75 A.P., vol. 16, 375.
76 *De la destruction de la noblesse en France* (1790), 26.
77 *Protestation motivée de M. de Vauquelin, né marquis de Vrigny député de la noblesse du bailliage d'Alençon*, 7.
78 A.P., vol. 16, 375.
79 A.P., vol. 16, "Déclaration du marquis de Laqueuille," 386.

principal sources of the nobility's decline and discredit. One outraged pamphleteer fulminated that those who had "acquired nobility by force of gold" were the "shame" of the second order and the reason for its "degradation." Had it not been for the scourge of venal ennoblement, he concluded, abolition never would have happened.[80] Another author stridently proclaimed that he only recognized "military nobility" and dismissed *anoblis* as "nothing but *roturiers*."[81] The upper nobility was attacked with equal vehemence. One writer denounced the courtiers as "slaves of favoritism" who, by their flattery and intriguing, had "mastered the weakness of the King."[82] Like the noble electoral assemblies and regimental committees, the protestors insisted on the need for equality among "true" nobles. "Above all," one urged, "let the families illustrated by titles, dignities, or other favors of the Court no longer be distinguished from those of other *gentilshommes*."[83] Rather than closing ranks in defense of their common interests, nobles continued to focus on the inequalities which divided them from one another. A year into the Revolution, the bitter rivalries of the Old Regime continued to undermine the unity of the nobility and shape its politics.

Merit in the new military constitution

Even as it tried to navigate the rapidly shifting tides of revolutionary politics, the military committee never lost sight of the noble officers' longstanding grievances about how social differences between them had resulted in the inequitable distribution of promotion. Their complaints exerted a powerful influence over the committee's new system of advancement, unveiled on 19 September 1790 and voted into law without dissent two days later. Alexandre de Lameth made this clear in his report on the proposed decree.[84] For the majority of military men, officers no less than soldiers, army life had offered nothing but "a continual burden of oppression, humiliation, and ingratitude" (71). Although *roturiers* had been unjustly excluded from the officer corps, Lameth admitted, provincial nobles had also suffered from social discrimination. Paraphrasing Saint-Germain, he drew a parallel between the plight of *roturiers*, barred from the officer corps by genealogical restrictions, and that of provincial noble officers, limited in their advancement by lack of sufficiently illustrious pedigree.

---

80 L. C. A. de Jassaud, *Invitation à la noblesse française* (Paris, 1790), 30.
81 *Les Derniers soupirs de la noblesse*, 8–9.
82 *De la destruction de la noblesse en France*, 7–8.
83 Jassaud, *Invitation à la noblesse française*, 30–1.
84 Alexandre de Lameth, "Rapport fait au nom du comité militaire sur l'admission dans l'armée et l'avancement militaire" (19 September 1790), *A.P.*, vol. 19, 70–6. Unless otherwise indicated, all citations in this section are from this report. Page numbers for citations from this source are noted in parentheses in the text.

> The rigid separation between soldiers and officers was reproduced between the two classes which formed this last-named group. While little-favored nobles consumed their life without advancement in the inferior grades, those of the Court shot past them, ... arrived promptly at the highest honors, and possessed them exclusively. What the first almost never obtained through their length of service, the courtiers received as if by right ... One's place was marked by birth. (71)

Convinced that Old Regime social inequalities had weighed just as heavily on officers as soldiers, the committee concluded that nobles would benefit as much as *roturiers* from the application of revolutionary meritocracy to the military. While the opening of careers to talent would end the professional privileges formerly enjoyed by nobles, this loss would be offset by the new possibilities for advancement they would henceforth enjoy. For the military committee, the revolutionary promise that citizens would be admitted to all "military employments" without distinction of birth meant not only that *roturiers* could now aspire to officer rank, but also that noble officers of modest means could now rise to the commanding positions formerly monopolized by the upper nobility. In this light, the new principle of meritocracy decreed by the Assembly did not appear to the committee as a dangerous revolutionary imposition, but rather as a long-overdue recognition of intra-noble equality.

Like the military nobility in its *cahiers* and regimental petitions, the military committee believed that seniority was the best way to safeguard equality and prevent birth, wealth, and influence from usurping promotions due to merit. Seniority would "close the door to unjust preferences, intrigue, and favoritism" and also keep officers from falling into an "excessive, humiliating, and dangerous dependence" on their military and political superiors (72-3). Like the War Council of 1788, the military committee believed that advancement through the subaltern grades (second lieutenant through captain) could safely be left to seniority, especially since the entrance examination it proposed to implement would guarantee the basic aptitude of all officers. But beyond the rank of captain, the importance and complexity of the officers' functions required "men distinguished by their talents" (73). If the advancement of such men was held up by the order of seniority, they would only arrive at these critical places of command with their "physical and moral forces" exhausted, or, worse, find them occupied by officers of mediocre capacity (73). Lameth thus recommended setting aside a portion of advancement to the superior grades for more rapid advancement by royal nomination. A third of lieutenant-colonels and colonels would be designated by nomination, as would half of all generals. But even with these provisions for royal appointment, two-thirds of colonelcies and half of generalcies would still be filled by seniority, an unprecedented concession to the provincial nobility.

The question of direct admissions to the officer corps posed a much greater challenge to the military committee as it sought to reconcile its notions of professionalism with the meritocratic principles of the Revolution. Whereas advancement reform during the Old Regime had always striven to approach the ideal of individual merit (by establishing equality of opportunity between noble officers), attempts to improve officer recruitment had always been based on the assumption that, when it came to placing untried adolescents in positions of command, what mattered most was family background. By abolishing birth-based distinctions, the opening of careers to talent left the army without a professional rationale of officer selection and even raised doubts about whether the direct recruitment of officers could continue in any form. Now that the Revolution had redefined merit as a quality possessed only by individuals, what could give a schoolboy the right to lead combat veterans? How could a young man who had never served presume to command soldiers who had risked their lives on the battlefield? This question had already been raised in June 1790, soon after the abolition of nobility.

> By what right can a young man aspire to the honor of command without having proven that he is worthy of it? Lacking personal actions ... [and] experience ... how dare he present himself and how dare you admit him?[85]

Although two prominent military writers of the Old Regime, Maurice de Saxe and Joseph Servan, had argued that the army would be better off if all military men began their careers as simple soldiers, the committee rejected this idea on professional grounds.[86] Flatly refusing to address the underlying question of principle, Lameth argued for the recruitment of officers directly from the educated classes because the army required personnel with a capacity for critical thinking. If cultivated subjects were forced to waste their youth as soldiers, most would shun military service and the army would end up with only worn-out, unimaginative commanders. While the army certainly needed experienced officers, especially in the subaltern grades, it required qualities of a different order in the higher ranks. It therefore required direct officer recruitment.

The issue of direct recruitment to the officer corps raised another difficult question which the committee had to address: what method of appointment was best suited to the preservation of political liberty? In his report to the Assembly, Lameth firmly rejected the traditional practice of royal nomination. Not only would the maintenance of this policy result in the *de facto* preservation of noble privilege, he warned, but also provide the executive with the means of

---

85 A.N. AD XVIII^{c}87, Emmery, *Idées présentées au comité militaire par M. Emmery, l'un de ses membres* (Paris, 26 June 1790), 17.
86 Maurice, comte de Saxe, *Les Rêveries, ou notes et commentaires sur les parties sublimes de l'art de la guerre* (Paris, 1763), 13–20; and Joseph Servan de Gerbey, *Le Soldat-citoyen, ou vues patriotiques sur la manière la plus avantageuse de pourvoir à la défense du royaume* (Switzerland, 1780), 128–9.

reconstituting absolutist authority. A potent "means of influence and corruption," the "arbitrary prerogative" of military appointment would allow the government to "augment its power" and erode liberty by buying the loyalty of the legislators themselves. But if Lameth pulled no punches in exposing the risks of an excessive concentration of power in the hands of the king, he was no less vehement in warning of the dangers of democratic excess. Allowing the soldiers to elect their own officers, Lameth insisted, was not only "destructive of all discipline," but also "contrary to all sound ideas of government." While embraced by short-sighted patriots like Dubois de Crancé as the key to creating a truly citizen army, the elective principle, if applied to the military, would result in the worst kind of despotism. To envision what would become of French liberty if the army were allowed to choose its own leaders, he reminded, one needed only to recall the example of ancient Rome where "emperors elected in the camps ... became the victims of their soldiers' caprices" and "the indiscipline of the army led to the oppression of the citizens" (72). In the realm of officer recruitment, Lameth concluded, monarchical and democratic extremes both led to the same fatal result.

The committee's search for a new mode of officer recruitment was further complicated by pressure from distinct groups (noble officers, bourgeois civilians, and plebeian non-commissioned officers), each advocating conflicting interpretations of revolutionary meritocracy. With the exception of isolated intransigents like the disgraced Guibert – who, in a last public pronouncement before his untimely death in 1790, warned the Assembly that the army would be lost if nobles did not retain their monopoly of officer rank – noble officers accepted the end of their birth-based professional prerogatives.[87] But they did so in the belief that revolutionary meritocracy did not rule out preference for the sons of officers. A new military school admissions policy issued by royal decree on 26 March 1790 – which actually *narrowed* the pool of potential applicants by reserving places for the sons of officers – had confirmed them in their view and given them reason to believe that the Assembly would adopt their interpretation.[88] On the other hand, most bourgeois had (in the *cahiers* of the Third Estate) expressly demanded an end to birth-based distinctions in officer recruitment. Although some had conceded that nobles or the sons of officers should take precedence, given equality of merit, most had opposed these sorts of distinctions. Yet, despite their democratic rhetoric, the bourgeois who drafted the Third Estate's *cahiers* never dreamed that artisans and peasants were capable of, or even interested in, becoming officers. For the most part, this was correct; few of the parish *cahiers*

---

[87] Guibert, "Lettre à l'Assemblée nationale publiée sous le nom de l'abbé Raynal" (10 December 1789), *Comte de Guibert: Stratégiques*, ed. J. P. Charney (Paris, n.d.), 670.

[88] A.G. Y^{a}57, Untitled *mémoire* (n.d.).

contained meritocratic demands of any sort. Equal access to the professions was simply not a concern of the French peasantry in 1789.[89] But one socially modest group within the Third Estate keenly desired to enter the officer corps: the non-commissioned officers of the royal army. The socially inflected meritocracy of the Third Estate *cahiers* offered little to these soldiers, who feared the prospect of competing for commissions with the sons of the bourgeoisie as much as they resented the genealogical barriers of the Old Regime. If special provisions were not made for promoting them into the officer corps, these veterans feared that the wholesale recruitment of young bourgeois would pose "great obstacles to [their] advancement."[90] In its work on officer recruitment, the committee had to reconcile these divergent interests while at the same time balancing revolutionary political concerns with professional necessity.

To establish a politically acceptable, professionally sound mode of officer recruitment that would satisfy noble officers, bourgeois civilians, and veteran soldiers, the committee ultimately adopted a composite system. It proposed to allocate the bulk (75 percent) of new officer commissions to young civilians who succeeded in a competitive, public examination. Respecting the principle of careers open to talent and avoiding the political pitfalls of entrusting the executive with power over appointments, this method also had a respectable professional pedigree. Before 1789, examinations had been used to select officers of the artillery, engineers, and the navy. A number of Old Regime military reformers had proposed extending this method to the army, and two respected authors, Joseph Servan and Lacuée de Cessac, repeated this recommendation in a published paper addressed to the committee.[91] The committee enthusiastically supported this idea. The vicomte de Noailles predicted that, just as they had made French engineer and artillery officers the envy of Europe, examinations would similarly enhance the infantry and cavalry cadres. Moreover, he argued, selection by examination would furnish officers recruited directly from civilian life with a legitimate title of preference. It would "advantageously dispose public opinion" and would "appear as a just reason for preferment over the large number of citizens who ... can only enter [the army] as soldiers."[92] Lameth reiterated these arguments in his report of 19 September on the new system of advancement. As well as constructing proof of

---

89 John Markoff, *The Abolition of Feudalism: Peasants, Lords, and Legislators in the French Revolution* (University Park, PA, 1996), 39.

90 A.G. $A^4$72. "Comité militaire: premier repertoire des pieces renfermées dans les cartons sous la côte A," no. 1904 (10 October 1790).

91 A.N. AD XVIII^{c}91, Servan and Lacuée de Cessac, *Projet de constitution pour l'armée des françois, présenté au comité militaire de l'Assemblée nationale par l'auteur du Guide de l'officier en campagne et par celui du soldat-citoyen* (n.d.), 30.

92 A.N. AD XVIII^{c}87, Noailles, *Troisième rapport du comité militaire, fait à l'Assemblée nationale, par M. le vicomte de Noailles* (Paris, 1 February 1790), 10.

"personal qualities," examinations would gradually improve the composition of the officer corps as promising new subjects with demonstrated "capacity" (72) and "talents" (75) replaced old officers whose only credentials had been parchment proofs of nobility. Examinations would procure young officers with "the brilliance of a polished education" (73), "theoretical knowledge," and an "aptitude to combine and reflect on the science of their profession" (71). Only one committee member, the marquis de Bouthillier, questioned the military benefits of examination. In a published dissenting opinion, he argued that examinations were not an ideal solution to the problem of officer recruitment because they could not measure the deeper qualities of character formed by one's early education. Since examinations could only test the kind of knowledge that money could buy, they would effectively "award preferences to wealth."[93] His warning, however, failed to sway the committee which recommended reserving three-quarters of all second lieutenancies for citizens who had passed a public examination; details about the administration and content of the examination were to be determined later.

In the actual event, revolutionary crises forced the abandonment of this system of recruitment before it was ever put into practice. It is thus impossible to know exactly how it would have affected the composition of the officer corps. Nonetheless, it is possible to get an idea of the kind of people the military committee expected to pass through the filter of examination by the underlying social assumptions embedded in their language. The terms employed by Lameth in his report – "brilliance," "polished education," "time of study," "theoretical knowledge," "aptitude to combine and reflect on the science of their profession" – all suggest that he assumed new officers would be recruited from cultivated families with the financial means to provide their children with formal schooling. In principle, this meant that the social pool of officer recruitment would be extended to encompass well-to-do social groups which had been excluded by genealogical barriers before 1789: *anoblis*, officeholders, professionals, bourgeois living from investments, and mercantile families. But unguarded pronouncements by members of the military committee, often voiced inadvertently while discussing less politically sensitive aspects of reform, suggest that landed families – not urban professionals or merchants – were expected to provide the majority of officers. In discussing leave policy, Emmery stated that the officers would have "properties" which required them to absent themselves each year to "preside over their harvests" or attend to their "domestic affairs."[94] Noailles, Wimpfen, and even Dubois de Crancé also wanted to require officers returning from leave to bring back with them new recruits from

---

93 Charles-Léon, marquis de Bouthillier, *Plan de constitution militaire* (Paris, 1790), 121–2.
94 *A.P.*, vol. 16, 495.

their region, an obligation which presupposed officers with sufficient local prestige to attract tenants and neighbors to the service. Bouthillier even assumed that officers would still be drawn mainly from families with traditions of military service. The officers he envisioned would not only have "affairs to direct and a fortune to administer," but would also be called to the profession of arms by "predisposition" and "honor."[95] Behind the deliberately bland formulations of Lameth's report lay the assumption that the officers of the future would not differ dramatically from those currently serving.

Although it believed that direct recruitment of young civilians by examination should provide the bulk of new officers, the committee recognized that the army also needed to promote personnel with "qualities acquired by experience" (71). To this end, it proposed reserving the remaining 25 percent of second lieutenancies for non-commissioned officers. Even during the Old Regime these veterans had been able to win commissions as *officiers de fortune* after years of exemplary service, but had never represented more than 10 percent of a regiment's cadre. In comparison, the committee's proposal to reserve 25 percent of new commissions for non-commissioned officers seemed like a substantial gain for them and a real move toward a more democratically composed officer corps. But close examination of the concrete mechanisms of promotion reveal this concession to be much less generous than at first appears. Only half of the places reserved for non-commissioned officers – a mere 12.5 percent of second lieutenancies – were to be awarded to seniority, and thus to the kinds of long-serving veterans who had been named *officiers de fortune* during the Old Regime. The remaining places were to be filled by non-commissioned officers designated by the vote of the regimental cadres. While the officers were free to use this prerogative (which they had demanded in their regimental petitions) to advance deserving veterans, they could also use it to admit their own relatives, their colonel's clients, or even young bourgeois who had joined the regiment with the promise of a commission. Thus, the committee's plan represented only a slight expansion (from 10 percent to 12.5 percent) of the possibilities for advancement long-serving soldiers had enjoyed during the Old Regime. If the non-commissioned officers wanted further democratization of officer recruitment, they could not expect much help from the military committee.

Before the new mechanisms of officer recruitment were to be implemented, the committee ruled that the mass of supernumeraries left over from reductions in the Maison militaire, the militia, and the successive downsizings of the line army would have to be reabsorbed. But to ensure that the advancement of serving officers would not be blocked by "this army of lazy and expectant officers,"

---

95 Bouthillier, "Rapport au nom du comité militaire sur la force et sur la solde de l'armée française" (19 January 1790), *A.P.*, vol. 11, 239.

it determined that only those with an "obvious right," "capacity," and "decided taste" for the military be readmitted as places became available (74). The rest would be retired forthwith. Nonetheless, many officers were recognized as having the right to reenter active service. The number of Old Regime supernumeraries deemed eligible for readmission was substantial: 93 supernumerary colonels, 45 majors-in-second, 634 captains, and 722 second lieutenants.[96] In addition, 376 captains, 184 lieutenants, and 184 second lieutenants whose places had been eliminated by the committee's own reorganization were also allowed to reenter the officer corps.[97] The reabsorption of these 138 superior and 2,100 subaltern officers, all with preferential rights to vacancies, promised to block new nominations to the officer corps for some time. In turn, this was sure to delay the placement of pages and military school graduates. As early as 16 February 1790 the war minister had complained of the "impossibility" of finding places for recent graduates of the military school.[98] All of these supernumeraries and students had to be absorbed before the new system of recruitment examinations could be put into practice. As the marquis de Bouthellier observed, the resulting backlog rendered "illusory the decree which has just consecrated [the Third Estate's] rights."[99] Had revolutionary events not conspired to destroy the Constituent Assembly's military constitution, it would have been a long time before the first bourgeois could have acceded directly to officer rank.

Even as it sought to recast the army to conform with the principles of 1789, the Assembly's military committee was determined to shepherd it through the revolutionary vortex with its professional integrity enhanced. In undertaking this task, the committee found it could use revolutionary meritocracy to make long-sought professional improvements. It used the abolition of hereditary distinctions to ensure that birth, favoritism, and wealth would no longer usurp the rights of merit at any level of the military hierarchy, a traditional ideal whose realization had been thwarted by Old Regime social structures. Revolutionary equality enabled it to break the Court's hold on superior ranks and allow officers currently confined to the subaltern grades to rise according to their merit. The abolition of

---

96 A.G. X^{c}1, "Etat des capitaines de remplacement avec réforme dans les troupes à cheval" (February 1791); A.G. X^{c}2, "Liste des sous-lieutenants de remplacement par ancienneté de date de sous-lieutenant qui ont droit à remplacement" (1 April 1791); A.G. Xc2, "Liste des sous-lieutenants attachés ... " (1 April 1791); *Recueil des listes des officiers des corps de cavalerie réformés de la Maison du Roi par ordre d'ancienneté pour servir au remplacement dans tous les autres corps* (1791); and *Recueil des listes des officiers des corps de l'infanterie réformés de la Maison du Roi ...* (1791).

97 *Règlement portant instruction aux colonels ou commandans des régimens d'infanterie française, allemande, irlandoise, et liégoise, qui sont chargés de mettre à exécution la nouvelle formation arrêtée par le roi* (1 January 1791).

98 A.G. Y^{a}161, "Lettre du ministre de la guerre à Reynaud" (16 February 1790).

99 Bouthillier, "Rapport au nom du comité militaire sur la force ... " (19 January 1790), *A.P.*, vol. 11, 239. See also, Anthoine's discourse of 30 May 1791, *A.P.*, vol. 26, 624–5.

genealogical testing made it possible to institute admissions criteria more relevant to professionalism than parchment proofs. As a social order, nobility was one of the great losers of 1789, but, as professionals, noble officers gained more than they lost. While they were stripped of their monopoly of officer commissions, a change whose practical effects would not have been felt for years, they won equality with the upper nobility, saw venality abolished, and could look forward to leading a more effective army. Through the efforts of the military committee, most of the serving nobility's prerevolutionary grievances were satisfied and the army remained in their hands.

3 The death and rebirth of the officer corps, 1790–93

Even as the National Assembly was putting the finishing touches on the new military constitution, the French army was coming apart at the seams. Insubordination on the part of their soldiers and charges of disloyalty leveled against them by political radicals undermined the officers' authority and weakened their will to persevere in the thankless task of attempting to maintain discipline. For many, the King's attempt to flee the country in mid-June 1791 was the final straw. Following the example of their sovereign, approximately 6,000 noble officers left the country during the last half of the year to take up arms against the Revolution. These departures confirmed the soldiers' distrust of their superiors and provoked new outbreaks of insubordination. Trapped in a vicious cycle of insubordination and emigration, the army seemed incapable of defending France from the growing threat of foreign military intervention and of maintaining order within the country itself. On the contrary, the military had become a major source of instability in its own right, promoting insecurity, eroding the authority of the government, and threatening to destroy the new constitution. Only by halting emigration and filling the gaps in the officer corps, the National Assembly realized, could military order be restored and the country spared from the horrors of anarchy and invasion. The path to stability – and, thus, the preservation of the Revolution's gains – ran through the army. As Antoine Barnave, chief political strategist of the moderate Feuillants, noted, "in this revolution, as in so many others, the final influence will be that of the armies."[1] Recruiting a new officer corps and rebuilding its authority became the key test of the constitutional regime's viability. These efforts would transform the social composition of the military profession and introduce the personnel who would lead the armies of the Revolution and Empire in nearly twenty-five years of unremitting warfare.

Insubordination and repression

In the summer of 1790, the army was rocked by a wave of troop mutinies that shattered the officers' authority and set in motion a series of events that would ultimately destroy the National Assembly's carefully constructed

---

1 "Lettre de Barnave à Théodore Lameth" (31 March 1792), *Œuvres de Barnave*, ed. Alphonse-Marc-Marcellin-Thomas Bérenger de la Drôme (Paris, 1843), vol. 4, 358–9.

3 Ministerial nomination slip proposing "sons of active citizens" as replacement officers in the 13th Infantry Regiment, July 1791, indicating the patrons supporting these young men's candidacies.

military constitution.² Ironically, it was the officers themselves who had given the first examples of insubordination in mid-1788 during the royal government's attempt to dissolve the *parlements*. When directed to crush popular demonstrations in favor of the *parlementaires* in Dauphiné and Béarn, officers refused to order their troops to fire on the crowds or resigned rather than carry out the repression. Signs that the officers' example of disobedience had spread to the troops began to appear when the army was directed to put down the subsistence riots that broke out in many regions during the harsh winter of 1788–89. Just as officers had resisted repugnant orders the previous summer, now soldiers refused to use force against their suffering compatriots. Discipline was further eroded by the frequent use of the army to maintain order in communities across France and to repress an upsurge of smuggling across the country's poorly policed frontiers. Deployed in small detachments, often under the shaky leadership of inexperienced junior officers, military units lost cohesion and became embroiled in divisive local struggles.³ Contacts with the politicized citizenry multiplied during the summer of 1789 as troops were transferred to the Paris area in preparation for the abortive royal *coup d'état* and then returned on a massive scale to internal policing duties in response to the Great Fear.⁴ During these troubled months, soldiers began to resist their officers' authority, although usually only by desertion. Although an uneasy calm returned during the winter of 1789–90, few officers believed that the bonds of discipline had been durably reforged.⁵

In the spring of 1790, insubordination returned to the army with a vengeance. This new burst of disturbances was characterized by increasingly direct confrontations between soldiers and officers. Most incidents were provoked by disputes over pay which, the soldiers claimed, had been illegally withheld from them. Fearful for their personal security and public safety, officers and municipal officials frequently met the soldiers' demands. When the officers resisted, however, the soldiers often seized the regimental pay chests. As summer approached, there was a tendency for these confrontations to become more violent. In April the soldiers of Maine infantry delivered their colonel to a lynch mob in the city of Bastia and stood by as he was murdered. The following month

---

2 The following discussion of insubordination is based on a variety of sources: Lucien de Chilly, *Le Premier ministre constitutionnel de la guerre: La Tour-du-Pin: les origines de l'armée nouvelle sous la Constituante* (Paris, 1909), 32–245; Henri Choppin, *Insurrections militaires en 1790* (Paris, 1903); Hartmann, *Les Officiers*, 124–78; and Scott, *The Response*, 46–97.

3 On these problems, see James N. Hood, "Revival and Mutation of Old Rivalries in Revolutionary France," *Past and Present*, 82 (1979), 82–115.

4 Between August 1789 and October 1790, the war ministry received at least 700 appeals for troops from jumpy local officials. Chilly, *Le Premier ministre constitutionnel*, 53.

5 Samuel F. Scott, "Problems of Law and Order during 1790, the 'Peaceful' Year of the French Revolution," *American Historical Review*, 80 (1975), 859–88.

the soldiers' committee of Touraine infantry, acting in conjunction with the National Guards of Lambesc, expelled their officers from the town for allegedly cutting off the ears of insubordinate soldiers. In Tarascon the committee of Loraine dragoons deposed their officers and appropriated the regiment's funds. By the end of the year, more than one-third of the regiments had experienced some form of insubordination. The mutiny was so widespread that La Tour-du-Pin, the war minister, deemed it a "menace to the nation itself."[6]

Although the exact causes of insubordination were complex, the officers had a simple explanation for the breakdown of their authority: outside agitators were leading gullible, but otherwise honorable, soldiers to defy their superiors. Dampmartin, a captain in Royal cavalry, claimed that the troops, "momentarily unfaithful to their pure, antique glory," had been "misled by apostles of insubordination." Each unit, he claimed, harbored "incendiary agents" who turned the soldiers against their officers.[7] Whether blaming radical journalists, meddling municipalities, National Guards, riotous civilians, anarchists, counterrevolutionaries, or, above all, Jacobins, officers perceived outside forces behind the revolt of their soldiers. For many officers, it was inconceivable that insubordination could stem from causes internal to the army itself.

This assumption dominated the efforts to reestablish discipline. Prominent generals thought that the spread of insubordination could be checked by isolating the army from civil society. Asked for their recommendations by La Tour-du-Pin in early 1790, the generals claimed that it was "essential not to let the troops become attached to the places where they are stationed" so that they would not develop close ties with civilian agitators.[8] But given the persistence of public disorder and the inability of the faction-ridden National Guard to cope with disturbances, the army could not be withdrawn from its policing duties.[9] In these difficult circumstances, the regimental officers did what they could to inoculate the soldiers against outside influences. They tried to prevent their troops from attending clubs, ordered them not to attend politically suspect plays, and censored their mail. The most common method employed by the officers to check the spread of what they perceived as the revolutionary contagion was to dismiss insubordinate soldiers and carefully screen new recruits. As a result of these operations, new enlistments dropped by more than 50 percent in 1790, and four to five times as

6 *A.P.*, vol. 16, 95.
7 Anne-Henri-Cabot, vicomte de Dampmartin, *Coup d'œil sur les campagnes des émigrés* (Paris, 1818), 5–6.
8 A.G. A^{4}60, "Lettre du marquis de Bouillé au ministre de la guerre" (5 February 1790). See also, A.G. A^{4}60, "Extrait d'une lettre écrite à Monseigneur par M. le chevalier de Fredy" (15 February 1790); and A.G. A^{4}61, Langeron and Rivou, "Mémoire" (27 February 1790).
9 On the National Guard as a nexus of local factionalism, Lynn A. Hunt, "Committees and Communes: Local Politics and National Revolution in 1789," *Comparative Studies in Society and History*, 18 (1976), 321–46.

many soldiers received dishonorable discharges as during a typical year before the Revolution.[10] These efforts to purge the army of potential troublemakers continued well into 1791. Between January and April 1791, the correspondence between Colonel Tourville of Auvergne infantry and his trusted adjutant-major, Poncet, was dominated by this subject. In February 1791 Tourville informed Poncet that the regiment had returned to a tenuous state of obedience, but only because of numerous dismissals. "Little by little," the colonel reported, "we are purging our bad subjects."[11]

These steps failed to check the insubordination and may even have exacerbated the problem by heightening the climate of confrontation within the regiments. Yet even as the crisis deepened during the summer of 1790, the National Assembly declined to act, reluctant to encroach upon a sphere (military discipline) it had expressly reserved for the executive just a few months earlier. On 4 June 1790 La Tour-du-Pin appeared at the bar of the Assembly to report that the military was falling into the "most turbulent anarchy" and that he was powerless to do anything about it.[12]

> Entire regiments have dared to violate the respect owed to the ordinances, to the King, to the order established by your decrees, and to their oaths ... I see in more than one corps the chain of discipline relaxed or broken; outrageous pretensions proclaimed without hesitation, ordinances without force, chiefs without authority, military strongboxes and flags stolen, royal orders arrogantly defied, officers disdained, vilified, menaced, driven away.

Worse, the soldiers had begun to form revolutionary committees, turbulent assemblies which not only organized resistance to the officers but also passed resolutions on political issues. If the Assembly did not rid the army of these deliberating bodies, the minister warned, France might suffer the same fate as Rome, degenerating into a "military democracy, a political monster that always devours the empire which produced it." Frankly avowing his powerlessness to restore military obedience, La Tour-du-Pin implored the Assembly to weigh in with its moral authority.

But occupied with the military constitution and hopeful that the upcoming Festival of Federation would restore good relations within the regiments, the military committee initially demurred. But the worsening of insubordination after the Federation convinced the committee that it had to act to save the army from disintegration.[13] Presenting its plan on 6 August 1790, Emmery proposed a

---

10 Scott, *The Response*, 81–2.
11 A.G. $X^b 168$, "Lettre de Tourville à Poncet" (18 February 1791).
12 La Tour-du-Pin, "Discours sur l'organisation de l'armée" (4 June 1790), *A. P.*, vol. 16, 95–6. All citations in this paragraph are from this report.
13 On the growing seriousness of insubordination after the Federation, see La Tour-du-Pin, "Mémoire relatif à l'insubordination qui se manifeste dans plusieurs corps de l'armée" (6 August 1790), *A. P.*, vol. 17, 640–1.

combination of conciliatory and repressive measures to end the disturbances once and for all.[14] Recognizing that the soldiers' charges of financial malfeasance had some foundation, Emmery called for inspectors to verify the regimental accounts. These inspectors would also be empowered to hear any other grievances the soldiers might have. To eliminate another source of tension, Emmery called for a halt to the summary dismissal of soldiers by their officers. Far from preserving the regiments from insubordination, he claimed, this "atrocious" practice was actually responsible for much of the underlying tension. To rectify the injustices which had been committed by overzealous officers, soldiers who had been dishonorably discharged since the Revolution would be amnestied. To give soldiers a means of peacefully expressing their complaints in the future, Emmery moved that all military personnel be allowed to petition their commanding generals, the war ministry, and even the National Assembly without having to obtain the permission of their hierarchical superiors. If they had a legal channel through which to voice their discontents, he reasoned, then the soldiers would no longer need to rebel. Finally, soldiers and officers would be directed to treat each other with "respect" and "justice." By "showing itself [to be] rigorously just," the Assembly could "calm everything."

Having recognized the legitimacy of many of the soldiers' grievances and offered redress, the committee intended to draw a line against further incidences of insubordination. Now that the soldiers had received justice, Emmery insisted on behalf of his colleagues, further acts of disobedience had to be severely punished. To this effect, soldiers accused of subsequent disciplinary violations would be treated firmly. If found guilty by a military court, they would not only be condemned to the ordinary penalties, but also be stripped of citizenship, declared "traitors to the *patrie*," and expelled from the army. The soldiers' committees would be suppressed immediately, Emmery continued, and the existing military laws (of the Old Regime) would be rigorously enforced until the promulgation of the new military constitution. The decree was "much applauded" by the Assembly and approved with scarcely a murmur of dissent.

Less than two weeks later, a mutiny of the three regiments stationed at Nancy put the Assembly's resolve to the test.[15] The town's garrison – Du roi infantry, Mestre-de-camp cavalry, and Châteauvieux Swiss – had experienced the same sorts of disturbances as the rest of the army: dishonorable discharges, confrontations between officers and soldiers, and the formation of committees. The first weeks of August, however, saw a marked rise in insubordination. On 1

---

14 Emmery, "Projet de décret relatif aux troubles qui règnent dans plusieurs corps de troupes" (6 August 1790), *A.P.*, vol. 17, 641–3.
15 This paragraph is based on William Baldwin, "The Beginnings of the Revolution and the Mutiny of the Royal Garrison in Nancy: *L'Affaire de Nancy*, 1790" (University of Michigan Ph.D. dissertation, Ann Arbor, 1973).

August soldiers of Du roi forcibly released a comrade who had been imprisoned for disobedience. Encouraged by this success, they demanded 200,000 *livres* in back pay, most of which was raised by the officers and frightened city officials. Soon thereafter, the two other regiments followed Du Roi's example. Recognizing neither military nor civil authority, the soldiers effectively controlled Nancy by mid-August. Although some deputies in the Assembly were eager to make an example of the rebels, others, fearing bloodshed, hesitated to enforce the decree of 6 August. Yet the revolt of the troops at Nancy ultimately proved too direct a challenge to the Assembly's authority to ignore. On 16 August the deputies unanimously approved the military committee's proposal to invite the King to adopt the "most efficacious measures" to restore discipline.[16] A number of officers were encouraged that the Assembly's strong stand would finally consolidate its authority and "begin the establishment of constitutional order."[17] After fruitless negotiations with the mutineers, the Assembly's forces under General Bouillé moved on the town. On 31 August they attacked and, after hours of bloody street fighting, subjugated the rebellious regiments. When word of the outcome reached the Assembly, the relieved deputies voted a decree of approval and thanks on 3 September.[18] The Assembly's decision to repress the Nancy mutiny by force not only signalled the deputies' rising impatience with military and, indeed, all revolutionary disorders, but also reflected their growing realization of the need for a stronger executive.

The Jacobins against the officer corps

Although the Assembly's forceful action against the mutiny at Nancy seems to have had the desired effect, resulting in a sharp drop in the incidence of insubordination during the winter of 1790–91, the military hierarchy soon found itself under attack from another quarter: the Jacobin movement. This hostility, increasingly apparent from early 1791 on, marked a sharp shift in the Jacobins' earlier attitude toward the officer corps. During the mutinies of the summer of 1790, local clubs had intervened to urge rebellious soldiers to return to obedience and protect the officers from their mutinous subordinates. After the action at Nancy, clubs across France had thanked Bouillé for his resolve.[19] Alexandre de Lameth, a Jacobin himself and no friend of insubordination, had even sought to enlist the

---

16 *A.P.*, vol. 18, 92–3.
17 "Lettre de Lafayette à Bouillé" (18 August 1790), Marie-Paul-Joseph-Roch-Ives-Gilbert de Motier, marquis de Lafayette, *Mémoires, correspondance, et manuscrits du général Lafayette, publiés par sa famille* (Brussels, 1837–39), vol. 5, 164.
18 *A.P.*, vol. 18, 530.
19 Michael Kennedy, *The Jacobin Clubs in the French Revolution: The First Years* (Princeton, 1982), 179–81.

clubs in the effort to maintain discipline after the repression. In a circular addressed to clubs across the country, Lameth urged provincial Jacobins to help "restore order and reestablish union" in the regiments.[20] In the autumn of 1790, therefore, the Jacobin movement seemed at one with the Assembly in its frustration with military insubordination. Yet within a few months, the Jacobin attitude toward the army had changed dramatically. Although they stopped short of advocating mutiny, the clubs denounced military tyranny, kept tabs on officers suspected of royalist leanings, and undermined the hierarchy by offering themselves as a powerful external authority to which soldiers could appeal. They also showed growing interest in military affairs, with the number of Jacobin petitions sent to the military committee increasing dramatically during the first months of 1791.[21] By the spring of that year, it was clear that Jacobin sympathies had shifted from the officers to the soldiers.

Jacobin hostility toward the military profession reached new heights in the spring of 1791 with their campaign to disband the officer corps and reconstitute it in a more democratic manner. The initial call for this measure – referred to as *licenciement* – was issued in January 1791 by the powerful Marseille club. Inviting its numerous affiliates to endorse its proposal, it initiated a movement of truly national scope. Dozens of clubs across France adhered to Marseille's appeal or adopted Lorient's more moderate call for the administration of a loyalty oath like that imposed on the clergy. On 25 April a prominent figure in the Paris club, the Third Estate deputy Gaultier-Biauzat, called for a commission to examine if *licenciement* could remedy the "inherent anti-patriotism of the army officers."[22] By approving this motion, the Paris club placed itself at the head of the provincial drive and stimulated a new wave of petitions. Over forty reached Paris between 20 May and 6 June, making the campaign for *licenciement* the single largest Jacobin lobbying effort during the tenure of the Constituent Assembly.[23]

The debate over *licenciement* consummated the split between moderates (who would soon break away to found the Feuillants) and radicals in the Paris club. While radicals called for the Assembly to take immediate action on the *licenciement* proposal, the moderates – led by the influential clubbists who also sat on the military committee (Lameth, Noailles, Beauharnais, and Broglie) – dragged their heels. Conflict at the 27 May meeting of the Paris club precipitated an open schism.[24] At this session, a radical clubist, Machenaud, accused the

---

20 Lameth, "Adresse de la société des amis de la Constitution de Paris aux sociétés qui lui sont affiliées" (10 September 1790), *La Société des Jacobins: Recueil de documents pour l'histoire du club des Jacobins de Paris,* ed. F. V. A. Aulard (Paris, 1889), vol. 1, 283–6.
21 A.G. A^{4}72, "Comité militaire ..."
22 *La Société des Jacobins*, vol. 2, 351.
23 Kennedy, *The Jacobin Clubs*, 189–193.
24 *La Société des Jacobins*, vol. 2, 453–5.

moderates of stalling. Describing the current noble officers as "ferocious and implacable enemies," he predicted catastrophe if they remained in charge of the army. A loyalty oath was insufficient, he argued, because it would not "cure them of [their] aristocratic gangrene." Machenaud accused the military committee of stalling and challenged it to make its report to the Assembly. After this stormy session, most of the committee members, as well as key moderate allies including Barnave, stopped attending the club. Their failure to shelve the issue of *licenciement* – a test case in the power struggle for the soul of the Jacobin movement – revealed to the moderates that they had lost their grip on the club, a revelation that precipitated their ultimate defection.

To maintain pressure on the military committee, the Paris Jacobins resolved to discuss *licenciement* at each of their meetings until the Assembly finally took up the issue. The clubbist and Third Estate deputy François-Paul-Nicolas Anthoine pronounced two discourses which, printed for public distribution, were intended to define the Jacobins' official position.[25] Anthoine held out little hope for legislative approval of the proposal. Noting that the committee was "composed of military men," he predicted that it would continue to defend the interests of the officers against the will of the nation. This was the root of the problem and the reason why *licenciement* was necessary. While the Revolution had unseated financiers, administrators, churchmen, and judges, the committee had conspired "to sacrifice everything to the army [and] everything in the army to the officer corps." In stark contrast to the rest of society, the military remained what it had been before 1789, a noble preserve. As long as the noble officers – "enemies of liberty and equality by education, system, and taste" – remained in place, revolutionary meritocracy would remain "cruelly illusory." *Licenciement* was the only way to rid the army of counterrevolutionary elements, shake up the hierarchy, and open the officer corps to talent. Anthoine received powerful support from Robespierre, who emphasized the "hideous contrast" between the liberalism of the Constitution and the archaism of the military institution. "You have destroyed the nobility," he thundered, "but the nobility still lives at the head of your army."[26]

As expected, the Assembly rejected *licenciement*. On 10 June a joint committee dominated by deputies who would help found the Feuillant club in July issued a strong recommendation against the measure.[27] Its reporter, the

---

25 Anthoine, *Discours sur le licenciement des officiers de l'armée de terre, prononcé devant la société des amis de la Constitution séante aux Jacobins ...* (2 June 1791); and *Nouveaux développemens sur le licenciement du corps des officiers de l'armée de terre, projet de décret, et réponse à M. Dubois de Crancé ...* (6 June 1791). All citations in this paragraph are from the first pamphlet.
26 Maximilien Robespierre, *Discours sur le licenciement des officiers de l'armée* (8 June 1791).
27 The committee was formed of several of the most important regular committees in the Assembly (constitution, diplomatic, military, reports, and investigations). Of its fifty-four members, thirty-five (65 percent) joined the Feuillant club in July 1791. Information on the membership of the joint committee is from Lemay, *Dictionnaire des constituants*.

military committee member Bureaux de Pusy, warned of the disastrous effects *licenciement* would have on "public tranquility."[28] He acknowledged that the Jacobins' doubts about the patriotism of certain officers had some basis in fact, but argued that *licenciement* would only exacerbate the trouble by casting the entire officer corps – constitutionalists along with counterrevolutionaries – under a cloud of suspicion. An inquisition targeting their political views would inevitably make mistakes: patriotic officers would be deprived of their positions and counterrevolutionaries would escape censure. Besides, experienced officers could not be replaced, especially at this juncture. Since the army's "instruction was almost totally destroyed" by two years of Revolution, it was the worst moment "to give as teachers and guides to our troops subjects without experience." To commission new officers from "the mass of citizens" would "consummate the disorganization of the army." So too would the massive promotion of non-commissioned officers. Not only were "the functions of these two classes of military men not the same," but, worse, to replace superiors by their subordinates would provide an incentive to mutiny. A "perilous measure that one would barely attempt in a moment of calm," *licenciement* was "an extremely imprudent, necessarily fatal enterprise" under current conditions.

Bureaux nonetheless recognized that something had to be done to address the widely-held suspicion that the officers were enemies of the Revolution. Many officers, he admitted, were troubled by the present state of affairs. Their disenchantment had two sources. For some, it flowed from "regret for the old order of things, remembrance of privileges which no longer exist, [and] perhaps even from the humiliation" of "finding themselves on the same level" as their former social inferiors. Officers of this sort, who did not appreciate that the Revolution had given them "equality with all those to whom they had been subordinated under the old social order," were probably incorrigible. But the majority, who did not share these views, could be redeemed. They had grown impatient with the Revolution only because they blamed it for the collapse of military discipline. Induced in error by rebellious soldiers who hid "their faults under the veil and name of patriotism," they "mistook for an effect of the Revolution the very indiscipline which the Constitution condemns." Such officers, who had been pronounced patriots until the troop mutinies of mid-1790, could be won back to the Revolution by the revival of subordination. To this end, Bureaux proposed an old remedy: extricating the army from civilian society by moving it into camps where "instruction and discipline" could be restored free from outside interference. To put to rest the suspicion that the officers were opposed to the new regime and remove all pretext for insubordination, they would be asked (like the clergy)

---

[28] All citations in the two paragraphs which follow are from Bureaux de Pusy, "Rapport sur l'état actuel de l'armée au nom des comités de Constitution, militaire, diplomatique, des rapports, et des recherches" (10 June 1791), *A.P.*, vol. 27, 104–8.

to swear a public oath to "the nation, the law, and the king." The Assembly's overwhelming support for these proposals signalled that the *licenciement* campaign had rebounded against its Jacobin sponsors by consolidating in the Assembly a majority in favor of restoring order.

Although they welcomed the Assembly's determination to bolster their authority and restore discipline, the new oath was a bitter pill for the officers to swallow, for it implicitly impugned their patriotism, professionalism, and honor.[29] They hesitated to accept blame for disorders which they saw as the work of outside agitators. Yet refusing the oath risked abandoning their places to ignorant civilians and rebels.[30] Recognizing the terrible choice the officers faced, a number of military noble deputies assembled to define a collective position to guide the army. Co-written by Bouthillier and Cazalès, their pamphlet acknowledged that the oath was a moral affront, but reluctantly conceded that refusal would invite disaster.

> An engagement of honor imperiously demanded after so many oaths can doubtless appear as insulting distrust of sensitive and courageous men; ... but the salvation of the *patrie* commands it ... It is not in this time of crisis and disorder, in these days of danger, that French officers will abandon the posts they have preserved and defended with so much patriotism, patience, and courage.[31]

The oath presented the officers with a momentous decision, a choice they believed critical to "the fate of France."[32] But as grave as their current dilemma was, an unforeseen turn of events was about to magnify their already excruciating crisis of confidence.

The King's flight and the end of the old officer corps

On the night of 20–1 June 1791, Louis XVI made an unsuccessful attempt to flee from France. This provoked a crisis in the army. Interpreting their sovereign's action as a repudiation of the Revolution, the officers began to abandon their posts, some resigning from military service and others crossing the frontier to swell the ranks of the *émigré* armies. Emigration confirmed the soldiers' doubts about the officers' patriotism and provoked a new wave of mutinies. In the resulting turmoil, many officers – both royalists and constitutionalists – were expelled, and others resigned in disgust at the general breakdown of authority. Emigration and indiscipline fed each other as the army descended into a state of chaos.

---

29 For an excellent discussion, see Hartmann, *Les Officiers*, 229–41.
30 Félix, comte de Romain, *Souvenirs d'un officier royaliste* (Paris, 1824), vol. 2, 109.
31 *Opinion de MM. de Cazalès et de Bouthillier, députés à l'Assemblée nationale, sur l'engagement d'honneur exigé des troupes* (June 1791).
32 "Lettre de Maiche" (16 June 1791), Pierre de Vaissière, *Lettres d'aristocrates* (Paris, 1907), 323.

The disintegration of the officer corps and collapse of discipline raised doubts about the stability of the new regime. If the government could not even control its army, how could it enforce laws or guarantee the security of persons and property? Insecurity was reinforced by fears that foreign powers were preparing a military riposte to the arrest of the King.[33] In the view of the Feuillant leaders who dominated national policy during this critical period, defense against invasion and the reinvigoration of government authority depended upon the restoration of order in the army. The revival of discipline would stem further emigration and perhaps convince some officers to return. The end of emigration would reestablish the soldiers' trust in their officers and rebuild hierarchical authority. With the army back in the hands of its leaders, it could be used against both internal agitators and foreign aggressors. "If the Revolution is to be ended," pronounced Alexandre de Lameth in July 1791, "it is above all to the discipline of the troops" that the government must attend.[34] For the Feuillants, the crisis provoked by the King's flight certainly posed a grave threat, but also presented an unparalleled opportunity. Having teetered on the brink of chaos and glimpsed in the abyss the specters of anarchy and invasion, perhaps the French would finally accept the necessity of strong government to restore public tranquility.

In the aftermath of the King's flight, the Assembly moved swiftly to assert its control over the army. To assure itself of the officers' loyalty in the new political context, the military committee proposed a revised version of the June oath that made no mention of the King. To administer the oath, the Assembly sent teams of *commissaires* (deputies of the Assembly invested with substantial powers and charged with carrying out urgent missions of national security) to France's strategic frontiers. Precursors of the Convention's representatives-on-mission, each team was empowered to adopt whatever measures were "necessary for public order and the security of the state."[35] A complementary decree authorized generals to cashier officers who refused the new oath, suspend those "whose conduct appeared suspect," and appoint replacements. They were additionally granted the power to militarize local National Guards for emergency service alongside the regular troops.[36] The Assembly approved these emergency powers without debate on 22 and 24 June 1791.

The *commissaires* soon began sending back reports which painted an unexpectedly reassuring picture. Although the Assembly had feared disorders of the

---

33 These fears were heightened by Emperor Leopold's Padua Circular (6 July 1791) and the Declaration of Pilnitz (27 August 1791). T. C. W. Blanning, *The Origins of the French Revolutionary Wars* (London, 1986), 84–9.
34 *A.P.*, vol. 28, 518.
35 Emmery, "Rapport sur la formule du serment à prêter par les militaires" (22 June 1791), *A.P.*, vol. 27, 408–12.
36 *A.P.*, vol. 28, 483.

worst kind – mutiny, counterrevolution, and invasion – the King's flight, according to the *commissaires*, had actually "engendered in all souls a new energy."[37] The *commissaires* at Besançon remarked on the "joy, unanimity, [and] enthusiasm" of the citizenry.[38] They moved on to Lons-le-Saulnier where they found public reaction equally reassuring. "Continual vigilance has not disturbed public tranquility," they wrote, "and it is with imposing calm that each citizen stands guard at his post."[39] The *commissaires* all reported, moreover that most officers were taking the oath. On 29 June the *commissaires* at Verdun informed the Assembly that the garrison's officers had all sworn loyalty.[40] On 3 July the *commissaires* at Vesoul wrote that all but one officer there had taken the oath.[41] One week later the Assembly learned that the officers of the 7th cavalry, commanded by Alexandre de Lameth's youngest brother Théodore, had unanimously "contracted the new engagement toward the *patrie*."[42] Summarizing the results of the *commissaires*' missions on 22 July, Alexandre claimed that the new oath had met with "complete success."[43]

This assessment was inaccurate and probably deliberately misleading. The *commissaires*' reports did not paint a true picture of the state of the army, for they were themselves part of the Assembly's effort to maintain public order. By emphasizing the good spirit of the citizens, the firmness of local administrations, the discipline of the soldiers, and the loyalty of the officers, the reports were calculated to reassure the nation that the Assembly had matters well in hand. In this moment of crisis, the Assembly could not afford to pronounce otherwise on the state of the country. An admission of instability might itself foment the kind of trouble the Assembly was desperate to avoid. The *commissaires*' reiterated descriptions of orderly National Guards, disciplined soldiers, and patriotic officers were "the best refutation of the pretensions of those who … dare to claim that we no longer have a public force."[44] In fact, not only had many officers refused to take the oath, but others had only sworn it conditionally, announcing their intention to resign if discipline did not improve.[45]

---

37 "Lettre des commissaires envoyés dans les départements du Nord, du Pas-de-Calais et de l'Aisne" (27 June 1791), *A.P.*, vol. 27, 562.
38 "Lettre de MM. les commissaires envoyés dans les départements du Doubs, du Jura, de la Haute-Saône et de l'Ain" (28 June 1791), *A.P.*, vol. 27, 669.
39 *A.P.*, vol. 28, 100.
40 "Premier compte rendu à l'Assemblée nationale par ses trois commissaires envoyés dans les départements de la Meuse, de la Moselle et des Ardennes" (29 June 1791), *A.P.*, vol. 27, 606–8.
41 "Lettre des commissaires de l'Assemblée dans les départements du Doubs, du Jura et de la Haute-Saône" (3 July 1791), *A.P.*, vol. 28, 5–6.
42 *A.P.*, vol. 28, 100.
43 *A.P.*, vol. 28, 511.
44 "Lettre des commissaires de l'Assemblée nationale dans les départements du Nord, du Pas-de-Calais et de l'Aisne" (3 July 1791), *A.P.*, vol. 28, 16.
45 Hartmann, *Les Officiers*, 274–5.

Moreover, fully one-third of the officers stationed in provincial garrisons were absent from their regiments, either on scheduled leave or without authorization. To inflate the rate of compliance, the *commissaires* counted all the absentees as "disposed to take the oath."[46] But careful study of regimental records has revealed these sunny pronouncements to have been pure fiction. By the end of 1791, 1,500 officers had resigned rather than swear the new oath.[47]

An even greater problem created by the King's flight was the massive emigration of officers, including thousands who had taken the oath. Although the first *émigrés*, the comte d'Artois and a handful of courtiers, had left France soon after the fall of the Bastille, most officers had welcomed the Revolution and remained at their posts. By the end of April 1790, only sixty-one officers had resigned their commissions or abandoned the army, a normal rate of attrition.[48] Emigration increased during the following months, prompted by the spread of insubordination and the Assembly's abolition of nobility in June 1790, but it did not reach crisis proportions until after the King's flight. Officers who had already been contemplating emigration – like the twenty-three in the 12th infantry who departed precipitously from the frontier town of Condé on the night of 23 June – took the King's action as implicit approval to cross the border.[49] For most officers, however, the decision to emigrate was taken only after much soul-searching, generally after they had already sworn the new oath. For those paralyzed by indecision or waiting to see how the situation would evolve, renewed insubordination was often the precipitant of emigration. No regiment was unaffected. Whether voluntary or forced, whether in large groups or individually, approximately 6,000 officers had left by the end of 1791, over 60 percent of the serving officers.[50]

At first, the military committee tried to put a bright face on the disintegration of the officer corps. Emigration, claimed Alexandre de Lameth, was a "fortunate crisis" which, by ridding the army of its most untrustworthy elements, would eliminate "one of the principal causes of trouble." The *émigrés* could be easily replaced by patriots who "would bring their love of the Revolution into the corps," thereby "reestablishing confidence" between the ranks.[51] But despite its outward confidence, the committee was well aware that the situation in the army was explosive. They knew that the *commissaires* "had seen almost everywhere

---

46 "Rapport de Chasset, au nom des trois commissaires envoyés dans les départements du Rhin et des Vosges" (31 July 1791), *A.P.*, vol. 29, 75.
47 Jean-Paul Bertaud and Daniel Reichel, *Atlas de la Révolution française*, vol. 3, *L'Armée et la guerre* (Paris, 1989), 26.
48 Hartmann, *Les Officiers*, 151.
49 This and other examples are found in Hartmann, *Les Officiers*, 251–326.
50 Donald Greer, *The Incidence of the Emigration during the French Revolution* (Gloucester, MA, 1966), 25.
51 Lameth, "Rapport des comités militaire et diplomatique sur les moyens de pourvoir à la défense extérieure de l'état" (22 July 1791), *A.P.*, vol. 28, 518.

great distrust on the part of the soldiers toward their officers" and realized that the oath had "not generally won them the confidence of their troops."[52] Emigration reinforced this climate of distrust, sometimes provoking the soldiers to take preemptive action against their allegedly treasonous superiors. The soldiers of the 17th infantry expelled their officers at bayonet point.[53] In the town of Avesnes, thirty-two officers of the 44th infantry fled after mutinous soldiers seized the regimental flags, commandeered the paychest, and issued petitions denouncing their superiors' lack of patriotism. Even in regiments which had not experienced emigration, the soldiers' suspicion of officers in general undermined hierarchical authority. Disgusted with the breakdown of discipline and frustrated at their impotence, many officers who had sworn the oath and accepted the constitutional regime decided to leave the army. The disloyalty of some officers had cast suspicion on all and made their position extremely precarious.

Grasping the mutually reinforcing relationship between emigration and insubordination, the committee urged the adoption of new penalties against both *émigré* officers and insubordinate soldiers which, if enacted together, might be able to break this vicious cycle.[54] According to the plan it presented on 21 July 1791, officers who emigrated would be pursued by military justice, as well as face the civil penalties to which all *émigrés* were subjected. For their part, soldiers implicated in insubordinate acts would also be dealt with sternly. The decree charged the agents of military justice to seek out "the instigators, authors, or principal culprits" of soldiers' movements. "Combined movements," defined as any deliberating assembly of soldiers, were outlawed, and non-commissioned officers were held personally responsible if the ringleaders were not identified. Finally, regimental disciplinary councils, composed exclusively of officers, were authorized to discharge soldiers convicted of "reprehensible conduct." To eliminate incentive to mutiny, the decree established a procedure for reinstating officers forced out by their soldiers and also froze the advancement of non-commissioned officers in insubordinate regiments. These measures – passed on 25 July over ineffectual Jacobin opposition to the harsh treatment reserved for soldiers and equally futile royalist complaints about the persecution of *émigré* officers – were intended to build a dike against the rising tide of military disorder.

But as insubordination reached new heights during the following weeks, this dike was quickly submerged. The 38th infantry expelled its officers, and soldiers of the 68th infantry actually seized the citadel of Arras. On 28 August 1791 the increasingly desperate committee responded by proposing a new law,

---

52 "Rapport de Biron au nom des commissaires envoyés par l'Assemblée dans les départements du Nord, du Pas-de-Calais, et de l'Aisne" (1 August 1791), *A.P.*, vol. 29, 89.
53 The examples in this paragraph are from Hartmann, *Les Officiers*, 263–5.
54 Emmery, "Projet de décret concernant la discipline militaire" (21 July 1791), *A.P.*, vol. 28, 469–71.

modeled after the infamous *loi martiale* (martial law), mandating the use of force against regiments that ignored three warnings to return to obedience.[55] Municipal officials were required under personal responsibility to summon all available forces (National Guards, *gendarmes* (personnel of the post-1789 equivalent of the *maréchaussée*, not to be confused with soldiers of the prerevolutionary Gendarmerie), and line troops) to put down rebellions. Mutineers who ignored the first two warnings risked harsh punishment: up to ten years on a chain gang. Those who ignored the third warning and had to be put down by force risked capital punishment. In approving the proposal, the most rigorous it had ever considered, the Assembly endorsed the committee's contention that the army required special laws and, in present circumstances, "striking examples" if it were to return to discipline.

As its tenure drew to a close, the Assembly grew increasingly apprehensive about the general state of disorder it was bequeathing to the Legislative Assembly. Accordingly, in its last days the Assembly adopted a series of measures – including the famous laws organizing the National Guard and curtailing the activities of the clubs – which, taken together, were intended to end the revolutionary unrest once and for all. Along with these historic decrees, the Assembly also considered a drastic proposal by the military committee for reviving hierarchical authority in the army. Presented by Wimpfen on 29 September, the last day the Assembly met, this measure would have effectively given officers unlimited disciplinary power over their subordinates. Condemning the "spirit of abstraction" which had led to the application of liberal civic principles to the army, Wimpfen insisted that it was "a being outside of society" and, as such, could not receive "general laws" without falling apart.[56] Military order rested on subordination which, in turn, depended on "the consideration attached to grades." Before 1789 military rank had drawn force from "the prejudice of birth," but the Revolution had destroyed this source of authority. The result was "such a leveling" that Wimpfen questioned whether it would ever be possible to revive hierarchy. The only hope lay in military laws which invested officers with "arbitrary authority." In accordance with this principle, Wimpfen proposed that the legislature invest commanders with what he termed "military dictatorship" – the power to punish subordinates "without form or process." The Assembly shrank at such a momentous step and rejected the plan. Yet, the fact that the committee dared to propose it shows how far the Assembly's attitude had evolved. In 1789 most deputies had seen passive obedience to the generals as the principle threat to the Revolution; two years later, many had come

---

55 Chabroud, "Rapport sur l'état d'insubordination, de révolte dans lequel se trouvent quelques-uns des corps de l'armée" (28 August 1791), *A.P.*, vol. 30, 4–5.
56 Wimpfen, "Rapport sur les délits et peines militaires" (29 September 1791), *A.P.*, vol. 31, 636–9.

to view insubordination as the primary danger to the Constitution, and some were even prepared to entrust the officers with virtually unlimited powers in order to save it.

Rebuilding the officer corps, 1791–93

The persistence of emigration dashed hopes for a quick return of order in the army. Many officers who had sworn the oath in the summer of 1791 had done so only to buy time to see how the situation would evolve. Continued insubordination and the inexperience of the new legislature did little to bolster their confidence. Whereas military nobles had accounted for nearly one-quarter of the old deputies, the Legislative Assembly was overwhelmingly composed of civilians from the former Third Estate. Its military committee reflected this shift; although it contained several career officers, like Mathieu Dumas and Lacuée, it was dominated by civilians.[57] Army officers expected little sympathy and even less understanding from this new body. Their worst fears were confirmed in December when the Legislative began to consider a pardon for the Nancy mutineers. To the officers, the Legislative Assembly appeared to be glorifying insubordination. Emigration spiked upward and continued through 1792, fueled by the declaration of war in April, renewed indiscipline (notably the massacre of General Dillon by his own troops), and popular violence directed at the captive King. Military emigration even persisted during the Convention, although on a much smaller scale because most of the old officers had already left. When it finally ceased in the year II (1793–94), 10,000 officers had either emigrated or resigned, almost the entire prerevolutionary complement of the active-duty officer corps.[58] These losses had to be made good if the army – and, indeed, the Revolution itself – were to be preserved.

The replacement of *émigré* officers began in June 1791 when the Assembly authorized generals to make emergency nominations. But as the scale of emigration became clear during the course of the summer, the military committee established a more systematic method of officer replacement. Voted into law on 6 August, it remained the basis of officer replacement until early 1793.[59] It was designed to reconstitute the officer corps as quickly as possible while avoiding

---

57 Pierre Caron, *Les Papiers des comités militaires de la Constituante, de la Législative, et de la Convention (1789–an IV)* (Paris, 1912), ix–xii.
58 The figures on emigration are from Greer, *The Incidence of the Emigration*, 112. The figures on resignations are from Gilbert Bodinier, "Les Officiers de l'armée royale et la Révolution," in *Le Métier militaire en France aux époques des grandes transformations sociales*, ed. André Corvisier and Jean Delmas (Vincennes, 1980), vol. 2, 67–8.
59 Emmery, "Rapport sur le mode de remplacement des officiers de l'armée" (1 August 1791), *A.P.*, vol. 29, 92–5.

two pitfalls – compromising professionalism by admitting unsuitable personnel and encouraging insubordination by promoting soldiers to replace the officers they had driven away. Accordingly, the law gave vacant lieutenancies and captaincies to the most senior officers in the branch and to experienced supernumeraries. The replacement of second lieutenants was handled slightly differently. In regiments where officers had left of their own accord, these positions were to be shared equally by the so-called "sons of active citizens" – in practice, educated young men recommended by prominent supporters of the constitutional regime – and veteran non-commissioned officers. But to discourage insubordination, three-quarters of vacant second lieutenancies in regiments which had expelled their officers were reserved for sons of active citizens. By attributing at least half of vacancies to young civilians of good family, the law sought to ensure the future solidity of the officer corps. Whereas the aging non-commissioned officers were "condemned to die in the inferior grades," Emmery explained, the sons of active citizens were "a sort of seed which fructifies." While the committee wanted to find replacements as quickly as possible, it never lost sight of how these operations would effect the long-term professional health of the officer corps.

As mid-level replacements, the war ministry eagerly sought seasoned supernumerary and retired officers who seemed loyal to the regime. Officers who had appeared unprofessional to the military establishment before 1791 – like those in the Maison militaire du roi – now seemed a precious resource. They came from a wide variety of backgrounds. Of eight such captains named to the 19th infantry in January 1792, one was a former militia captain, another was a hussar lieutenant, the third had served in the Gendarmerie, the fourth had been an officer in the Prussian army, the fifth was a former Garde du corps du roi, the sixth was a supernumerary captain and former deputy, the seventh had been a militia lieutenant, and the eighth cited no services at all.[60] Excepting this last nominee, what they had in common was past service as officers in units which had remained open to *roturiers* during the Old Regime. As the rare non-nobles with officer commissions, these men were positioned to advance rapidly during the Revolution; 203 became generals, including three future war ministers (Servan, Schérer, and Dubois-Crancé).[61] But the appointment of these outsiders, many with dubious military credentials, engendered resentments which sometimes broke out in insubordination. For example, the second lieutenants of the 58th infantry opposed the nomination of two former *gendarmes* as lieutenants "under pretext of their youth," a euphemism for their lack of experience.[62] Hostility to

---

60 A.G. X^{b}168, "Feuille de nomination, 19ème régiment" (12 January 1792).
61 Information on replacement officers who became generals is from Six, *Dictionnaire biographique des généraux*.
62 A.G. X^{b}784, "Lettre du ministre de la guerre au commandant du 58ème régiment d'infanterie" (17 April 1792).

the replacements, often perceived as privileged, non-military intruders, was even more pronounced toward the sons of active citizens named to vacant second lieutenancies. It is to them that we will now turn our attention.

The military committee had originally intended to leave the choice of the replacement second lieutenants to the military establishment. Nominees were to be proposed by the regimental colonels, screened by the commanding generals, and approved by the war minister.[63] In practice, however, civilian patronage quickly made itself felt in the selection process. Deputies, local politicians, courtiers, and revolutionary celebrities were able to have their own protégés nominated. In fact, patronage became so important that aspirants who neglected to enlist influential support almost all failed in their attempts to secure nomination. This *ad hoc* patronage system soon became institutionalized. By early 1792, ministerial nomination forms were redesigned to include a column headed "recommended by" which was assiduously filled in, often with multiple names.

Not everyone was comfortable with this method of selection. Deputies who distrusted the executive feared that counterrevolution might be able to perpetuate itself in the officer corps if ministers were allowed to nominate whomever they pleased. Without guarantees of the patriotism of the nominees, the political regeneration of the officer corps might be compromised and the Revolution threatened. It was necessary to guide the minister's discretion by demanding "severe proofs of the aspirants' patriotism."[64] These wary deputies proposed that would-be replacements be required to furnish certificates of patriotism from their local administration and proof of service in the National Guard. Without such restrictions, they warned, the sons of active citizens might be drawn exclusively from "the children of nobles."[65]

Other deputies, however, believed that professional considerations alone should dictate the choice of replacement officers. If nobles and the sons of officers made the best replacements – as military deputies like Mathieu Dumas, Jaucourt, and Viénot-Vaublanc were prepared to believe – then so be it; their nomination should be expedited, not hindered by patriotic nonsense. They feared that requiring certificates would force nominees to beg for signatures, foster intrigue, and bog down the entire replacement operation. Requiring National Guard service, moreover, would exclude military school students and regimental volunteers, those best prepared to become officers. Viénot-Vaublanc argued that the volunteers ("educated people who have served in several campaigns") and military school students ("the sons of poor parents, of former officers"), merited special consideration. "It would be useful," he claimed, "to admit into the armies

---

63 *A.P.*, vol. 29, 92–5.
64 Albitte, "Rapport au nom du comité militaire sur les remplacements à faire dans l'armée" (31 October 1791), *A. P.*, vol. 34, 535–7.
65 *A.P.*, vol. 29, 94.

young citizens exercised in tactics from childhood and consecrated, in a manner of speaking, to this sole object."[66] In the end, the Assembly settled on a compromise: while instituting tests of patriotism (National Guard service and certificates of patriotism), it gave the war minister the actual authority to appoint replacements.[67] In practice, the political criteria of eligibility did little to constrain the minister's choice.[68]

To a certain extent, the sons of active citizens resembled the Old Regime officers whom they were replacing. Nomination records for the 332 sons of active citizens named to a fourteen-regiment sample show that 10 to 20 percent were noble.[69] These figures are probably low because some nominees did not advertise their social origins. For example, the son of "high and mighty lord L. H. F. Colbert, chevalier, comte de Colbert, colonel d'infanterie, chevalier de Saint-Louis, lieutenant du Roi du comté nantais" was noted simply as Ambroise Colbert.[70] Other sons of active citizens, like Aiguillon (11th infantry), Lubersac (13th infantry), Barbuat de Maison Rouge (17th infantry), Daboville (24th infantry), Menou (35th infantry), Bruneteau de Sainte-Suzanne (36th infantry), and Cadet de Vaux (46th infantry) all bore names familiar to the officer corps of the Old Regime. At least 15 percent of the sons of active citizens came from military families, and 9 percent had served briefly as subaltern officers before the Revolution or had attended a military school. Although their numbers fell in later nominations, especially during the Convention, a substantial minority of sons of active citizens were young military nobles who had been destined for the profession of arms before 1789.

Whether noble or *roturier*, military or civilian, almost all of the sons of active citizens were educated young men from "*honnête* [socially and morally upstanding]" families. Although the hazards of socio-professional classification have been amply demonstrated, I will present such an analysis to give a rough idea of the

---

66 Viénot-Vaublanc and Choudieu speaking before the Legislative Assembly (1 February 1792), *A. P.*, vol. 38, 61.

67 For these requirements, see the successive modifications to the basic replacement law (6 August 1791) which were passed on 13 November 1791, 11 December 1791, 7 March 1792, 15 April 1792, and 24 August 1792.

68 "Lettre de M. Duportail, ministre de la guerre, concernant l'état nominatif des sujets nommés aux sous-lieutenances" (1 December 1791), *A. P.*, vol. 35, 506.

69 The lesser figure represents the percentage of confirmed nobles in the officer corps. The greater figure represents confirmed nobles as well as those with traits suggestive of nobility, such as the *particule* or fathers who had been officers before 1789. The sample is composed of the following infantry regiments: 11th (A.G. Y^b374); 17th (A.G. Y^b380); 23rd (A.G. Y^b386); 35th (A.G. Y^b398); 40th (A.G. Y^b404); 44th (A.G. Y^b409); 46th (A.G. Y^b411); 59th (A.G. Y^b425–6); 61st (A.G. Y^b428–9); 68th (A.G. Y^b432); 70th (A.G. Y^b433); 81st (A.G. Y^b446); 82nd (A.G. Y^b447); and 105th (A.G. 2 Y^b271–5).

70 A.G. Personnel Dossiers, Series 91/47, Colbert, "Extrait du registre des baptêmes de l'église paroissiale de Saint-Eustache à Paris" (31 August 1763).

social milieu from which these young officers were recruited.[71] Of the 367 sons of active citizens for whom I could identify family occupations (just over 10 percent of the total number), most came from relatively elevated social strata. 199 (54 percent) came from Old Regime military or robe families, 118 (32 percent) and 81 (22 percent) respectively. The remainder came from families in administration (9 percent), local government (6 percent), commerce (11 percent), and the professions (3 percent), as well as an important contingent of proprietors and *rentiers* (those who lived from investment income) who listed no vocation (15 percent). Only a handful came from the peasantry and the artisan classes. These figures are open to a number of critiques. The emphasis on families with traditions of public service may be exaggerated since the existing biographical dictionaries focus primarily on legislators and generals.[72] And the families themselves tended to emphasize their service credentials, believing it would help secure places for their sons. Finally, this, like all socio-professional analyses, simplifies the complex trajectories of individuals and families. If the career of someone like Simon Gabriel Canuel, royal notary, intendant of Monseigneur de Maupeou, and father of Simon Canuel (a replacement officer named in 1792) resists classification, it is nonetheless clear that his family – like those of all sons of active citizens – enjoyed a social existence above that of most of the French. The replacement operations of 1791–93 definitively ended the traditional equivalence between the terms "officer" and "noble," but did not result in social leveling.

The patronage system reinforced the tendency toward elevated social recruitment, since only well-established families could secure the backing of prominent adherents to the constitutional regime. While most patrons were deputies, military men, or both (notably liberal military nobles like Broglie, Lafayette, Lameth, and Noailles), other illustrious personalities, ranging from members of the royal family to revolutionaries like the abbé Grégoire and Condorcet, participated in the recommendation process. The system was unabashedly nepotistic. To give just one illustration, of the 332 sons of active citizens named to the fourteen-regiment sample, at least 24 (7 percent) were related to deputies. A far cry from the open admissions examinations projected in 1790 (but perhaps similar in its results), the patronage system limited the recruitment of sons of active citizens to young men connected to powerful political and military figures.

---

71 On the problems of socio-professional analysis, see Simona Cerutti, *La Ville et les métiers: naissance d'un langage corporatif* (Paris, 1990), 7–11.
72 The following works were used to identify the professional milieux of the sons of active citizens: Louis Bergeron and Guy Chaussinand-Nogaret, *Grands notables du Premier empire*, 23 vols. (Paris, 1978–95); Lemay, *Dictionnaire des constituants*; Adolphe Robert, Edgard Bouloton, and Gaston Cougny, *Dictionnaire des parlementaires français*, 5 vols. (Paris, 1889–91); and Six, *Dictionnaire biographique des généraux*.

The nomination slips drafted by the war ministry and surviving letters of recommendation make it possible to advance several conclusions about the nature of this patronage. Legislative and military patronage, together over 95 percent of recommendations during the constitutional monarchy, essentially monopolized the replacement process until 1793, when its aggregate share dropped to about 80 percent.[73] Deputies used patronage to spread the spoils of the Revolution to family, friends, and neighbors at home. Colonels also proposed replacements, generally indicating young men related to officers in their regiments or those serving as regimental volunteers.[74] With the formation of Pache's radical ministry in October 1792, however, both legislative and military patronage lost ground to a new force, the Parisian sectional movement whose leaders (Danton, Santerre, and various section presidents) furnished 20 percent of recommendations in the early Republic. Yet, in the overall replacement operation, they left only a faint impression: recommendations from the Paris sections amounted to only 4 percent of all patronage.

The letters of application and recommendation sent to the war ministry offer a blend of traditional and revolutionary justifications which gives the impression that the Revolution's message of individual meritocracy had not been fully absorbed by the upper strata of French society. The arguments mobilized in these letters fall into two general categories: political and familial. The nature of political argumentation changed abruptly after the destruction of the monarchy on 10 August 1792. Before that time, applicants stressed their loyalty to king, constitution, and the law; order was the order of the day. Only two weeks before the fall of the monarchy, for example, one young man declared his "respectful attachment to his [majesty's] person and the constitution," and his "entire submission to the law."[75] Others touted their muscular commitment to law and order, for example citing service against the Nancy mutineers.[76] One candidate's father even noted that his son had distinguished himself "by containing popular demonstrations and urging misguided citizens to return to order."[77] Those pursuing Lafayette's patronage in particular sought to play upon his

---

73 During the constitutional monarchy, patronage was constituted in the following way: legislators (46 percent), military officers (30 percent), legislator-officers (7 percent), ministerial personnel (15 percent), the Paris sections (1 percent), and unknown (1 percent). During the Republic, patronage was constituted in the following way: legislators (47 percent), military officers (26 percent), ministerial personnel (6 percent), the Paris sections (18 percent), and unknown (3 percent).

74 The Old Regime practice of taking on young men as volunteers, an apprenticeship similar to the *cadets-gentilshommes*, continued in the regiments through 1793 with the approval of the war ministry. A.G. $X^b 784$, "Lettre du ministre de la guerre Servan au commandant du 11ème régiment d'infanterie" (18 July 1792).

75 A.G. Personnel dossiers, Series 91/47, Martelet, "Lettre de Martelet au ministre de la guerre" (22 July 1792).

76 See Lefevre of the 24th infantry, A.G. $X^b 170$, "Feuille de nomination" (1 October 1791).

77 A.N. D XV 1, "Lettre de Syprien" (n.d.).

well-known hatred of the Jacobins. One condemned the "monstrous faction," while another boasted of his "hatred of faction."[78] After the fall of the monarchy, however, a language of republican patriotism replaced the rhetoric of constitutional order. Justifications like "distinguished himself during the arrest of the King" (Aunesse), "forced to leave his corps because of [his] patriotism" (d'Angerville), "member of the Society of Friends of the Constitution" (Destouel), "captain of the Marseille volunteers at the affair of 10 August" (Liautaud), and "has not ceased to present, under its sweetest guise, love of liberty and equality to the people" (Robert) distinguish the republican letters from those of the constitutional monarchy.[79]

Under the constitutional monarchy, applicants also cited qualifications which may be termed familial. These included a family's stature, its wealth, the education which it had been able to provide, and, whenever possible, its hereditary services to the state. Few letters from 1791–92 lacked a statement boasting of the good reputation enjoyed by the applicant's family. To take them at face value, one would have to conclude that the sons of active citizens all came from families which, whether "upstanding," "very well-regarded," or "honorable," all commanded "general esteem."[80] Aspirants clearly believed that belonging to distinguished families would help demonstrate their suitability for officer rank. Some applicants also indicated their wealth, claiming that they "will have all [they] need to meet all the extraordinary expenses of the profession [they] desire to embrace."[81] More frequently, they cited education, a term implying good upbringing as well as formal schooling. Rare was the applicant who did not claim to have "received the best education," "an honest and cultivated education," or "a very careful education."[82] Finally, despite the Revolution's rejection of hereditary social distinctions, applicants cited family service as a title of admission to the officer corps, just as military aspirants had done during the Old Regime. One recommendation announced that the candidate would make a fine officer because he was "related to a captain in the regiment and had several cousins [serving] as officers in other corps."[83] Others pointed to long family traditions of military service, as did Corvisart de Warigny who came from "a poor, ancient family which

---

78 A.N. C 358, "Lettre Outreguin, sous-lieutenant chasseur du bataillon de la Place royale de Paris à Lafayette" (1 July 1792); and "Lettre de Gallet à Lafayette" (5 July 1792).
79 A.G. $X^b 126$, "Etat des citoyens qui demandent des sous-lieutenances et qui ont fourni toutes les pieces exigées par la loi, années 1792 et 1793."
80 A.G. $X^b 174$, "Feuille de nomination, 36ème régiment" (22 October 1791).
81 A.G. Personnel dossier, Series 91/47, Voysin, "Lettre de Voysin au ministre de la guerre" (n.d.). Voysin, the brother of a Third Estate deputy, claimed personal wealth of 30,000 *livres*.
82 A.G. $X^b 174$, "Feuille de nomination, 36ème régiment" (22 October 1791); A.N. D XV 1, "Mémoire pour solliciter une sous-lieutenance de cavalerie" (1792); and A.G. $X^b 174$, "Feuille de nomination, 24ème régiment" (15 September 1791).
83 A.G. $X^b 170$, "Feuille de nomination, 24ème régiment" (1 October 1791).

has distinguished itself in the military."[84] Some applicants based their demands even more explicitly on the rationale of hereditary merit. The elder Tricotel, a former militia officer, argued that "the services and military talents of the father are the son's best recommendation."[85] Another letter claimed that the father, an engineer named Arlet, "merits by his civic qualities and attachment to his duties ... that his son be placed."[86] The emphasis on family standing, wealth, and education, as well as the persistence of the notion of hereditary merit, reveals that the revolution in social distinction proclaimed on the night of 4 August was less complete than one might expect.

By mid-1793 approximately 3,250 sons of active citizens and a slightly smaller number of senior non-commissioned officers had been named to vacant second lieutenancies. The two groups contrasted sharply. Although disproportionately urban and literate, compared to the French population as a whole, the non-commissioned officers were generally of more modest birth than the sons of active citizens. After all, they were veterans who had voluntarily enlisted at a time when service as a soldier was not held in high esteem. Socially resembling the rank-and-file from whom they were drawn, the non-commissioned officers named to the officer corps as part of the replacement operations were forty years old, on average, and two-thirds had already served for at least twenty years at the time of their nomination.[87] It was their influx that was largely responsible for the democratization of the composition of the officer corps between 1791 and 1793. In contrast, the seemingly inclusive term "sons of active citizens" actually concealed a fairly rigorous social selection. Well-off, well-educated, and well-connected, the sons of active citizens were seventeen years younger on average than the non-commissioned officers and differed sharply from their grizzled counterparts. Believing it "indispensable" to retain a cadre of socially elevated young men from whom superior and general officers could be drawn after the revolutionary troubles had subsided, the military hierarchy insisted that the "balance between these two classes of subjects be constantly maintained."[88]

The recomposition of the officer corps from these disparate groups – young elites, on the one hand, and aging career soldiers, on the other – created a new axis of tension within the army. In the eyes of the non-commissioned officers, the sons of active citizens were privileged dilettantes. One fifteen-year veteran

84 A.G. X^b186, "Feuille de nomination, 68ème régiment" (n.d.).
85 A.N. D XV 1, "Demande de Tricotel" (1792).
86 A.N. D XL 28, "Lettre de F. T. Arlet au lieutenant-général Marassé" (22 June 1792).
87 These statistics are derived from a sample composed of the 384 non-commissioned officers named as replacement second lieutenants in the infantry regiments designated in footnote 69.
88 A.G. X^b125, "Lettre du ministre de la guerre au citoyen Lacuée, adjudant-général à l'armée du Pyrénées" (25 December 1792).

described them as "inept children, without pronounced patriotism, without military knowledge."⁸⁹ The non-commissioned officers were insulted that the Assembly distrusted them to the point of giving them mere schoolboys as peers and superiors.⁹⁰ The veterans regarded the young newcomers as "protégés who ... carry off the fruit of their services and the hope of their fortune."⁹¹ From their point of view, the sons of active citizens were no improvement over their former noble superiors. Some soldiers may have even preferred to serve under the noble scions of military families, rather than young bourgeois fresh out of school or their father's home. Lieutenant-Colonel Dampmartin, admittedly a biased source, claimed that "the soldiers liked the officers of birth and viewed with indifference the parvenu officers; the retirement of the former and the advancement of the latter afflicted them."⁹² Even if (as seems more likely) they had no particular love for the nobility, the non-commissioned officers were no more inclined to accept the sons of active citizens. They often expressed their frustration in angry letters to the war ministry. One such letter, written by the non-commissioned officers of the 44th infantry, denounced the professional commitment and patriotism of the sons of active citizens. "None have arrived; they probably emigrated. Such are the men whom you prefer to the brave veterans of the regiment."⁹³ Sometimes the non-commissioned officers took direct action against the sons of active citizens. In January 1793, to cite just one incident, the non-commissioned officers of the 70th infantry expelled Valéry Voysin, the rich brother of a deputy.⁹⁴

After Dumouriez's *coup* attempt in April 1793, civilian authorities began to heed the non-commissioned officers' complaints. Noting "the general discontent and disgust" produced by these nominations and fearing that they gave generals "a

89 A.G. MR 2018, Claude Vézu, "Mémoire sur les abus qui se commettent à l'armée par le citoyen Vézu, chef du 3ème bataillon de Paris" (1793).
90 A.N. D§1 26, "Lettre de Binet, sergent-major au 42ème régiment d'infanterie, connu des citoyens Charbonnier et Escudier, tous deux députés du Var à la Convention, aux représentants du peuple" (21 April 1793).
91 A.N. AF III 158, "Lettre de Lhoir, lieutenant au 2ème bataillon de la 52ème demi-brigade à la commission militaire des Cinq-Cents" (10 Fructidor V).
92 Anne-Henri-Cabot, vicomte de Dampmartin, *Mémoire sur divers événemens de la Révolution et de l'émigration* (Paris, 1825), vol. 1, 150. Necker expressed a similar view when, in reaction to the abolition of nobility in June 1790, he wrote that the soldiers, "far from being wounded by the brilliance of the people to whom they consecrate their labors, they are often happy to receive its reflection" *A.P.*, vol. 16, 387.
93 A.G. X^{b}178, "Lettre des officiers et sous-officiers du 44ème régiment au ministre de la guerre" (n.d.).
94 A.G. Personnel dossier, Series 91/47, Voysin, "Lettre de Voysin au ministre de la guerre" (14 February 1793). For other examples of conflict between non-commissioned officers and the sons of active citizens, see A.G. X^{b}785, "Lettre du ministre de la guerre au commandant du 1er régiment d'infanterie" (20 December 1792); and A.G. X^{b}791, "Lettre du Xavier Audouin aux représentants du peuple près l'armée d'Italie" (30 Brumaire II).

means of taking over the army," the representatives-on-mission to the Army of the Ardennes annulled some nominations.[95] Surveillance committees also issued denunciations. The one at Saint-Brieuc condemned the nomination of Palasne-Champeaux, son of a deputy to the Constituent Assembly. Although the young man lacked the maturity and talents to be an officer, he had still obtained a commission, no doubt through "the continual servility of [his] father in the antechambers of the under-ministers." Moreover, the elder Palasne-Champeaux was "a rabid federalist," and the son was already exhibiting the same "arrogance as ... his father, with those whom he dares regard as his inferiors."[96] In the opinion of many republicans, the constitutional monarchy had succeeded all too well in finding officers capable of replacing their aristocratic predecessors. For this reason, the sons of active citizens suffered disproportionately from the purges of politically suspect officers conducted in 1793 and the year II.[97] Yet, despite this attrition, those who escaped the purges or won reinstatement after Thermidor would find themselves well-placed to succeed in the military profession during the Directory and Empire.

The officers of the National Guard volunteer battalions, 1791–93

Another group of socially favored officers who would go far in the armies of the Directory, Consulate, and Empire came from the battalions of National Guard volunteers formed in three successive levies between the summer of 1791 and the fall of 1793. The first volunteer battalions were created in response to the King's flight. On 21 June 1791 the National Assembly called upon the departments to raise battalions to maintain internal order and defend the frontiers from expected invasion.[98] Events appeared to warrant the mobilization of these citizen-soldiers. Shaken by insubordination and emigration, the regular army could not be relied upon to support the regime or to defend the country effectively. Given the uncertainties of the internal political situation and the likelihood of foreign invasion, the creation of a fresh army commanded by officers who had the confidence of their men was seen as an absolute necessity. After the declaration of war in April 1792, the Assembly urgently repeated its appeal for the formation of volunteer battalions as reinforcements. Although their service was intended to last only for the duration of the emergency, military requirements and political considerations eventually led to their unification with the professional army. The assimilation of

---

95 A.N. AF II 232, "Arrêté des représentants du peuple, commissaires à l'armée des Ardennes, qui annule toutes nominations aux emplois militaires faites par les généraux de l'armée" (14 May 1793).

96 A.N. AF II 9, "Les membres composant le comité de surveillance renouvellé par les sections de Saint-Brieuc au citoyen Bouchotte, ministre de la guerre" (8 October 1793).

97 From 700 to 1,300 officers were suspended between June 1793 and April 1794. Bertaud and Reichel, *Atlas*, 22; and Lynn, *Bayonets*, 84–7.

98 For the military committee's initial proposal to form volunteer battalions, see *A.P.*, vol. 27, 393–5.

the volunteers into the regular military structure added a new element to the reconstituted officer corps.

Two structural differences – the organization of the battalions along territorial lines and the designation of their officers by election – distinguished the volunteers from the regular army and lent their cadres particular characteristics. The battalions were recruited from and maintained close ties with their home departments. In fact, the battalions were usually recruited from even smaller areas, generally from a single urban center or several contiguous rural districts. Their constituent companies were drawn from even more narrowly circumscribed areas ranging in size from a district to a single commune. Usually companies were raised "in isolation" in their communities of origin and were only formed into battalions when they reached the frontier.[99] Generally, the authorities charged with organizing the battalions respected the integrity of the different communities which had furnished companies. Officials who tried to shuffle volunteers between the companies could face stiff resistance. For example, the agents responsible for forming the 1st battalion of the Allier were opposed when they tried to transfer personnel between companies. These officials, who included two Old Regime army officers, wanted to redistribute the experienced volunteers not only to give "to each company the same military resources and forces," but also to "stifle all spirit of locality." The volunteers, however, resisted vigorously. "The majority of volunteers loudly demanded ... that the companies be formed by district. The agents vainly pointed out the flaws of such an organization but, fearing a fatal schism, preferred to bend to the will of the majority."[100]

Others, however, saw military value in encouraging a spirit of locality among the volunteers. One of these, Lieutenant-Colonel Oudinot of the 3rd battalion of the Meuse, one of thirteen volunteer officers destined to become a marshal, insisted on "the importance of maintaining and nourishing the union and spirit of fraternity which constitute the force of the national battalions." He warned that this spirit would "suffer from the admission of strangers."[101] In practice, Oudinot's view usually prevailed. The internal organization of most battalions reflected the desire of towns and villages to keep their companies distinct and under the leadership of their own officers.

In conjunction with territorial organization, the method of designating the officers and non-commissioned officers – democratic election by the volunteers themselves – ensured that the battalions would remain firmly in the hands of local

---

99 A.G. X^b126, "Circulaire de la commission aux conseils d'administration" (15 Thermidor III).
100 A.G. X^v4, 1er bataillon de l'Allier.
101 A.G. X^w67, "Lettre d'Oudinot aux administrateurs du département" (28 November 1791). The other marshals who were elected as officers in National Guard volunteer battalions were Brune, Davout, Jourdan, Kléber, Lannes, Maison, Masséna, Molitor, Mortier, Mouton, Suchet, and Victor. And even Napoleon himself was elected to high rank in a Corsican battalion.

elites. Complementary political and practical motives dictated the adoption of election as the means of choosing officers for the volunteer battalions. Since the volunteers were temporarily activated National Guards, which all elected their officers, it was politically impossible for the Assembly to curtail their right to vote for their own leaders. This consideration was bolstered by pragmatic ones. It was expected that the prospect of gaining an officer's commission by winning election would bring forward large numbers of eager volunteers. "Competition for the places [of officer]," one ministerial official remarked, had "marvelous effects, and it is doubtful that without this vehicle, the volunteers would have flocked to the armies in the way they did."[102] Election also resolved administrative problems which threatened to delay the completion of the battalions. The war ministry could have appointed the officers itself, but this would have gone against the revolutionaries' characteristic distrust of executive authority and also required much research, correspondence, and paperwork. Already overwhelmed with trying to find replacements for the thousands of regular army officers who had emigrated, the war ministry's personnel office was in no position to assume this additional burden. Letting the volunteers elect their own officers would allow the ministry to concentrate on its other pressing affairs.

Yet, while confirming the volunteers' right to choose their commanders, the Assembly instituted safeguards to ensure that the battalions were provided with competent leadership. Volunteer officers of all ranks were to have served in either the National Guard or the regular army. To ensure competence at the higher levels, the Assembly also required that at least one of the commanding lieutenant-colonels in each battalion had served as a captain in the regular army. In part because of these eligibility requirements, but also because most communities contained willing veterans whom the volunteers were happy to have as their leaders and instructors, about one-third of the officers elected had previously served in the army.[103]

The voting procedure reinforced the spirit of locality inherent in the territorial organization of the companies and battalions. The election of the company-grade officers – a captain, a lieutenant, and a second lieutenant – was carried out within the company itself, always apart from the rest of the battalion and under the direction of a municipal official. For these elections, the Assembly adopted the same mode of voting it had designed for civil elections. If the first two ballots did not produce an absolute majority, a runoff would be held between the two leading candidates. As in civil elections, some companies dispensed with these formalities and named officers by acclamation.[104] These electoral assemblies of friends,

---

102 A.N. AF III 152ª, "Conscription."
103 Bertaud, *La Révolution armée*, 70.
104 For a useful summary of revolutionary voting procedures, see Patrice Gueniffey, *Le Nombre et la raison: la Révolution française et les élections* (Paris, 1993), 273–321.

relatives, and neighbors generally chose as officers men whose expertise, social position, wealth, or force of character commanded respect in their civil communities. This manifested itself in an important percentage of unanimous votes (22 percent), votes decided by a margin of at least 90 percent (35 percent), and the infrequency of elections close enough to require a second round of voting (9 percent).[105] The election of the battalion officers – two lieutenant-colonels and a quartermaster – was to be conducted separately by companies according to the same procedure. The nomination of battalion officers was often divisive, but even these contestations concealed a high degree of consensus within the individual companies. Although the 1st battalion of the Charente inférieure elected its quartermaster by only 56 percent of the vote (169 of 301), six of its eight companies cast unanimous or near-unanimous votes. The 1st, 2nd, 5th, and 7th companies all unanimously designated a volunteer named Boujou, who ultimately won the election. The 3rd company gave him 84 percent of its suffrage. The 6th and 8th companies, however, each cast unanimous votes for their own candidates, Roux la Prudence and Bigondeau, respectively. The 4th company accorded another candidate, La Rue, over 60 percent of its vote.[106] The community-based recruitment of the companies could thus be a source of division within a battalion by infecting it with local feuds and personal rivalries. In such instances, a compromise might be reached by choosing an outsider, as happened at the formation of the 1st battalion of the Mayenne et Loire.[107]

But more typically the logic of advancement discouraged the election of candidates from outside the voting company to fill its vacancies. This is because the promotion of an insider procured advancement for other members of the group. When the 8th company of the 1st battalion of the Aisne had to elect a new captain, it used its choice to unleash a cascade of promotions. By naming the company lieutenant captain, the second lieutenant lieutenant, the sergeant-major second lieutenant etc., the replacement of a single officer resulted in advancement for five additional volunteers. These promotions were all decided by unanimous votes.[108] One volunteer reflected bitterly on this inward-looking practice which, in his view, perpetuated a narrow spirit of corporatism opposed to the proper sentiment of self-effacing virtue. "Each company will naturally follow the bent of the human heart which leads it to isolate itself in a corps, and to regard the posts

---

105 A.G. X^v2–21 and 31–3. These figures are based on the systematic analysis of the archives of 430 National Guard volunteer battalions, about half of the total number of battalions levied between 1791 and the year II. All election transcripts giving exact vote-counts were used, producing a sample of 302 elections. For a more detailed discussion, see my article, "Démocratie et professionalisme: l'avancement par l'élection dans l'armée française, 1760–1815," *Annales historiques de la Révolution française*, 310 (1997), 601–25.
106 A.G. X^v9, 1er bataillon de la Charente Inférieure.
107 Claude Petitfrère, *Les Bleus d'Anjou (1789–1792)* (Paris, 1985), 161.
108 A.G. X^v3, 1er bataillon de l'Aisne.

left to its nomination as a property that would be humiliating and against its interest to transport elsewhere, [a tendency] directly opposed to the spirit of the Constitution."[109] By providing a self-interested reason for choosing candidates for promotion from within the group, advancement by election reinforced the insularity of units that were already united by ties of family and community.

These elections produced a corps of volunteer officers composed of local notables. In his statistical survey of the social composition of the volunteers of 1791, Jean-Paul Bertaud found that company-grade officers were generally recruited from groups which enjoyed wealth and standing in their communities.[110] About 60 percent classified themselves as merchants, professionals, administrators, or students. The volunteers' propensity to choose notables as their officers was especially pronounced in the case of the lieutenant-colonels who commanded the battalions; of these, at least half were noble. In large part, this was due to the requirement that one of the battalion's lieutenant-colonels had to have served as a captain in the regular army, a position effectively reserved for nobles during the Old Regime. But nobles also won election because of the social deference some continued to enjoy after 1789. Battalions chose as their commanders local nobles with no military experience whatsoever, men like Louis-Marie-Joseph de Fay de Quincy, son of the lord of Chignolles (3rd battalion of the Aisne), and Michel-Louis Rigaud de l'Isle, son of an ennobled merchant (4th battalion of the Drôme).[111] Considerations of social status played an equally important role in the choice of non-noble lieutenant-colonels: Bertaud found that fully 80 percent were local notables. The volunteer officers of 1792 came from similar social backgrounds, with the sole difference that nobles now formed a negligible element among the lieutenant-colonels.[112] The elected cadres of the volunteer battalions reproduced local solidarities, divisions, and hierarchies in a formal military structure. The elites who dominated the battalions constituted a large pool of socially distinguished officers, many of whom were destined for brilliant professional futures. This would not have surprised Barnave who had postulated that, in any territorially based military system, "the senators of the provinces and the officers of the army are from the same families."[113]

Those who received their commissions as part of the effort to rebuild the officer corps between mid-1791 and the end of 1793 – the sons of active citizens, non-commissioned officers, and National Guard volunteer officers – would provide the backbone and much of the higher leadership of the republican and Napoleonic

109 A.G. X^{V}1, Cazotts, lieutenant au 7ème bataillon de volontaires du Côte d'Or, "Réflexions sur le remplacement des emplois vacans dans les bataillons des gardes nationales volontaires."
110 Bertaud, *La Révolution armée*, 65–71.
111 Commandant Georges Dumont, *Les Bataillons de volontaires nationaux, 1791 (cadres et historiques)* (Paris, 1914), 387 and 405.
112 Jean-Paul Bertaud, "The Volunteers of 1792," in *Reshaping France: Town, Country, and Region during the French Revolution*, ed. Alan Forrest and Peter Jones (Manchester, 1991), 172–3.
113 Barnave, *Œuvres*, vol. 2, 48.

armies. 962 of the 2,248 generals (43 percent of the total) who would serve the Revolution and Empire achieved officer rank in one of these three capacities.[114] But among them, certain groups were clearly favored. In the lead with 486 generals (about 22 percent) were the volunteer officers, local elites who had benefited from immediate election to high rank. Close behind them, as the non-commissioned officers had feared, were the sons of active citizens. Blessed with wealth, education, social prestige, and family connections, these young men had key advantages in the competition for advancement. At least 173 became generals (about 8 percent). If we also include the 203 mid-level nominees (generally Old Regime supernumeraries) who became generals, then these operations yielded 376 generals, over 16 percent of all general officers of the Revolution and Empire. Superior cultural, social, and economic resources were not, however, the only reason for the success of the volunteer officers, sons of active citizens, and supernumeraries. The demographics of the recomposed officer corps ensured that the older non-commissioned officers would wear out as the wars ground on, while the others, most of whom were still in the prime of life, would remain. Given these considerations, it is not surprising that only one hundred of the older, more plebeian non-commissioned officers promoted as part of the replacement operations of 1791–93 ever reached the rank of general (a little over 4 percent). While ending the noble domination of the military profession, the revolutionary reconstruction of the officer corps did not lead to dramatic social leveling. In contrast to the former non-commissioned officers, the National Guard volunteer officers, sons of active citizens, and supernumeraries constituted a distinct pool on which later regimes would draw to staff the highest ranks of the army.

114 The figures in this paragraph are all derived from Six, *Dictionnaire biographique des généraux*.

4 Republican meritocracy in the nexus of war, civil strife, and factionalism

Upon taking power on 21 September 1792, the Convention had to face daunting, concurrent challenges. While striving to defend France against internal and external enemies, it also had to restructure the state along republican lines. As an institution both essential to the national defense and ideologically tainted because of its historic links to monarchy and nobility, the army stood at the junction of these two, often conflicting, aims. In keeping with its political mandate, the Convention rid the military of its Old Regime vestiges and purged the handful of noble officers who still remained. But this was just the beginning. Viewing them as incompatible with egalitarian and virtuous republicanism, it also abolished the system of officer recruitment and promotion adopted by the Constituent Assembly in 1790. The Convention therefore had to rebuild the entire career structure of the military profession, an endeavor that would not only have to pass the test of ideological purity, but also meet the challenges of warfare, civil strife, and political infighting. With the spring campaigning season approaching, the army would have to be reorganized quickly and put on a war footing. With entire regions of the country slipping into open counterrevolution, its subordination to the central government would have to be assured. And most significantly, factionalism in the Convention itself was politicizing the process of military reform, turning the army into an object which Girondins, Montagnards, and Hébertistes would fight to control. Despite the imminence of invasion and civil war, it was ultimately this struggle for power within the republican ranks which most strongly influenced the form republican military institutions would take.

The uneasy place of merit in the republican revolution

From the beginning the men who carried out the republican revolution in 1792 were less interested in the question of merit than their predecessors in 1789. In part, they could afford to be nonchalant because the first revolution had already secured civil equality and opened careers to talent. But perhaps the more fundamental reason for their relative unconcern was that their revolution, at least initially, was dedicated to highly risky, purely political objectives: overthrowing a centuries-old monarchy, replacing it with a republican form of government, and defending it against counterattack. As they struggled with the consequences of their momentous deed in the immediate aftermath of 10 August, the revolutionaries scarcely had time to consider the secondary question of merit's place in the

4 Official record of the election of an officer in the 39th Infantry Regiment, 28 Pluviôse II. The text indicates that the officer being replaced had been cashiered for accepting a position in a Federalist battalion of Toulon.

new polity. To the extent that merit figured at all in their public pronouncements, it typically appeared as an established principle whose final victory had been secured by the demise of the monarchy. By bringing an end to the tyranny of "kings, ministers, and the civil list," one Parisian orator proclaimed, the republican revolution had "eliminated the source of corruption." With the destruction of the Court, "effort would replace intrigue," and merit would triumph naturally, effortlessly, and painlessly.[1] A perfect meritocracy would be the automatic consequence of the republican revolution.

In practice, however, things were not so simple. Once confronted with the challenge of converting their rhetoric of opposition into a workable framework of government, the deputies of the Convention began to encounter contradictions between the meritocratic ideals of 1789 and their vision of the nascent republican polity. Their attempts to restructure existing meritocratic institutions along egalitarian and democratic lines would entail a fundamental reworking of the military profession.

One of the dangers of the current mechanisms of military meritocracy, from a republican point of view, was that they were predicated on the intervention of a superior authority – a king, minister, commanding officer, or examination board – to make selections. It had been against precisely this kind of executive power that the men of 10 August had risen, and they were determined not to revive it in any way. To do so, particularly in the army, could threaten the very existence of the Republic. To vest an individual with power over military careers, warned Saint-Just, was to "reestablish monarchy" which would take root "wherever the executive power disposes of the honor and advancement of the armies."[2] The Constituent Assembly (a republic in all but name according to some) had already confronted this problem when considering the reform of advancement in September 1790. But the means of promotion it had adopted – which preserved an important role for royal nomination – suggests that, despite their concerns, the deputies of the National Assembly were ultimately more willing to trust monarchs and ministers than their successors in the Convention would be. In the Convention, the objection that meritocracy risked reviving monarchical-style authority would not be so easily dismissed.

A second concern of republicans was that the practice of meritocracy necessarily involved making distinctions between citizens and distributing them within a scale of ranks. While the various individual qualities of merit – experience, technnical knowledge, courage, leadership, and genius – were all admirable in themselves and, indeed, had to be encouraged if the Republic were to survive, any

---

[1] "Discours de M. Gonchon, orateur des hommes de 1789," (16 August 1792), *Réimpression de l'ancien Moniteur*, no. 231, vol. 13, 437–8.
[2] *A.P.*, vol. 57, 458.

formal system for bringing them forth was bound to foster unacceptable inequalities. This threat was especially salient in the case of officers recruited directly from civilian life. The Constituent Assembly had faced this problem when determining a new method of entry-level officer selection, but its solution – competitive examinations measuring general education – flew in the face of republican egalitarianism. Denounced as making wealth the key to admission, the Convention condemned the examination for fostering a new "aristocracy" and consequently abolished it.[3] In the Republic, where "equality ought to preside all institutions," even superior knowledge was suspect.[4]

Republicans also believed that meritocracy, as traditionally conceived, implied a concept of personal motivation at odds with their ideal of a virtuous polity. Ever since the seventeenth century, when young nobles had been expected to strive to merit their privileged status, meritocratic institutions had sought to stimulate effort by appealing to the individual's desire for ranks, honors, and distinctions. This aim had become increasingly important in the successive reforms of advancement after the Seven Years' War and was further reinforced by the Constituent Assembly's military constitution. Republican virtue, however, looked to a different source of motivation than the individualistic one traditional meritocratic institutions (whether of the Old Regime or early Revolution) sought to tap. Described by Robespierre as the "soul of the Republic," virtue was that "magnanimous devotion" to the common good that rejected "stupid vanity" and instead "subsumed all private interests in the general interest." The virtuous citizen of the Republic was not spurred to action by the thought of personal gain, but rather by the hope of advancing the common cause. Meritocracy, in appealing to "egoism" and encouraging the selfish pursuit of "frivolous distinctions," thus perpetuated the flawed moral inclinations French society had received "under despotism."[5] Would it be possible to formulate a new conception of meritocracy which avoided the pitfalls of tyranny, inequality, and ambition?

Dismantling the meritocratic institutions of the old order

Before attempting to build mechanisms of officer recruitment and promotion compatible with republican polity, the Convention first had to dismantle objectionable military institutions it had inherited from the previous regimes. Naturally, the Convention sought to extirpate everything which recalled the old

---

3 A.N. AF II 199, "Lettre de Bossut au Comité de salut public" (8 Messidor III).
4 Garnier des Saintes speaking before the Convention on 11 February 1793, *A.P.*, vol. 57, 451.
5 Maximilien Robespierre, "Aux Amis de la constitution, sur les circonstances actuelles," and "Lettre de Maximilien Robespierre, membre de la Convention nationale de France, à ses commettans," in *Œuvres de Maximilien Robespierre, avec une notice historique, des notes, et des commentaires*, ed. Laponneraye (New York, reprint, originally published 1840), vol. 2, 19, 90, and 95.

monarchy. The law of 28 November 1792 abolishing "signs of royalty" was followed by a succession of decrees ordering the deroyalization of the military.[6] Officers of the regulars were ordered to exchange the white uniform of the Bourbons for the blue of the National Guard. They were also required to relinquish their old brevets of rank, which bore royal commissions, as well as epaulettes, decorations, and buttons embossed with monarchical marks. Those who failed to comply risked dismissal.[7] Regimental flags were scrutinized for offending signs, and even service records were altered to conform to the new political orthodoxy. For example, the indication "King's Own Regiment" was changed in the personnel registers maintained by the war ministry to "Regiment of the Tyrant" to extirpate the memory that the soldiers of the Republic had once served a king.

Especially shocking to republican sensibilities were the honorific distinctions of the monarchy, particularly the Cross of Saint-Louis. This royally bestowed honor was not only a visible sign of the reciprocal bonds which had once attached the officer corps to the king's service, but also a vestige of an honor-based motivational system which, in encouraging ambition, struck directly at the republican ideal of a virtuous and egalitarian polity. Accordingly, one of the Convention's first acts, taken on 15 October 1792, was to abolish the Cross. Although it had been awarded to long-serving *roturier officiers de fortune* as well as nobles, the decoration was, in the eyes of republicans, nothing more than "a stain on a uniform," the sign "by which kings branded their slaves."[8]

This was not, however, the only fault republicans found with military decorations. If royal provenance had been their only objection to the Cross, then the Convention could have replaced it with a politically acceptable decoration – one which was "simple, made for republicans, and capable of inspiring *émulation* without exciting envy" – as several officers suggested.[9] But all such plans were rejected out of hand because, in the view of the legislators, honorific orders of any sort violated republican equality by establishing distinctions between citizens. Decorations, moreover, encouraged self-interested instincts – ambition, pride, and honor – that were incompatible with the virtue republicans sought to inculcate. When kings had distributed their "ridiculous lot of titles and cordons" to

---

6 *Loi tendant à faire éffacer tous les emblèmes de la royauté* (28 November 1792).
7 A.N. AF II 14, "Comité de la guerre, séance du 19 November 1792;" A.N. AF II 198, "Arrêté du 24 August 1793;" and A.G.X^{b}126, Prat Desprez, "Exposé succinct des travaux du bureau de nomination aux emplois des officiers de l'infanterie" (28 June 1793).
8 *A.P.*, vol. 52, 505.
9 A.G. Y^{a}208, "Décoration militaire" (24 October 1792); "Sur le remplacement de la Croix de Saint-Louis par une decoration militaire;" and "Copie de la lettre écrite par le citoyen Gautier, adjudant-général commandant la 10ème division au citoyen président de la Convention nationale" (2 October 1792). See also, A.N. DXV2, "Demande de Chancel, colonel-adjudant-général de l'armée du Nord aux commissaires du pouvoir exécutif pour la décoration militaire" (5 September 1792).

their lackeys, Chenier recalled, "it was the pride of a single man flattering the vanity of several." The Republic could not move too quickly, he urged, to replace "these little indulgences of *amour-propre*, this 'honor' that Montesquieu called the basis of monarchies," with "love of the *patrie*, glory, and virtue."[10] Bestowed by a monarchical-type authority, establishing distinctions of status, and fostering a spirit of egoism, decorations were rejected as fundamentally antithetical to the Republic.

In keeping with its commitment to equality, the Convention made a concerted effort to blunt hierarchical distinctions within the army. Officers of all ranks, from generals to second lieutenants, were viewed with suspicion and subjected to political surveillance. Cowed by the threat of dismissal, imprisonment, or execution, the officers were reduced to silence during the Convention and effectively prevented from asserting a distinct professional identity. To weaken their hold over the army, they were stripped of all power over the advancement of their subordinates. To leave the officers with such authority, warned Bernard-Facos Lidon, was to see the soldiers inevitably transformed into "clients of faction and servitude."[11] At the same time, the rank-and-file (now known by the designation citizen-soldiers) were invited to play an unprecedented role in the internal direction of the army. In each combat unit, the Convention established administrative councils which were to carry out supervisory functions that had previously been the responsibility of the officers. The members of these councils – nine soldiers and four officers under a preliminary regulation, and then fifteen soldiers and eight officers according to the definitive law – were designated for six-month terms by the vote of the soldiers themselves. Disciplinary regulations were also rewritten to equalize the treatment of officers and soldiers, and the disciplinary councils, charged with upholding these regulations and hearing appeals in each unit, were reorganized along democratic lines to prevent abuses of power.[12] To give the soldiers a further means of resisting their officers' expected machinations, the soldiers were allowed to appeal over the heads of their superiors to outside, civilian authorities: municipalities, clubs, representatives-on-mission, and even the Convention itself.

More than merely efface the officer and limit his power, the Republic virtually made a cult out of the common soldier. As a citizen who sacrificed wealth, comfort, and even life itself for the good of the nation, the soldier exemplified the austerity and selflessness of republican virtue. "He repulses the enemy, preserves his *patrie* from the yoke of domination and, through his valor, confidence,

---

10 A.N. AD XVIII^{c}288, *Discours prononcé à la Convention nationale par Chenier* (15 Brumaire II).
11 A.N. AD XVIII^{c}308, *Projet d'organisation de la force armée de la République française, présenté au nom du Comité de défense générale par Bernard-Facos Lidon, député de la Coreze, membre du Comité de la guerre* (n.d.).
12 Lynn, *Bayonets*, 74–5 and 104.

firmness, and devotion, is the model of the true republican."[13] An ideal citizen, the soldier of the Republic deserved to enjoy, to the greatest extent compatible with his military duties, the civic rights which he was defending. This notion was not new in 1793. First voiced by military reformers during the Old Regime, it had, to a significant extent, been realized in practice through the military reforms of the Constituent Assembly. But the Republic went even further, according soldiers rights unprecedented for the time and, in certain ways, unimaginable today. The most striking of these was the right of inferiors to elect their hierarchical superiors, what Saint-Just called the "civic right" of the soldier.[14] But there were others as well, like the right to marry without first obtaining official permission, that also tended to level the inequalities of military society.[15] As exemplary citizens, moreover, soldiers were now encouraged to take part in the political life of the nation, something the Constituent Assembly – in banning them from clubs and restricting their voting rights – had shown itself loath to do. The Convention, in contrast, made special efforts to involve soldiers in the political life of the nation. It ordered copies of the *Bulletin des lois* posted in military camps, distributed political journals to the troops, encouraged club attendance, and even attempted to draft a "manual for the troops which would contain all the laws relative to their rights and duties."[16] As the "people of the armies," the soldiers were celebrated in republican rhetoric, while the officers, vilified in official discourse and forced to protect their precarious position by becoming as unobtrusive as possible, faded into the background.[17]

Nothing signalled the leveling of hierarchy, the weakening of distinctions between soldiers and officers, more sharply than the abolition of direct nominations to the officer corps. In a republic of equals, it was no longer acceptable for some citizens to begin their careers directly as officers while the rest were obliged to begin their service in the ranks. Rather, all should enter the army at the bottom of the hierarchy, as simple soldiers. Republican military writers hammered home this point. With us, wrote the anonymous author of a republican military constitution, "no one can aspire to any place without having passed through all the subaltern grades, beginning with that of soldier."[18] "If you are all equal," exclaimed the commander of a Parisian National Guard volunteer battalion, "then

---

13 A.N. AD XVIII°288, Bouquier, *Rapport et projet de décret formant un plan général d'instruction publique*, 2.
14 *A.P.*, vol. 57, 458.
15 *Loi, qui en dérogeant au reglèment du 1er juillet 1788, autorise tout militaire à se marier sans la permission de ses chefs* (8 March 1793).
16 A.N. AF II 232, "Lettre du représentant du peuple Gasparin au Comité de salut public," (13 May 1793). On the political education of the republican army, see Bertaud, *La Révolution armée*, 194–229, and Marc Martin, "Journaux d'armées au temps de la Convention," *Annales historiques de la Révolution française*, 210 (1972), 567–605.
17 A.N. AF II 211, "Le Comité de salut public aux représentants du peuple près les armées" (II).
18 A.G. MR 2018, "Constitution militaire de la République" (n.d.).

begin by the *métier* of soldier before arriving at officer rank, and if you have merited it, you will be rewarded with advancement."[19] The elimination of direct officer nomination and its consequence, the unification of the hierarchy of non-commissioned and commissioned grades into a single continuum of ranks, was the most durable feature of republican military meritocracy. Although the extraordinary rights granted to soldiers would be whittled away, republican opposition to the direct nomination of officers would remain unshakable. A lone attempt to reinstitute it was made in the year VII (1797–98), but was soundly rejected for tending to "reestablish aristocracy in the armies."[20] It was not until Napoleon's seizure of power that young men from good families would once again be able to become officers directly without having to pass through the ranks.

With the elimination of direct commissions, specialized military education lost its *raison d'être*. It was probably doomed in any event because of its origins in the Old Regime's system of noble privilege. Before 1789, recalled the Montagnard legislator and educational reformer Romme, military schooling was designed to "favor the ambition of a class of men who regarded all honorable posts in the state as their patrimony."[21] Barère put it more bluntly. To get into a royal military school, he claimed, one had to be descended from "some feudal brigand, some privileged scoundrel, some ridiculous marquis, some upstart baron or court hanger-on."[22] The administrators of the military school tried to defend it against these attacks. Since early 1790, they reminded, admissions to the school were no longer based on pedigree, but rather on the military services of the applicants' fathers. Perhaps this change had made little difference at first, they admitted, but now that the rapid turnover of personnel in the army had "raised to officer rank many non-commissioned officers and soldiers who are absolutely without fortune," it was "all the more necessary to reserve such aid for this class of citizens."[23] This argument – that the emigration of the nobility had opened military education to good republican soldiers who had risen through the ranks – did not satisfy the Convention. For the deputies, military education was incompatible with republicanism not only because of its past association with noble privilege, but also because any form of professional education tended to inculcate a particularist outlook, revive corporate identity, and, ultimately, resurrect "caste."[24] Although specialized instruction might be necessary in the technical branches, as

19 A.G. MR 2018, "Mémoire sur les abus qui se commettent à l'armée, par le citoyen Vézu, chef du 3ème bataillon de Paris" (n.d.).
20 A.N. AF III* 274, "Procès-verbal de la Commission militaire des cinq-cents" (18 Brumaire VI).
21 A.N. AD XVIII^{c}290, Romme, *Rapport sur l'instruction publique considerée dans son ensemble*, 4–5.
22 Cited in H. C. Barnard, *Education and the French Revolution* (London, 1969), 142.
23 A.N. AD XVIII^{c}290, *Fondation des écoles militaires de la République* (1793), 14; and A.G. Y^{a}161, "Lettre du ministère de la guerre à Perard," (21 September 1792).
24 A.N. AD XVIII^{c}288, C. F. Daunou, *Essai sur l'instruction publique*.

in military engineering where it was deemed "absolutely indispensable," the Convention refused to allow it in an egalitarian army where everyone began as a simple soldier and learned by doing.²⁵ Military schooling for infantry and cavalry officers was consequently abolished on 9 September 1793.

It is true that the Convention briefly attempted to establish a republican military school, the Ecole de Mars, but even this short-lived experiment illustrates the fundamental republican opposition to direct recruitment and specialized officer education.²⁶ Founded on 13 Prairial II (1 June 1794), the Ecole de Mars was intended to "form entirely republican defenders of the *patrie* and revolutionize the youth." Although its 3,000 students, recruited among the "children of *sans-culottes* serving in the different armies" and the rural poor, would receive a veneer of instruction in the military arts, and a handful would be selected for more intensive training in the technical branches, the institution's primary aim was to teach its students republican values.²⁷ Even the technically minded director of engineering at the school, Bizot-Charmois, believed that, at most, the school might "cast some germs of knowledge into the imagination of the young students." He did not complain about the modesty of this instructional goal because he recognized that the main purpose of the school was a moral one – to "form *mœurs* [habits, morals, and social comportment], character, and virtues appropriate to republicans."²⁸

In keeping with republican egalitarianism, matriculation at the Ecole de Mars would under no circumstances provide graduates with titles to officer rank. Barère explained that

> this national education furnishes neither privilege, nor any particular title to placement. In the royal military school, one acquired the right to be placed as an army officer, without having learned to be one; here, one learns above all to be a citizen, to be a soldier, to obey the laws, to love the *patrie*, and to await its call. The man of the Republic ought to train himself, receive education, and improve himself without any other ambition than that of becoming a good citizen ... He must not announce any pretention, he ought to wait in his honorable solitude for the Republic or his fellow citizens to call him to occupy a place.²⁹

This pronouncement was not just rhetorical sugar-coating applied to make the revival of military education palatable to the Convention. Rather, it announced an inflexible policy which was enforced by successive republican regimes.

---

25 A.N. AF II 199, "Rapport par la Commission de l'organisation et du mouvement des armées de terre aux représentants du peuple composant le Comité de salut public," (22 Thermidor III).
26 The only work on the Ecole de Mars remains Arthur Chuquet, *L'Ecole de Mars* (Paris, 1899).
27 A.N. AD XVIII^c288, Barère, *Rapport fait à la Convention nationale au nom du Comité de salut public dans la séance du 13 Prairial sur l'éducation révolutionnaire, républicaine, et militaire, et décret sur la formation de l'Ecole de Mars* (13 Prairial II).
28 B.G., in-fol 287, Bizot-Charmois, "Plan d'instruction militaire destiné aux élèves de l'Ecole de Mars" (8 Thermidor II).
29 A.N. AD XVIII^c288, Barère, *Rapport ... sur la formation de l'Ecole de Mars*.

Although, with the school's closure in Brumaire III, the students were sent back to their homes and ordered to await military call-up like their peers, some attempted to parlay their experience at the Ecole de Mars into an officer's commission. On each occasion, their demands were rejected in no uncertain terms. One former student, Chauveau, who dared to request an officer's commission was sharply rebuked. "The intention of the Convention," he was informed, "was not to privilege the students of the Ecole de Mars by violating in their favor the hierarchy and the rights of their brothers-in-arms."[30] Another student, Pierre-François Jerome, was chastised even more severely. "Thousands of your comrades are fighting," the curt ministerial response reproached, and you "have done nothing to become an officer." "We are not here to renew privilege."[31]

Factionalism and republican military reorganization

Ridding the military of institutions linked to the social and political practices of the old order was only the first step on the path of republican military reform. More difficult was the task of providing the military profession with new structures not only consonant with the egalitarian and democratic principles of the new polity, but also capable of providing the Republic with the means of preserving itself from internal and external threats. And, as if balancing the demands of ideological purity with those of military necessity were not enough of a challenge, the Convention had to undertake this task while in the throes of a bitter factional struggle between Girondins and Montagnards for control of the state.

While it is axiomatic that, in revolutions, the organization of the armed forces is never politically neutral, this was never more evident than during the Convention's consideration of comprehensive republican military reform. Adopted in the Montagnard-dominated war committee on 1 February 1793 and presented to the full legislature six days later by its principal author, Dubois-Crancé, the plan called for two dramatic changes: the unification of the volunteer battalions with those of the former royal army – in new units called *demi-brigades*, to be composed of two volunteer and one regular battalion – and the creation of a new system of advancement – reserving two-thirds of promotion to a democratic form of election and the remaining one-third to a redefined notion of seniority.[32] These radical proposals provoked two weeks of heated debate which pitted notable Montagnards, led by Dubois-Crancé and Saint-Just, against prominent Girondin orators. The factional coloration of the debate suggests that more was at stake in the proposed reorganization than just the ideological and

---

30 A.N. AF II 201, "Arrêté du 6 Floréal III."
31 A.G. X°1, "Rapport présenté à la Commission de l'organisation et du mouvement des armées de terre: bureau du personnel de la cavalerie" (6 Nivôse III).
32 A.N. AF II 14, "Comité de la guerre, séance du 1er February 1793."

military consequences of unification and electoral advancement. Rather what hinged on these specific points of republican military reform was control of the army, the state, and, ultimately, the course of the Revolution. Even in the face of foreign invasion and civil war, it was the life-or-death struggle between Girondins and Montagnards that most strongly determined the precise manner in which general republican ideals would be translated into concrete military institutions.

Debate in the full Convention began on 7 February with a discussion of the proposed unification of the volunteers with the former royal army, an operation that would come to be known as the *amalgame*.[33] The Montagnards argued that this measure was both militarily and politically necessary. From a military perspective, the existing fragmentation of French forces into hundreds of battalions generated intolerable confusion. Administrative oversight had broken down, corruption was rife, magazines were empty, and critical locations on the frontier were undefended. Thanks to recent levies, the Republic did not lack defenders. But scattered across France in over 600 disparate units – volunteer battalions, regular regiments, free companies, legions, and others – they lacked cohesion and uniformity. Indeed, even the war ministry had no clear idea of the number and nature of the forces at its disposal. To regain control over this anarchic situation, it was necessary to carry out a general recensement and reorganizaton. In addition, unification was militarily necessary because the volunteers lacked expertise which only the line could provide. All these administrative and tactical problems could be solved by fusing the two armies.

Politically, the Montagnards argued, unification of the regulars and volunteers was needed to efface the last traces of "aristocracy" in the line army. Saint-Just warned that, as long as the army remained apart from the nation, "an armed corporation, the last dangerous debris of the monarchy," it would menace the Republic.[34] And as long as its officers retained a distinct corporate identity, Dubois-Crancé added, they would perpetuate the spirit of "aristocracy." Only unification could dispel the "noble spirit" which still haunted the line units and continued to make even plebeian officers who had risen from the ranks believe that they belonged to a "different caste" from their soldiers.[35] The integration of the army into the nation and the extinction of the last sparks of the old noble ethos could only be assured by submerging it in a sea of patriotic volunteers, the nation in arms.

While praising these high ideals, the Girondins raised a number of practical objections to the Montagnard plan. Led by Buzot, they argued that, at the present juncture, unification would demoralize and disorganize the army by transforming the healthy competition between volunteer and line officers into a bitter rivalry for

---

33 For a more complete discussion, see my article, "Démocratie et professionalisme."
34 *A.P.*, vol. 57, 457.
35 A.N. AD XVIII^{c}307, *Rapport sur l'embrigadement des armées au nom du Comité militaire, par le citoyen Dubois Crancé* (13 Frimaire II).

advancement. Such divisions would cripple military effectiveness at the very moment when the monarchical powers were poised to descend upon the Republic. Furthermore, the displacement of battalions, turnover in personnel, and administrative changes involved in such a sweeping reorganization would compromise the army's capacity to wage war. Although unification appeared beneficial in the long run, admitted the Girondins, present military conditions demanded its postponement. The law actually enacted on 21 February 1793 adopted their position by suspending the execution of the plan. For their part, the Montagnards, fearing the outcome of the reorganization if carried out by the just-installed war minister Beurnonville, suspected of Girondin sympathies, also welcomed the delay. Several months later, however, only days after the expulsion of the Girondins from the Convention and the replacement of Beurnonville by the radical Bouchotte, Montagnard deputies would describe the suspension of unification as the work of a "conspiratorial faction" and have it lifted.[36]

Having resolved the question of unification by means of this temporary compromise, the Convention turned to the second point of contention, military election. The Montagnards argued that election was both a political right and a professionally sound mode of selection. Politically, Dubois-Crancé claimed, granting soldiers the right to elect their superiors was a long-overdue act of justice. Having set aside his self-interest in order to defend the nation, the citizen-soldier had an even stronger title to the conservation of his rights than the ordinary citizen. To this end, it was necessary to "shape everything according to the great principle of equality, that administrators only hold their positions by the free choice of the administered."[37] Not merely the rights of the individual citizen-soldier, pursued Saint-Just, but even the very survival of the Republic depended upon the adoption of electoral advancement. It alone could eliminate from the army the influence of "all powers foreign to the spirit of popular independence" and guarantee the "liberty of the people." To leave advancement in the hands of generals or ministers, he warned, would allow them to constitute personal military clienteles with "civil war, usurpation, and military government" the inescapable outcome. Only a democratic system of electoral advancement, he concluded, could prevent an ambitious leader from using the power of promotion to wrest the army's loyalties away from the nation.[38]

The Montagnards also touted the military advantages of this system. According to Saint-Just, it was absolutely necessary to perfect meritocracy and reinforce discipline. Who more than the soldiers could be counted on to make discerning choices? After all, their very survival ultimately depended upon the

36 "Lettre des représentants Lesage-Senault et Duhem, commissaires à l'armée du Nord" (8 June 1793), A.P., vol. 66, 234.
37 A.P., vol. 57, 359.
38 A.P., vol. 57, 457–8.

wisdom of their votes. Who was in a better position than they to judge the "conduct, bravery, and character of those with whom they have lived?" Advancement by election would "multiply the force" of the army by "honoring only virtue, courage, and merit." Far from fomenting insubordination, as some had claimed, election would actually "reestablish discipline" by ensuring that the soldiers had confidence in their officers' abilities and patriotism. This new kind of republican discipline, based upon respect, trust, and informed consent, would make the army an extraordinarily effective fighting force.[39]

As with their objections to unification, the Girondins did not challenge the Montagnards' political arguments for electoral advancement, but, taking up the criticisms formulated by the military committee of the Constituent Assembly, opposed it on the grounds that it would interfere with the proper functioning of the army. According to them, the Montagnards were mistaken in believing that election would favor merit. On the contrary, election would open the door to intrigues and the promotion of ambitious incompetents. The accession of such people to officer rank would disgust experienced soldiers, violate their rights to advancement, and subject their careers to an unacceptable degree of insecurity. By promoting those unworthy of the honor, election would generate resentment and cleavages within the officer corps at a time when its undivided attention was needed for the war effort. Furthermore, if their careers were at the mercy of their subordinates' good will, the officers would overlook disciplinary infractions, or worse, court the soldiers' suffrage by countenancing even the most outrageous lapses of good conduct. Yet, as the debate progressed and it became clear that the majority in the Convention wanted some kind of electoral advancement, the Girondins were forced to moderate their initially uncompromising opposition. Isnard, Genissieu, Vergniaud, and Salle put forward an alternative system of electoral advancement based on cooption, but this attempt at compromise came too late. The system of democratic electoral advancement presented by Dubois-Crancé two weeks earlier was decreed without amendment on 21 February 1793.

The method of electoral advancement adopted instituted a two-stage voting procedure, combining presentation by the inferiors and cooption. When a position of sergeant, second lieutenant, lieutenant, or captain fell vacant, the company with the opening was to assemble to proceed with the election. All those in grades below that being filled were allowed to vote. They could only choose candidates from the rank immediately inferior to the one being filled, thereby ensuring gradual advancement. Although the law did not clearly indicate if candidates had to be chosen within the voting battalion itself, or rather, if the choice could be extended to the entire *demi-brigade*, the war ministry soon interpreted the law as

[39] *A.P.*, vol. 58, 457–8.

restricting the selection of candidates to the voting battalion.⁴⁰ The voting procedure was modeled after that employed in the primary assemblies. Voting was to take place by secret ballot, illiterate soldiers were allowed to designate a comrade to transcribe their choices, and soldiers absent for military reasons could vote by mail. Immediately after the voting, the three oldest soldiers capable of reading and writing were to count the ballots and determine the three leading vote-recipients. Then these candidates were to be presented to an assembly of all the personnel in the battalion of the grade to be filled. This assembly was to select one of the candidates in a vote of their own. Although the superposition of this cooptive selection over a genuinely democratic vote drew some criticism, notably by Robespierre who denounced it as "an incomplete election which participates in two opposing systems, the choice by the superior and the choice by the subaltern," the law did provide a means for the lower assembly to overrule the upper one. A candidate who had been proposed and rejected three times would receive promotion automatically if presented a fourth time.

By leaving the battalions intact and distinct within the *demi-brigade*, Dubois-Crancé's method of unification would have perpetuated the tendency for the vote to designate members of the electoral community. In the regular battalion of the *demi-brigade*, elections were to be conducted within the company, a group of professional soldiers bound by hierarchical discipline, *esprit de corps*, and common experience. In the case of the volunteers, voting was to take place in units which, as we have seen, mirrored the civil communities in which they had been raised. These professional and civil solidarities, sufficient in themselves to favor the selection of candidates from within the unit in which a vacancy had occurred, were reinforced by the self-interested logic of advancement. Throughout the 1790s, officers complained that voting companies only chose candidates from their own ranks, "under the abusive hope of obtaining a more eminent [grade]" for themselves.⁴¹ Of course, suffrage was not influenced solely by group loyalty and ambition; considerations of competence and charisma also shaped electoral choices. But given a range of reasonably qualified candidates, the organization of the *demi-brigades* and the vote by company encouraged the designation of postulants from within the electoral group.

The new law on advancement contained another significant innovation, however, that drew little comment during the Convention's debates. This was the provision granting one-third of all advancement to seniority defined not as *time served in one's present grade*, but rather as *time of one's total military service*. This

---

40 A.G. X^{b}786, "Lettre du ministre de la guerre au conseil d'administration du bataillon de dépôt du 104ème régiment" (16 July 1793).
41 A.N. AF II 207, "Lettre du conseil d'administration de la 91ème demi-brigade" (4 Germinal III). For similar complaints, see A.G. X^{b}791, "Lettre de Xavier Audouin au commandant de la 4ème demi-brigade" (4 Frimaire II); and A.G. MR 2008, "Vues sur l'infanterie françoise."

change gave a marked advantage to the personnel of the former royal army who had many years of service as soldiers and non-commissioned officers to their credit. Under the traditional definition of seniority as time in the grade, they would have generally been outranked by the volunteer officers and sons of active citizens because these two categories of personnel had been commissioned directly in 1791 and 1792 when the promotion of non-nobles in the regular army was still impeded. Redefined as length of overall service, however, seniority favored the veterans of the line army over the volunteers and sons of active citizens, the majority of whom had only entered the military profession after 1789. This was the purpose of the change. In his report to the Convention, Dubois-Crancé emphasized "the advantages of this system for veteran troops over newly raised corps."[42]

Given these formal provisions and likely comportment, how would these organizational and advancement reforms have affected the composition of the officer corps, had they been implemented as proposed? Although the plan's Montagnard backers spent much time praising the patriotism of the volunteers and warning against the aristocratic spirit which still prevailed in the line army, the proposed system of advancement actually favored the regular officers. By replacing seniority in the grade with seniority of total military service, the plan virtually ensured the regulars this portion (one-third) of advancement, a proportion which corresponded exactly to their numerical importance within the *demi-brigade*. In addition, since advancement by seniority applied to vacancies within the entire *demi-brigade*, the law ensured the regulars automatic, cross-over promotions into the volunteer battalions. These were not the only benefits enjoyed by the regulars under the new system. Although election would seem to have favored the more numerous volunteers, the organization of the vote by company and battalion, in conjunction with the self-interested logic of electoral advancement, ensured that the regulars would also monopolize all promotions by election within their own battalion. Electoral advancement would take place separately within the battalions and, moreover, be distributed evenly across the *demi-brigade*. This was the conscious intention of the plan's author. In an address to the regular army, Dubois-Crancé summarized the advantages which it would enjoy under the new system.

> (1) The regular battalion will have all the vacant places in its battalion, by either election or seniority ...
> (2) Furthermore, this battalion will have almost all the vacant places due to seniority in the other two battalions since the rights of seniority roll across the whole *demi-brigade* ... [43]

42 *A.P.*, vol. 57, 361.
43 Dubois-Crancé, "Addresse à l'armée," reprinted in Colonel Théodore Jung, *Dubois-Crancé (Edmond-Alexis-Louis): mousquetaire, constituant, conventionnel, général de division, ministre de la guerre* (Paris, 1884), 368–9.

In principle, then, by awarding the regulars all advancement by seniority (one-third) and all advancement by election within their own battalion (two-ninths), the law guaranteed them five-ninths of all promotions, a share nearly double what a strictly proportional division of advancement would have given them, and also ensured that they would soon take over positions of command in the two volunteer battalions.

While the ostensible military aims of the *amalgame* – uniformity, administrative simplification, and the redistribution of expertise throughout the armed forces – were straightforward responses to the military situation of France, the political intentions of the Montagnard plan were less evident. If, as their orators claimed, the point of the reform was to infuse the former royal army with the patriotic spirit of the volunteers, why did the mechanisms of advancement give preferential treatment to the regulars at the expense of the volunteers? Why did the system allow regular officers to cross over into the volunteer battalions (by seniority of service) without providing the volunteers opportunities to move into and exert their influence over the line battalion? Clearly the plan of advancement proposed by Dubois-Crancé would have produced effects at odds with its avowed political purpose. To understand this gap between rhetoric and reality, we must situate the military reorganization in its broader political context, the Girondin–Montagnard power struggle.

The fundamental political purpose of the reorganization was to disarm the Girondins by removing the volunteer battalions from departmental control and incorporating them into the regular army, under the authority of professional officers and the war ministry. The Montagnards viewed the volunteers as a potential Girondin military force. The volunteers were led by local notables, suspected of hostility towards the preeminent role of Parisian radicals in national politics and, consequently, to the Montagnards who sought to propel themselves into power with the aid of the Parisian popular movement. Furthermore, the departmental authorities "never ceased to control by correspondence ... the battalions they formed."[44] Even if not overtly pro-Girondin, the volunteers were an unpredictable, independent military force, a parallel army free from the control of the central military administration. For some time, the Montagnards had suspected that, in the event of open conflict, the volunteers might turn against them. As early as June 1792, Robespierre had opposed a Girondin-backed plan for the establishment of a volunteer camp near Paris, insisting that it would serve the purposes of the "enemies of equality" who intended to "master the capital."[45] In December 1792, Marat warned that a new gathering of volunteers at Paris was intended "to contain the [Parisians] by terror, massacre their most energetic deputies, and carry

---

44 Bertaud, *La Révolution armée*, 66.
45 Cited in *La Société des Jacobins*, vol. 3, 668.

off the Capet family by force." The volunteers responded to Marat's "calumnies" with wall posters proclaiming their "profound disgust" for the "so-called people's friend."[46]

The Montagnards' fear of the volunteers was not without foundation. Shocked by the September Massacres, which had demonstrated the power and violence of the Paris commune, a number of deputies had called for the formation of a departmental guard, a "force sent by all the departments," to restore order in Paris and protect the Convention from intimidation by Parisian militants. The principal advocate of this measure was Buzot, the Girondin leader and future Federalist, who argued that the creation of such a force was necessary if the Convention wanted to remain "independent of the men who want to eliminate the deputies of the provinces, who imagine that the representatives of the nation have come only to be the slaves of certain Parisian deputies."[47] His call was supported by other Girondin deputies like Lasource, who accused the Parisian militants of violating the unity of the Republic by imposing their will on the rest of the nation.

> I fear the despotism of Paris, and I do not want those who control opinion in that city ... to dominate the National Convention and all of France ... The influence of Paris must be reduced to one eighty-third like all the other departments; I will never submit to its yoke; I will never let it tyrannize the Republic.[48]

Other deputies, such as Barbaroux, another Girondin who would be proscribed along with his colleagues in June, accused the Parisian radicals of usurping powers delegated exclusively to the representatives of the nation. "I see in Paris a disorganizing commune which sends *commissaires* into all the parts of the Republic to command the other communes, which delivers arrest warrants against the deputies of the Legislative Body and against a minister, a public man who belongs not to the city of Paris, but to the entire Republic."[49] Montagnard accusations notwithstanding, the Girondins' attack on Paris was not an expression of "federalism." Rather, they wanted to restore the unity and indivisibility of the Republic by reducing the independent power seized by the Paris Commune and thereby permit the Convention to exercise undivided sovereignty on behalf of the whole nation.[50] In Girondin eyes, Paris, not the provinces, was in revolt against the nation.

---

46 *Réponse au numéro 69 de Marat, soi-disant l'ami du peuple, par les citoyens-soldats des bataillons nationaux casernés à Paris* (Paris, n.d.).
47 *A.P.*, vol. 52, 127.
48 *A.P.*, vol. 52, 130.
49 *A.P.*, vol. 52, 135.
50 M. J. Sydenham, *The Girondins* (London, 1961), 32–3 and 197–8. Although the literature on the Girondins has been growing rapidly in recent years, the question of Girondin attitudes toward decentralization is far from settled.

Throughout the autumn of 1792 and into early 1793, local administrations echoed these sentiments. For example, in November 1792 the department of the Finistère warned the Paris sections that

> the only enemies which we have left are within your walls; chase out all these agitators of the people who lead it into insurrection only to enslave it ... We demand that our representatives enjoy full liberty. We are prepared to march in order to ensure it ... A single city will not lay down the law for the whole Republic.[51]

Saber-rattling of this sort was countered by equally incendiary rebuttals issued by the Paris sections, as well as by a number of provincial Jacobin clubs.[52] The latter, however, were divided among themselves, with some clubs supporting the idea of forming a departmental guard to restore the Convention's authority and freedom of action.[53] Given the uncertainties of the political situation, it was only prudent for the Montagnards to regard the volunteer battalions as a potential Girondin instrument of civil war.

They did not, however, see the line army in the same way. The nobility had largely abandoned or been driven from the officer corps. By early 1793, they accounted for no more than 10 percent of its strength.[54] They had been replaced in large part by former soldiers and non-commissioned officers of the old royal army, men who had proven their attachment to the Revolution time and time again. They had already rejected counterrevolution by refusing to follow Lafayette in his attempted putsch, just as they would reject Dumouriez's blandishments in May 1793. Owing everything they had – rank, status, dignity, and pay – to the Revolution and largely uninvolved in the arcane power struggles setting Girondins against Montagnards, these were men who could be relied upon to execute the Convention's orders. "The soldiers are all good, loyal Frenchmen," proclaimed Dubois-Crancé, "veritable *enfants de la patrie* [children of the nation, true patriots]."[55] But given the principled republican opposition to any form of government nomination, as well as the uncertainty about which faction – Girondin or Montagnard – would actually end up controlling the government, it was impossible for the Montagnards to suggest appointing officers of the line army directly in positions of responsibility in the new *demi-brigades*. The challenge for the Montagnards was to create a system of advancement that would

---

51 *A.P.*, vol. 53, 104.
52 See the address delivered to the Convention by the president of the *Assemblée générale des sections* on 19 October 1792 and the "Adresse de la Société des amis de la liberté et de l'égalité de la ville d'Auxerre," *A.P.*, vol. 52, 582, and 663.
53 See the "Adresse des Amis de la liberté et de l'égalité de la ville de Lisieux", the "Adresse des Amis de la liberté et de l'égalité de la ville d'Alençon" and the "Adresse de la Société des amis de la liberté et de l'égalité de Brives," *A.P.*, vol. 52, 663–4.
54 Lynn, *Bayonets*, 71–2.
55 *A.P.*, vol. 58, 359.

promote this particular category of personnel without making this preference explicit. Thanks to the ingenious articulation of its provisions for unification with its purposefully constructed system of advancement by election and seniority of service, Dubois-Crancé's plan brilliantly accomplished just that. Defusing republican fears of executive authority by eliminating all government intervention in advancement and pronouncing no formal preferences, it nonetheless amounted to an automatic mechanism for favoring a certain category of military personnel, deemed sympathetic to the Montagnard cause. Far from being based on fear of the political sentiments of the line army, Dubois-Crancé's comprehensive reorganization sought to use it to shackle the quasi-autonomous volunteers, remove them from departmental control, dilute their locally dominated cadres with a constant infusion of plebeian officers from the former royal army, and subordinate them to the central military administration. In sum, the law of 21 February 1793 was intended to reestablish the central government's monopoly of armed force and ensure that it was managed by obedient officers.[56]

Factionalism and the reimposition of centralized control

In the short run, the passage of Dubois-Crancé's law on republican military reorganization did little to strengthen the Convention's grasp over its armed forces. Although the armies of the Republic numbered more than 500,000 men on paper in the spring of 1793 and, thanks to a series of extraordinary levies, would surpass 750,000 by year's end, the government had little effective control over them. As the formation of *demi-brigades* had been suspended, the volunteer battalions of 1791 and 1792 retained their independent existence, those of the former royal army remained scattered, and the formation of new units – the National Guard volunteer battalions of 1793, the battalions of *fédérés* (other units of patriotic volunteers who offered to march to the front), and the various requisition battalions formed by the levy of 300,000 and the even larger *levée en masse* (the levy in mass, theoretically subjecting all physically fit French males to military service) added to the chaos. The proliferation of these heterogenous units, their frequent displacements, their officers' ignorance of administrative procedure, and the inevitable "fog of war" all conspired to defeat the government's efforts to gain an accurate picture of the forces at its disposal. "No registers, no money, no

---

56 For almost a century, most scholars have advanced a different interpretation of the *amalgame*, accepting Dubois-Crancé's claim that its primary aim was to inject the patriotic spirit of the volunteers into the politically suspect line army. To my knowledge, the first historian to make this claim was Jean Jaurès in his essay *L'Armée nouvelle*, ed. Jean-Noël Jeanneney, 2 vols. (Paris, 1992 [1915]). For a more recent "Jaurèsian" interpretation which places greater emphasis on the technical rationale of the *amalgame*, see Jean-Paul Bertaud, "Le Recrutement et l'avancement des officiers de la Révolution," *Annales historiques de la Révolution française*, 210 (1972), 513–36; and Bertaud, *La Révolution armée*, 92–9, 158–60, and 166–92.

accounting," was how one frustrated staff officer described the state of administration in his division.[57] Even the war ministry admitted that it did not have a clear idea of the "number of combat units," let alone the number of troops, their logistical requirements, and their cost.[58] On top of this administrative confusion, the defection of General Dumouriez on 5 April 1793 intensified fears about the loyalty of the officers. Something needed to be done quickly to get a handle on the situation.

When the news of Dumouriez's treason reached Paris, the panicked Convention voted to send to the armies representatives-on-mission – deputies vested with nearly unlimited powers to dismiss, arrest, and even execute political suspects. Chosen from among the most energetic men of the Mountain (at least thirty-two of thirty-seven), they were directed to eliminate "all the obstacles which have hindered the success of the armies of the Republic."[59] The practice of sending legislators armed with extraordinary powers to the armies was not new in 1793. The Constituent Assembly had reacted in this way to the King's flight, as had the Legislative Assembly after the declaration of war and again after the fall of the monarchy. But these were just emergency responses to particular crises. Unlike these precedents, the Convention's decision to send representatives-on-mission to the armies represented a systematic attempt to reimpose state control over the Republic's military forces. By its decrees of 8 and 9 April 1793 the Convention gave them extensive powers to investigate the state of military administration, as well as authority to "suspend, dismiss, replace, and arrest" incapable or corrupt functionaries and all other "disturbers of public order." They were also instructed to "exercise the most active surveillance" over the agents of the war ministry, generals, officers, and soldiers, and were empowered to cashier those deemed to be incompetent. If any were suspected of complicity in Dumouriez's treason or "any other plot" tending to threaten "the security of the nation" or promote "the disorganization of the armies," the representatives-on-mission were empowered to deliver them to the revolutionary tribunal. In sum, the representatives were given "unlimited powers" to effect "all the measures of public safety that the circumstances require."

Their most notorious function in this regard was to identify and replace politically suspect officers. Acting on denunciations offered by a variety of

---

[57] A.N. AF II 14, "Lettre de Girault, capitaine-adjudant-major au Comité de salut public" (letter received by the Comité de la guerre on 15 Brumaire II).

[58] A.N. 138 AP 4, "Mémoire sur le département de la guerre" (n.d.).

[59] *Décrets de la Convention nationale, qui déterminent les pouvoirs des représentants du peuple, députés vers les armées* (8 and 9 April 1793). All citations in this paragraph are from this decree. For a list of the representatives-on-mission, see *Décret de la Convention nationale, contenant la liste des représentans du peuple, députés près les armées* (12 April 1793). Information on their political leanings is from Alison Patrick, *The Men of the First French Republic: Political Alignments in the National Convention of 1792* (Baltimore, 1972), 317–39.

sources, the representatives had dismissed about 1,300 officers by April 1794.[60] Many denunciations came from hierarchical subordinates, like the sergeant-major of the 42nd infantry who charged his commander with "blocking the advancement of the non-commissioned officers."[61] Other denunciations reveal close relations between the troops and revolutionary civilians. Nicholas Houel, a junior officer in the 68th infantry and former president of the Jacobin club at Cambray, urged the representatives – in the name of "the patriots of the city and corps" – to "consult the testimony of the soldiers" and "strike with your justice and anger the traitors who vex us." His appeal must have carried some weight, because fourteen of his unit's officers, many of them noble, were arrested by representative Le Tourneur "on suspicion of disloyalty" only four days later.[62] The cadres of entire units – like the 21st cavalry and 55th infantry, charged with making treasonous suggestions of surrender during the siege of Landau – were drummed out of the army in public ceremonies. To the "applause" of the troops, representatives La Coste and Beaudot cashiered and arrested over forty "aristocratic" officers from these units and replaced them with "*sans-culottes*" – in most cases, soldiers from the units themselves.[63]

The representatives-on-mission were also charged in September 1793 with carrying out the general expulsion of nobles from the officer corps, a measure that had long been demanded by the radical press and Hébertiste-dominated war ministry. Although the Committee of Public Safety spared certain officers in the technical branches, whose expertise was judged essential to the war effort, this measure ended the traditional link between nobility and military service once and for all. By 1794, nobles accounted for no more than 3 percent of the officer corps.[64] Yet, while nobles were singled out for particularly harsh treatment, by this time no officer was above suspicion. Even volunteer officers who had been elected by their men could find themselves denounced by their former supporters.[65]

---

60 Bodinier, "La Révolution et l'armée," 203.
61 A.N. D§1 26, "Lettre de Binet, sergeant-major au 42ème régiment, connus des citoyens Charbonnier et Escudier, tous deux députés du Var à la Convention aux représentants du peuple" (21 April 1793).
62 A.N. D§1 16, "Lettre de Houel, lieutenant au 68ème régiment d'infanterie, ex-président de la Société des amis de la Constitution de Cambray" (2 September 1792); and A.G.X^{b}186, "Etat des nominations faites en execution de l'ordre des représentants du peuple Drouet, Jure, et Dar ..." (6 September 1793).
63 Archives municipales de Strasbourg, Affaires militaires 4°76, "Procès-verbal des opérations des commissaires des représentants du peuple La Coste et Beaudot, chargés de mettre à éxécution leur arrêté du 22 de Pluviôse relatif au 21ème régiment de cavalerie et au 1er bataillon du 55ème régiment d'infanterie" (3 Ventôse II).
64 Lynn, *Bayonets*, 67. On the purge of politically suspect officers in general, see 77–87.
65 For an example, see A.N. D§1 28, "Lettre du chef de bataillon et officiers du 3ème bataillon des volontaires nationaux de la Seine inférieure en garnison à Lorient aux représentants du peuple" (4 May 1793).

Although best known for their political surveillance of the officer corps, the representatives-on-mission were also concerned with a broad range of more mundane, but perhaps more essential, matters of military administration and organization. They spent much of their time trying to decipher the finances of the volunteer battalions and line regiments, take stock of the state of magazines and supply depots, speed the procurement of material and horses, and improve logistical arrangements. They were also responsible for supervising the levy of new conscripts, their incorporation into the armies, and the reconstitution of battalions which had been taken prisoner or decimated by combat. It was under their watch, moreover, that the long-delayed formation of *demi-brigades* was finally given the go-ahead. But, taking account of the actual deployment of the battalions, their feelings toward each other, and the capacities of individual officers, the representatives did not always follow the prescribed mode of unification.[66] In some *demi-brigades*, they simply juxtaposed one line with two volunteer battalions, leaving them intact and distinct just as the original plan had mandated. But in other *demi-brigades*, they shuffled the constituent companies, in effect forming entirely new battalions, or even broke up the companies altogether, distributing their men throughout the entire *demi-brigade*. In armies where there was a shortage of line units, the representatives did not hesitate to form *demi-brigades* exclusively from volunteer battalions. These operations were far from uniform, but, thanks in part to their very diversity, were all the more effective in mixing personnel from the line and volunteers. Although approximately 24 percent of the line and 20 percent of the volunteer battalions escaped incorporation and retained an independent existence, the *amalgame* was effectively complete by the beginning of the year IV. But by this time, new circumstances were making necessary a second fundamental military reorganization.

Although the representatives-on-mission restored a measure of control to the Convention, the medicines they employed against the malady of administrative chaos and disloyalty were arguably worse than the disease itself. The spirit of denunciation their presence nourished not only weakened hierarchical discipline by offering the soldiers a powerful means of resisting and even coercing their officers, but also created a destabilizing climate of distrust in which jurisdictional conflicts and factional rivalries flourished. The arrival in the armies and provinces of these omnipotent emissaries from Paris armed obscure local hatreds with new, fatal weapons.[67]

---

66 The conclusions which follow are based on an examination of the formation of fifty randomly selected *demi-brigades*, as well as Jean-Paul Bertaud's useful, unpublished manuscript, "Tableau d'organisation des demi-brigades conformement au décret du 12 août 1793, an II–an IV."

67 Some of the best work on the interplay between representatives-on-mission and local hatreds has been done by Colin Lucas. See his *The Structure of the Terror: The Example of Javogues and the Loire* (Oxford, 1973); and his article "The Rules of the Game in Local Politics under the Directory," *French Historical Studies*, 2 (Fall 1987), 345–72.

The advent of the representatives-on-mission also brought to the periphery conflicts which dominated at the center. The power struggle between the Parisian *sans-culotte* movement and the Convention was gradually extended to the armies in the form of endless sniping between the agents of the Hébertiste-dominated war ministry, jealous of its independence, and the representatives-on-mission, eager to restore the authority of the legislature.[68] The agents were instructed to spy on the representatives, sometimes refused to recognize their authority, and, on at least one occasion, imprisoned one. The Convention retaliated, directing the representatives to keep an eye on the ministerial agents and arrest them if necessary. In a revealing instance of the destabilizing interplay between Parisian politics and military affairs, one general, denounced by the representatives-on-mission as a "former procurer's clerk who owed his rank only to intrigue," was defended by his patron, the war minister Bouchotte, on the grounds that "presumptions in favor of his morality and courage exist in his section and among many enlightened *sans-culottes*." The representatives struck back by urging the Committee of Public Safety to "survey Audouin and Prosper Sijas," two important radicals in the war ministry about whom the representatives had "conceived suspicions."[69] Naturally, the officers found themselves caught in the middle of this tug-of-war.

Thus, hostility between representatives-on-mission and ministerial agents was more than just a war of words. The conflict that existed at the heart of the revolutionary French state had a corrosive effect on the composition and morale of the officer corps. The confusion of powers produced a situation in which it was "not rare to see the Committee of Public Safety, the representatives of the people with the armies, the minister, the generals, the commanders of corps, and councils of administration each make a different nomination to the same position."[70] In this chaotic and ultra-politicized environment, moreover, outrageously unqualified men were named to high rank by ministerial agents and representatives alike, competent officers were dismissed from the service on the flimsiest charges, the principle of gradual advancement from rank to rank was frequently violated, and arbitrariness masquerading as political purity was often the key to rapid advancement. Officers who persisted in the military career, but refused to play the political game, were reduced to a fuming, but impotent silence. This wearing struggle was finally brought to an end in the spring of 1794. The violent repression of the

---

[68] This murky situation is described with admirable clarity by Howard G. Brown, *War, Revolution, and the Bureaucratic State: Politics and Army Administration in France, 1791–1799* (Oxford, 1995).

[69] A.N. AF II 234, "Lettre de Bouchotte au général Jourdan" (30 1er mois II); and AF II 238, "Lettre de Duquesnoy, représentant du peuple près l'armée du Nord, au Comité de salut public" (13 Frimaire II).

[70] A.N. AD XVIII^c308, Dubois-Crancé, *Rapport et tableau des officiers-généraux, adjudants-généraux, et commissaires des guerres qui doivent être en activité de service la campagne prochaine dans les armées de la République* (III).

Hébertistes in March, which had already decapitated the war ministry both figuratively and literally, was followed several weeks later by the suppression of the ministry itself and its replacement by twelve executive commissions attached directly to the Committee of Public Safety. With authority over the army increasingly concentrated within the Committee of Public Safety, the arbitrary powers of the representatives-on-mission were reduced as well and a degree of stability began to return to the military profession. But great damage had already been done.

Despite the success of its efforts to reimpose a degree of control over the military, however, the Convention still lacked authority over advancement which had been reserved for election and seniority by the law of 21 February 1793. This renunciation of government power had been voluntary, motivated by ideologically driven republican fears of executive authority. But pressure to revise the law and restore a measure of government discretion over advancement began to build as the ill-effects of seniority of service and election became increasingly obvious. Within a month of the implementation of the Dubois-Crancé advancement law, concerned officers and legislators had already begun to warn of its dire consequences. Offering no other guarantee of an officer's aptitude than sheer persistence in the army (or, worse, inability to hold down another job), reported the abbé Grégoire and Jagot from their mission in early 1793 to the Army of Italy, seniority of service favored "old soldiers without intelligence" at the expense of talent. The resulting accession of illiterates to positions of command was producing a "frightening disorder" in military administration and inciting "disturbances" among the officers. It was necessary, they concluded, to revise the law immediately to require that all officers be able to read and write.[71] This was not done. A year later representative Pflieger, on mission to the Army of the Moselle, had to relate the disastrous consequences of this inaction. Promotion to high rank, he claimed, had been monopolized by "old quarter-masters, horseshoe-makers, trumpet majors, master tailors, musicians, and old brigadiers – all people who have never been in a position to acquire true military expertise." Most were illiterate, and many were notable for their "crapulous conduct, presumption, and stubbornness, the inevitable result of their ignorance."[72] Advancement by election was also attacked, although its detractors trod more cautiously, partly out of fear of denigrating such a hallowed revolutionary institution and partly because its results were probably not as uniformly appalling as advancement by seniority of service.

---

71 A.N. D§1 25, "Lettre des représentants du peuple Grégoire et Jagot au Comité de la guerre" (14 March 1793).

72 A.G. X^{c}3, "Lettre de Pflieger, représentant du peuple chargé de la nouvelle organisation de la cavalerie près l'armée de la Moselle, aux citoyens représentants du peuple composant le Comité de salut public de la Convention nationale" (11 Germinal II).

The Dubois-Crancé law was also criticized because it left the government powerless to advance merit. Although the Convention and its representatives with the armies could exclude the incapable and purge the treasonous from the officer corps, its republican distrust of the quasi-monarchical institution of government-bestowed advancement left it without a means of recognizing superior talent and rewarding faithful service. The first calls to reinstitute a means for the government to do this came from the war ministry. Self-interested motives underlay the ministry's lobbying effort. Not only would the return of government-directed advancement restore a *raison d'être* to the ministry's personnel bureau, which had been reduced to filling out forms and expediting correspondence since the implementation of Dubois-Crancé's system of advancement, but also augment the power of the radical militants who dominated the ministry by allowing them to exercise patronage within the officer corps. Naturally, these were not the arguments the radical minister Bouchotte put forward to the Convention. Rather, he invoked traditional utilitarian arguments about the need to promote *émulation* by offering "encouragements" and the equally important need to offer "just" recompense for services rendered.[73] These claims were advanced even more forcefully by Bouchotte's outspoken lieutenant, the defrocked priest and *sans-culotte* activist, Xavier Audouin. In his letters to the Convention, Audouin expressed "perplexity" at the absence of any means of "according advancement to citizens who had truly distinguished themselves" in the service of the *patrie*.[74] Although the Convention ostensibly bowed to these demands, issuing a decree on 27 August 1793 reestablishing the principle that soldiers "would be rewarded for their acts of heroism by advancement in grade," it delayed instituting concrete mechanisms for putting this ideal into practice.[75] Having relinquished the power to make promotions, the Convention was not about to hand it over to the radicals in the war ministry.

It was not until the balance of power had tipped against the Parisian radical movement and its allies in the war ministry that the Convention finally felt confident enough to alter the mode of advancement. First, the mounting evidence that the Dubois-Crancé law favored illiteracy spurred the Convention to establish filters against the promotion of those who could not read or write. Its decree of 27 Pluviôse II mandated that, from the grade of corporal on, all French soldiers

---

73 A.G. X^{b}786, "Lettre de Bouchotte au Comité militaire" (26 June 1793); see also his letter of 21 July, in the same carton, in which he urged the Convention to authorize him to reward "useful actions" with advancement.

74 A.G. X^{b}126, "Lettre du citoyen Audouin, ajoint au ministre de la guerre de la 6ème division, au Comité militaire de la Convention nationale" (21 July 1793). See also his letters of 5, 25, and 26 Brumaire II in A.G. X^{b}791.

75 *Décret de la Convention nationale, du 27 août 1793, portant que les soldats françois seront recompensés de leurs hauts faits par un avancement en grade.*

had to be literate. The Convention, however, rejected a more rigorous proposal that all illiterate soldiers currently invested with officer rank be forced to resign their commissions.[76] Many representatives-on-mission, however, were not satisfied with this minimal safeguard. Some began to take steps on their own authority to ensure the quality of promotions within their own jurisdictions. In Floréal II, for example, the representatives-on-mission with the Army of the Moselle instituted military juries to verify that personnel proposed for promotions were actually capable of fulfilling the responsibilities of their new grade.[77] Similar *ad hoc* arrangements were probably instituted in other armies as well.

It was only several months later, however, that the Convention approved a new advancement law restoring to the government some authority over promotions. Attributing one-third of advancement to seniority of service, one-third to election (according to the procedures defined by the Dubois-Crancé law), and one-third to government designation, the revised law on advancement was presented to the full Convention on 1 Thermidor II (19 July 1794) by Bertrand Barère.[78] Aware that the restoration of government discretion represented a break with republican principle and threatened to turn the deputies against the proposal, Barère took great pains to distinguish it from the similar systems that had existed under the monarchy. It was true, he admitted, that "kings and ministers" had relied on this "powerful mechanism" to "perpetuate the life of despotism." And it was also true that "injustices and intrigues" had always attended this practice, wherever it had been employed. But since the French people had thrown off the royal yoke and established a republican government, the vices that had corrupted the institution no longer existed. Now that France had an "enlightened government," a truly "national representation," it had become possible to restore the prerogative of advancement to the Convention. In granting promotions, the Convention would not be investing itself with a monarchical-style power. Rather than elevating it above and setting it apart from the nation, the ability to bestow recompense would finally enable it to "execute the decrees of public opinion" and "revolutionize glory." Rather than using this prerogative to increase their own authority, the deputies "would consider themselves honored to be called upon by the people to appreciate men rendered obscure by their fortune or rank." Acting not as despots, but rather as conduits of the national will, the representatives could be entrusted with the power of advancement. "National justice" imperatively demanded it. The Republic could no longer stand by passively as "the feeble or

---

76 A.N. AD VI 43, *Rapport fait au nom des Comité de salut public et de la guerre, par Merlin (de Thionville)* (27 Pluviôse II).
77 A.N. AF II 206, "Arrêté des représentants du peuple près l'armée de la Moselle" (27 Floréal II).
78 A.N. AD VI 43, Barère, *Rapport et projet de décret présentés au nom des Comités de salut public et de la guerre sur les places à decerner par la Convention nationale aux défenseurs de la patrie qui se seront distingués par de traits de bravoure* (1 Thermidor II).

modest citizen was punished for his virtues, the man of genius for his talents, and the intrepid soldier for his bravery." Consequently, the decree specified that the proportion of advancement attributed to the Convention would be used, first and foremost, to repay the nation's debt for heroic deeds already performed. If, after this, places still remained at its discretion, the Convention could use them for utilitarian ends – to encourage merit actively by granting them to soldiers distinguished by "their principles, conduct, and talent." By describing the new system of advancement as a necessary means of realizing the national will and by emphasizing its non-motivational, recompensive function, Barère succeeded in making the proposal palatable to the Convention which adopted it without opposition. This first compromise with republican principle would not be the last.

5 The politics of professionalism during Thermidor and the Directory, 1794–99

The Directory has long suffered from a reputation for indecision and ineffectiveness, but, at least in the case of the military, this is not entirely merited.[1] Finding itself burdened with a bloated, disordered, and arbitrary military establishment inherited from the Convention, the Directory dared to undertake a comprehensive reorganization which, although highly unpopular, was necessary to instill order, stability, and regularity in the army. It instituted a new system of advancement which returned authority to the military hierarchy, even while it conserved fundamental egalitarian changes made in 1793. It also carried out a drastic consolidation of under-strength units and a correspondingly severe reduction of redundant officers. Although this downsizing alienated many personnel and provoked a divisive debate over the criteria of retention, this operation must be considered a success since it provided Bonaparte with the military units and cadres he would employ to such effect during his rule. The Directory's accomplishment is all the more impressive since its work of reform was plagued by all manner of obstacles. Corruption, economic stagnation, fiscal chaos, and the ongoing war crippled the logistical administration and led to demoralizing shortages for the troops in the field. Political infighting led to instability at the highest levels of government, politicization of military reform issues as rival factions vied for control of the armed forces, and, ultimately, the direct involvement of the army in these struggles. Marked by the structural transformation of their profession, career instability, dearth, and politicization, the Directorial years were difficult ones for the officer corps. But these trials would also lay the basis for a rejuvenated and changed military profession.

Digesting the legacy of the Convention

The reign of Terror left a bitter legacy of fratricidal hatred which swept across France in the weeks following Robespierre's demise. This wave of reaction against the perceived excesses of the Convention, the so-called White Terror, affected military no less than civil society. "The charlatanism of greasy hair and *carmagnoles* [a popular dance, associated with the *sans-culottes*, that was fashionable during the Terror] is over," a reconverted Dubois-Crancé proclaimed. "Let us finally learn to

---

1 A notable exception is Albert Goodwin, "The French Executive Directory – A Revaluation," *History*, 22 (1937), 201–18.

Récapitulation

	Officiers conservés	Officiers réformés	Total
Infanterie de bataille	9790	1449 5	
Infanterie légère	2670	1139	15634
	12460		
Carabiniers	72		
Cavalerie de bataille	550	150	
Dragons	720	340	1170
Chasseurs	936	348	
Hussards	504	318	
	2786		

12460 (Grades d'Infanterie)
2786 (of. de Troupes à Cheval)
15246 Commandés

Total des réformés 16804.

F.A.H.2

5 The original ministerial estimate of the number of officers who would lose their places as a result of the Directory's military downsizing, the second amalgame, Brumaire IV.

apply with justice the recompense due to merit. That is true equality." During the previous two years, he continued, this truth had been forgotten or willfully ignored. Wielding political orthodoxy like a weapon, "avid and immoral intriguers" had lorded it over the officer corps. "Just like our former feudal nobles under the Old Regime," Dubois-Crancé mused, drawing on memories that the Revolution had not effaced, "certain beings who called themselves exclusive patriots considered it an injustice not to be named colonels by the age of 20."[2] The turbulent *sans-culottes* who had risen to high rank under the "disorganizing system" of Robespierre, one ministerial recommendation concluded, had to be removed from the officer corps.[3]

The machinery of the Terror was thrust into reverse. Armed with the law of 21 Germinal III (10 April 1795), which authorized them to dismiss personnel who had "participated in the horrors committed under the Tyranny," the Thermidorean representatives-on-mission began to purge the army of its most pronounced terrorists.[4] Representative Gillet dismissed one captain on the simple suspicion that he had "owed his advancement only to the intrigue of the conspirators Hébert, Ronsin, Vincent, and Manuel, with whom he was closely linked."[5] Another officer was cashiered because he had reportedly said that "only the guillotine can save the Republic."[6] At the same time, hundreds of officers dismissed during the Terror began to demand reinstatement.[7]

But the reaction against terrorism in the officer corps soon came under fire. Its methods, critics charged, were as arbitrary as those employed before 9 Thermidor and only served to perpetuate the climate of fear and instability which had undermined military professionalism during the Terror. Even officers who demanded "the punishment of *égorgeurs* [a Thermidorean term for those associated with the most violent excesses of the Terror]" and the removal of personnel who owed their places to "the tyranny of Robespierre" recognized the need to expedite this divisive housecleaning and return to a system of regular advancement "which eliminates arbitrariness." A purge, in their view, was not an end in itself, but rather the necessary prelude to a new order in which the course of military careers would be governed by wise laws "assuring gradual advancement to merit."[8]

---

2 A.N. AD XVIII^{c}318, Dubois-Crancé, *Rapport et tableau des officiers généraux, adjudants-généraux, et commissaires des guerres qui doivent être en activité de service la campagne prochaine dans les armées de la République* (II).
3 A.N. AF II 200, "Rapport du Comité du personnel de l'artillerie et du génie au Comité de salut public" (14 Fructidor III).
4 A.G. X^{b}126, "Copie de l'arrêté des représentants du peuple près les ports et côtes de Brest et de l'Orient" (10 Floréal III).
5 A.F. II 209, "Arrêté du représentant du peuple Gillet, près l'armée de Sambre et Meuse" (2 Frimaire III).
6 A.N. AF II 205, "Rapport au Comité de salut public" (28 Floréal III).
7 See the numerous petitions contained in the alphabetically organized cartons in A.N. AF III 145.
8 A.N. AF II 210, "Lettre de la 25ème demi-brigade à la Convention nationale" (8 Germinal III).

Calls for a new system of advancement capable of protecting military careers from politicized civilian interference began to make themselves heard after Thermidor. One of the most influential advocates of this idea was General Louis-Antoine Pille, the Burgundian protégé of Carnot appointed to head the war sections of the Committee of Public Safety. As a former *commissaire des guerres* under the Old Regime who had been elected commander of a National Guard volunteer battalion in 1791, Pille was well equipped to carry out both his administrative and military responsibilities. What he had seen from his quasi-ministerial perch infuriated him: the representatives-on-mission were continuing to cashier officers, assign replacements, and make promotions at a furious pace. These arbitrary interventions, he reported to the Committee of Public Safety, were undermining the morale and good composition of the officer corps.[9] Tending to "annul the mode of advancement established by the law," they generally ignored the rights of seniority, benefiting instead incapable subjects with "no other title of eligibility than the interested recommendation of an administration or authority." As a result, "discouragement" was spreading among the "good and experienced officers, who understand neither intrigues nor how to serve a party." To end this, it was not only necessary to "halt further nominations by the representatives of the people," but, more importantly, to adopt a new law on advancement and "maintain its exact observation."

The termination of the representatives' power of nomination in Floréal III (April–May 1795) paved the way for the reinstitution of normal advancement procedures. But did the army actually possess such procedures? Many thought that the existing legislation on advancement – the law of 21 February 1793 as modified by the decree of 1 Thermidor II – was no less detrimental to military well-being than the arbitrary interventions of the representatives. Even the representatives-on-mission to the armies had noted the ill-effects of Dubois-Crancé's system of advancement and called for changes. Yet, despite the imposition of literacy requirements, the establishment of military juries in certain armies, and enhanced government discretion over promotions, this system was still in force. Before 9 Thermidor, only a handful of officers had dared to criticize it. But now that the Terror had ended, ushering in a more open climate of public discourse and lifting the cloud of suspicion under which the officer corps had labored, complaints began to pour into the Convention from the armies.

Much of the criticism concerned the unorthodox definition of seniority – time of total service – that Dubois-Crancé's law had imposed. As even the Hébertiste war ministry admitted in June 1793, Dubois-Crancé's law had "totally reversed" the order of seniority.[10] Under this system a freshly promoted officer

---

9 A.N. AF II 199, Pille, "Rapport présenté au Comité de salut public" (22 Floréal III).
10 A.G. X^b786, "Lettre de Xavier Audouin au commandant du 6ème régiment d'infanterie" (8 June 1793).

would be ranked within his new grade not by the date of his promotion, but rather by the date of his initial entry into military service. Thus, a soldier promoted to second lieutenant after having served in the ranks for thirty years (itself a good indication that he had been judged unfit for greater responsibilities) would very likely become the most senior second lieutenant immediately. This would all but guarantee him the next vacant lieutenancy to be filled by seniority, and so on up the hierarchy. Explaining this system to the incredulous members of the Thermidorean Committee of Public Safety, a war section report noted that "if he has the most seniority of service, the last officer to be promoted to a grade becomes the first among those of the same rank and the first in line for advancement to a superior rank."[11] Although the abbé Grégoire was exaggerating when he claimed that "a corporal could become a lieutenant-colonel in three months" under this system, the redefinition of seniority ensured extremely rapid advancement to long-serving soldiers of the Old Regime. For example, in the 40th infantry, a sexagenarian named Louis Denis, who had joined the royal army as a common soldier in 1759, rose from sergeant to captain between 27 August and 11 November 1793.[12] In regiments hard-hit by battle losses or political suspensions, it was not uncommon to find entire cohorts of officers promoted two steps in the hierarchy – from sergeant to lieutenant, or from second lieutenant to captain – in a single day.[13]

Cases such as these elicited a storm of protest. The critics charged that seniority of service destroyed military effectiveness and fostered discontent by promoting age, illiteracy, and incompetence at the expense of vigor, instruction, and merit. Even veterans well positioned to benefit from seniority of total service, like Sergeant-Major Binet of the 42nd regiment, warned that it was harming the army by promoting ignorant officers instead of the "best instructed."[14] Typically, the disgruntled petitioners were better educated and more socially elevated officers – often the sons of active citizens and young notables elected directly to positions of command in the National Guard volunteer battalions – whose career profiles effectively excluded them from promotion by seniority of service. While self-interest may have been their principal motivation, they always couched their complaints in general, professional terms. Pierre Galdou, a young staff officer in the 5th military division, complained that seniority of service benefited "ignorant old men, ... veterans who do not know two words of their *métier*." In favoring these officers, he continued, the Convention had only sought to extend its "justice" and "generosity" to a class of "estimable

11 A.N. AF II 200, "Rapport du 9ème commission au Comité militaire" (19 Vendémiaire III).
12 A.G. Y^{b}404, "Contôle des officiers: Soissonais, 40ème régiment."
13 A good example is found in the 68th infantry, whose cadres were decimated by a spate of political suspensions. A.G.^{b}432, "Contôle des officiers: Beauce, 68ème régiment."
14 A.N. D§1 26, "Lettre de Binet."

citizens" whose careers had suffered from the genealogical barriers of the Old Regime. But in its war to the death with the "crowned brigands" of Europe, the Republic could not afford this luxury. What the army needed in wartime were "young officers who, spending entire nights studying their profession, have made it a duty to acquire the knowledge which can alone merit them the confidence and esteem of their fellow citizens." Like many of the well-educated critics of seniority of service, Galdou called for a new system of advancement based on *concours*, competitive examinations which would not only test knowledge, but also encourage studiousness.[15] Lieutenant Espardeilles of the 1st battalion of the Landes echoed Galdou's complaints. In a letter to the Convention's military committee, he warned that seniority of service was advancing only "men without instruction" and causing "much discontent" among the younger officers.[16] Captain Delon, a son of an active citizen currently serving as *aide-de-camp* to General Moncey, was another officer who denounced the "abuses of the current mode of advancement."[17] Highlighting differences between veteran soldiers and young men from better backgrounds who had been commissioned directly, seniority of service brought into sharp relief differences of age, class, education, and professional profile.

The post-Thermidorean outcry against electoral advancement was even more widespread. Far from producing good choices and reinforcing the soldiers' confidence in their officers, as the plan's Montagnard supporters had assured, military election, the critics charged, had fostered poisonous divisions, promoted incompetent intriguers, and destroyed hierarchical subordination. According to Quartermaster Colombet of the 95th *demi-brigade*, elections were "always preceded by cabals" in which "turbulent" soldiers "used a thousand means" to capture the suffrage of their peers and secure promotion to ranks for which they were totally unqualified.[18] In one case, the wife of a candidate reportedly bought wine for the voting assembly who, their "heads heated with drink," elected her husband and other men "without military knowledge" to the places they sought.[19] To continue electoral advancement, claimed Lieutenant Arnauld of the 22nd *demi-brigade*, would only "increase the number of idiots" and "give the

---

15 A.G. MR 1160, "Opinion sur les abus qui se glissent dans les armées de la République et sur les moyens à prendre pour les corriger, par Pierre Galdou, sous-lieutenant adjoint au citoyen Quenin, adjudant-général dans la division du Mont-Libre no.5, aux représentants du peuple composants le Comité militaire" (27 January 1795).
16 A.N. AF II 200, "Minute de la lettre d'Espardeilles, lieutenant au 1er bataillon des Landes, au Comité militaire" (22 Fructidor II).
17 A.N. AF II 200, "Minute de la lettre de Delon, aide-de-camp du général Moncey, au Comité militaire" (17 Vendémiaire III).
18 A.G. MR 2008, "Lettre du citoyen Colombet, quartier-maitre trésorier de la 95ème demi-brigade aux citoyens membres composant le Comité militaire" (1 Frimaire III).
19 A.N. AF II 14, "Lettre de Girault, capitaine-adjudant-major, au Comité de salut public" (n.d.).

Republic officers and non-commissioned officers unworthy of commanding free men."[20] To the critics, an even greater drawback of electoral advancement was its corrosive effect on discipline. Officers who sought election, they charged, courted the suffrage of their subordinates by promising to overlook their disciplinary transgressions. Under this system, complained a volunteer officer,

> an ambitious man, a deceiver, is sure to win promotion, while the true soldier will be left behind. The reason is quite simple: the first gains the soldier's friendship by fomenting his vices, while the second attracts his hatred by reprimanding or punishing him ... Whoever desires advancement is obliged to relax his service by turning a blind eye to a thousand things which ought to be punished. In consequence, this gives rise to indiscipline and insubordination.

Because it was "conducted by the soldier," the existing system of electoral advancement was "totally contrary to the good of the service."[21] By placing the officers' careers in the hands of their subordinates, the existing system of electoral advancement tended to invert the military hierarchy by transferring power from the superiors to the inferiors.

After Thermidor, the way was open for the Convention to remedy these drawbacks. In Germinal III (March–April 1795), François Aubry, a former Old Regime artillery officer who had been readmitted to the Convention after having been imprisoned for protesting the expulsion of the Girondins, proposed a new law on advancement.[22] This was necessary, he argued, because the existing system – containing the "germ of independence, arbitrariness, and anarchy" – was "false in its principles" and "dangerous in its results." Since its inception, it had been denounced not only by professional military men, but also by its most fervent legislative supporters once they had witnessed its disorganizing influence. But knowledge of these complaints, he claimed, had been suppressed by the "tyranny" of the old Committee of Public Safety. Now that liberty had been restored to the legislators, it was time to approve a new system of advancement that would finally "place the well-instructed officer where his knowledge carried him, the courageous soldier where glory called him, and the aged veteran ... where confidence and justice" summoned him. To recognize these three kinds of merit and to "reconcile the rights of the government with democratic principles," Aubry presented the following plan. One third of promotions would be reserved

---

20 A.N. AF II 210, "Lettre d'Arnauld, lieutenant dans la 22ème demi-brigade au Comité de salut public" (30 Prairial III).
21 A.N. AF II 210, "Lettre de Lecomte, adjudant-major, 1er bataillon des Côtes du Nord au Comité de salut public" (16 Prairial III).
22 A.N. AD VI 43, *Projet de loi sur le nouveau mode d'avancement militaire pour les troupes de la République, présenté au nom du Comité militaire par F. Aubry, député du département du Gard* (Ventôse III).

for government nomination, a necessary prerogative that the "delirium of principles" had stripped from its hands. But to ensure that these decisions would be "sheltered from intriguing and abusive preferences," they would have to be approved by the Convention and publicized in print. The next third would be selected by military election. But the method of election Aubry proposed was far different from the democratic system approved in 1793. To ensure "the maintenance of subordination," the right of the inferiors to present the candidates for promotion was eliminated and replaced by a system of co-option similar to that which had been used by the corporate bodies of the Old Regime. The officers of the rank to be filled were to present three candidates to their hierarchical superiors, who would choose one for promotion. Aubry had even wanted to add a further mechanism – examination by a military jury of all officers designated for promotion in this manner – to reinforce hierarchy and ensure the quality of candidates, but this idea was rejected in the military committee.[23] The remaining portion of advancement was allotted to seniority in the grade, thus ending the disastrous experiment with seniority of total service. A final provision of the law permitted generals-in-chief of the armies to grant extraordinary promotions to soldiers who had "distinguished themselves in war by brilliant actions." Adopted without dissent on 14 Germinal III (3 April 1795), the new system of advancement was a marked retreat from the republican extremes of 1793 and the year II. Yet, while it reinforced the government's prerogative of promotion and replaced democratic election with a corporate form of co-option that strengthened hierarchical authority and gave the officers a say in the recruitment of their peers, the new law remained faithful to bedrock republican principle by declining to reinstitute direct officer recruitment and a system of honorific distinctions. Those who wanted to become officers would still have to begin their careers as common soldiers and could expect only the inner satisfaction of having furthered the interests of the Republic as a reward for their services.

The second *amalgame* and the "purge" of the officer corps

Flawed as it had been, Dubois-Crancé's system of advancement was still not the most pressing military problem the Thermidoreans had inherited from the Convention. This was rather a massive surplus of officers who clogged advancement and absorbed scant resources the financially strapped Republic could ill afford to squander. The levies of 1793 and the year II had increased the size of the army to at least 750,000, and the officer corps had grown apace. But, while death, desertion, and the slowing of new recruitment had reduced effectives to about 400,000 by the beginning of the Directory, all vacancies in the officer corps

---

23 A.N. AF II 15, "Comité militaire, séance du 17 Ventôse III."

had continued to be filled so that it remained at the maximum size it had reached at the height of the Terror. The problem was exacerbated by the redundant nominations of representatives-on-mission, as well as the Convention's decision to reinstate officers who had already been replaced while prisoners of war, blockaded in besieged cities, hospitalized, or unjustly suspended. As early as the spring of 1793, far-sighted observers had predicted that, if nothing was done, "we will soon have more officers than soldiers."[24] But these warnings were not heeded. Already in the year II, observers found decimated battalions where all vacant officer slots had continued to be filled – including one in which twenty-seven officers commanded only three soldiers.[25] Although precise figures were unavailable at the time, the war ministry estimated two years later that there was one officer for every four soldiers.[26] The army of the Republic had grown far more top-heavy than the royal army had ever been.

At the same time, the government's difficulty in funding the war effort was becoming more acute. With the lifting of price controls on 4 Nivôse III (24 December 1794), the value of government scrip collapsed, creating chaos within the military administration and making it impossible for the government to provide supplies or meaningful pay to the troops. Efforts to print more money to bolster the government's sagging purchasing power only exacerbated this inflationary cycle. From all the armies of the Republic, frantic letters arrived detailing their desperate plight.[27] One of these, from the chief military administrator attached to the Army of the Rhine-and-Moselle, began by warning that "all the services in the army will be annihilated" if the "lack of funds" was not immediately remedied.[28] As things currently stood, the troops were running out of bread and more could only be obtained by requisitioning grain from the home departments. Setting up a regular system for purchasing bread from dealers was out of the question because of the "exhaustion of the [army's] treasury." Meat rations would run out in twenty days, which would inevitably provoke the "most violent murmurs among the troops." But because of the lack of metal currency, there could be no solution to this problem. And not only men, but also horses, were going hungry. The only solution was to "send to the rear a portion of the cavalry"

---

24 A.G. MR 2018, "Mémoire sur les abus qui se commettent à l'armée, par le citoyen Vézu, chef du 3ème bataillon de Paris" (1793).
25 A.N. AD XVIII^{c}307, *Rapport sur l'embrigadement des armées au nom du Comité militaire, par le citoyen Dubois-Crancé* (13 Frimaire II). See also his inspection report in A.N. AF II 198, "Lettre de la Commission d'organisation et du mouvement des armées de terre au Comité de salut public" (forwarded on 18 Messidor II).
26 A.N. 138 AP 4, "Mémoire sur le département de la guerre." (n.d.).
27 Countless examples can be found in the relevant cartons of the B series at the A.G., as well as in the cartons containing incoming correspondence in the AF III series at the A.N.
28 A.G. B^{2}48, "Lettre du commissaire ordonnateur en chef au citoyen Desaix, général-en-chef de l'armée du Rhin-et-Moselle" (22 Ventôse IV).

and distribute it in the French countryside, obviously an unacceptable situation for an army on the point of beginning a new campaign. And the transport service attached to the army was in a state of chaos, counting only 300 horses when 2,400 were needed. Such dearth, moreover, was disastrous for discipline, wrote General Vandamme, a divisional commander attached to the same army.

> Our army is disgusted because it is poorly paid ... The officers, the generals, to what are they reduced? They depend on the soldier, they cannot stop him from pillaging, from stealing; they are reduced to living with him. Thus by this misery, by this abasement, the disgusted officer is without authority and courage. The soldier disdains and cannot respect him.[29]

To its credit, the Directory acknowledged the magnitude of the crisis – characterizing the military administration as a system which was "incoherent and disordered in its totality as well as its individual parts" – and determined to take firm steps to address the problems.[30]

It had been obvious for some time that firm action was needed to give the army a cost-efficient and militarily sound organization. Consequently, as its last act, the Thermidorean Committee of Public Safety approved a drastic consolidation of under-strength units and a corresponding reduction of officer strength. Known as the second *amalgame*, the Directory confirmed this measure on 18 Nivôse IV (8 January 1796) and largely succeeded in carrying it to completion within a year.[31] As originally planned, the second *amalgame* represented the largest wartime downsizing ever undertaken. The 952 existing battalions were to be consolidated into 140 new *demi-brigades* of three battalions each. As a result, 532 battalions were to be dissolved and their cadres of officers and non-commissioned officers made redundant. A similar consolidation of the cavalry was to eliminate 145 squadrons, reducing their number from 323 to 178. As a result of these operations, the war ministry estimated, officer strength would be reduced from 32,046 to 15,242, a reduction of over 50 percent. In practice, however, the reductions were even greater because the units proved substantially more understrength than expected. Each *demi-brigade* of new formation required eight old battalions, on average, to form its three new, full-strength battalions. In extreme cases, like the 4th *demi-brigade* which required no less than twenty-two battalions to achieve its full complement of soldiers, the extent of consolidation was even greater.[32] The impact on the officer corps was profound. About 25,000 lost

---

29 A.G. B²48, "Lettre du général Vandamme au représentant du peuple Woussen" (12 Ventôse IV).
30 A.G. B¹³ *31, "Lettre du Directoire exécutif au ministre de la guerre" (8 Frimaire V).
31 *Arrêté relatif à l'organisation de l'armée de terre* (10 Brumaire IV), and *Arrêté du Directoire exécutif, concernant l'organisation générale de l'armée* (18 Nivôse IV).
32 A.N. AF III 144ª, "Second rapport fait par le citoyen Petiet, ex-ministre de la guerre, au Directoire exécutif, sur l'administration de son département" (3 Vendémiaire VI).

their places, a bloodletting even greater than the demobilization of 20,000 which accompanied the end of the Napoleonic wars in 1815. The reabsorption of the supernumeraries, moreover, slowed the pace of advancement to a crawl.[33] For example, during the two years following the second *amalgame*, not a single officer received promotion in the 39th *demi-brigade*.[34] The climate of professional insecurity created by the second *amalgame* would dominate the mentality of the officer corps for the duration of the Republic.

Many officers, however, detected a silver lining in the cloud cast by the second *amalgame*. In their view, the dramatic downsizing of cadres presented a golden opportunity to purge the officer corps of the incompetence, illiteracy, and immorality with which it had been infected during the Convention. "The storms of the Revolution have not destroyed talent and virtue," wrote Inspector-General Krieg, an Old Regime career officer whose single-minded professionalism had allowed him to weather the Terror largely unscathed. "For a time, the eruptions of the volcano covered these treasures with ashes, but ... they will be revealed to the enlightened eye of the government which will surely distinguish them."[35] Now in full retreat from his earlier egalitarianism, Dubois-Crancé voiced the hopes of many officers when he confidently predicted that the second *amalgame* would produce a "corps of chosen and purified officers."[36] But consensus ended there. As the prospect of reductions loomed, sharp differences of opinion emerged over the aims and methods of the impending purge. Although all expected downsizing to improve the composition of the officer corps, there was little agreement on what this would mean in practice. What kind of officer corps did France need? What kind of professional qualities should officers possess? What was the selection procedure best suited to achieving these ends? What, in the final analysis, constituted true merit? At stake in these questions was not only the reinvigoration of professionalism and French military power, but also the careers of individuals and groups. Realizing this, the officers lobbied for methods of reduction likely to favor their own careers. These interventions, in which considerations of professionalism and self-interest mingled, highlight the internal fault lines of the officer corps the Directory had inherited from the Convention.

The purge debate brought out differences between veterans from modest social milieux who had begun their careers as soldiers in the royal army and

---

33 A.N. AF III 144ª, "Etat comparatif du nombre des officiers titulaires existans au commencement du ministère et au 1 Thermidor [V]" (3 Vendémiaire VI). Jean Vidalenc, *Les Demi-solde: étude d'une catégorie sociale* (Paris, 1955), 33.
34 A.G. $X^b 260$, "Lettre du conseil d'administration de la 39ème demi-brigade d'infanterie de ligne au citoyen Scherer, ministre de la guerre" (1 Ventôse VII).
35 A.N. AF III 145ᵇ, General Krieg, "Quelques observations sur les vices existans dans l'état militaire de la République" (26 Fructidor IV).
36 A.G. MR 2018, Dubois-Crancé, "Du licenciement des armées à la paix et de la force armée à tenir sur pied" (20 Thermidor IV).

younger men from more elevated social circumstances who had been commissioned directly as sons of active citizens and National Guard volunteers during the period 1791–93. The latter group was markedly more enthusiastic about the purge than the former. Officers like Jean-Baptiste Simon – a merchant's son from the Seine-et-Oise who had relinquished a lieutenancy in his local volunteer battalion to accept a commission in the line army as the son of an active citizen – was just one of many who petitioned the government to use the downsizing to remove the disgraceful personnel who had invaded the officer corps during the Convention. Rarely "firm, educated, disinterested, or truly refined," officers of this vintage owed their ranks only to "the impolitic law on advancement of 21 February 1793." By "sacrificing the most eminent grades to seniority of service and the choice of the soldiers," Simon fulminated, "the frightful regime of Robespierre forced merit to hide itself and languish, totally forgotten."[37] Seniority of service, wrote Urbain Arnaud, a young Provençal who had been elected lieutenant in the 2nd battalion of Marseille in 1791, had all too often benefited "old soldiers who didn't even have the experience that their seniority should have given them."[38] For men like Lieutenant Lhoir, who had been elected directly to officer rank at the formation of the 1st battalion of Ile-et-Vilaine, advancement by election was no better. Whereas the volunteer battalions of 1791 – composed of the "elite of ardent and enlightened youth, friend of persons and properties" – had chosen a corps of "meritorious officers" to lead them, the military elections carried out in the line army under the law of 21 February 1793 had produced far different results. They had elevated to officer rank a "crowd of incapable individuals, driven by false principles of republicanism, who mistook license for liberty and regarded submission to the laws of discipline as the shameful attribute of servitude." By means of "cabals" and "flattery," "vile louts, ranting soapbox politicians from the Paris sections, and a swarm of deserters" had insinuated themselves into the officer corps. Soon, the "well-bred" officers of 1791 had found themselves swamped by a "crowd of *sans-culottes*, ... the dregs of the officers vomited into the armies by the regime of the Terror."[39] In the estimation of the sons of active citizens and volunteer officers, the Convention, by making age and demagoguery the keys to advancement, had compromised both the proficiency and dignity of the military profession.

In their estimation, the only remedy was to conduct the reduction of cadres by *concours* (competitive examination), a method which would not only

---

37 A.N. AF III 158, Jean-Baptiste Simon, "Idées rapides sur la nouvelle organisation et sur la réforme des officiers" (14 Thermidor V).
38 A.N. AF III 210, "Lettre d'Arnaud, lieutenant à la 22ème demi-brigade, au Comité de salut public" (30 Prairial III).
39 A.N. AF III 158, "Lettre de Lhoir, lieutenant au 2ème bataillon de la 52ème demi-brigade, à la Commission militaire" (10 Fructidor V).

eliminate ignorance and immorality, but also (and not coincidentally) favor the careers of the better-educated officers who demanded it. *Concours*, they argued, would filter out the illiterate, uneducated, and unmotivated, leaving behind an officer corps of serious young men filled with "knowledge," "genius," and "enlightenment." The "best method for discovering and encouraging talents," *concours* would also inject a new spirit of diligence, studiousness, and striving into the officer corps. It would, predicted Lieutenant Lhoir, "foster zeal and love of work," as well as "stimulate genius" and "all the martial virtues."[40] If *concours* were instituted, mused Lieutenant Lemaitre, the son of a former feudal agent who had been elected to the rank of sergeant in the 1st battalion of the Cher in 1791, the "officers would rush to cultivate the knowledge necessary to become well-instructed military men."[41]

By filtering out intellectual incapacity and stimulating greater professionalism, *concours* would also raise the social level of the officer corps and encourage the sons of good families to take up the profession of arms. The influx of "drunkards, incompetents, immoral men, ... intriguers, and pillagers" during the Convention had discouraged young men of bearing from seeking out military careers.[42] This was only to be expected since anyone concerned about his honor would hesitate to accept a place among such disreputable colleagues. By screening out these kinds of people, wrote Adjutant-Major Lecomte, the son of a fief-holding doctor who had been elected sergeant in the 1st battalion of the Côtes-du-Nord in 1791, *concours* would make "all places honorable" and "*honnête*" men would "no longer fear having men without *mœurs* and conduct as brothers-in-arms."[43] To exclude socially unacceptable officers, Simon even recommended that the examination boards administering the *concours* enquire into what officers "were before serving." Only then would the officer corps "recover its former splendor," and a new "aristocracy" of "merit" and "good *mœurs*" take its rightful place at the head of the army.[44]

These aggressive calls for the removal of propertyless and plebeian elements from the officer corps did not go unchallenged. Recognizing that a purge by *concours* would favor the educated and well-to-do newcomers at their own expense, veteran officers who had risen from the ranks of the former royal army lobbied the legislature to institute a different criterion of selection, experience as

---

40 Ibid.
41 A.N. AF III 182, "Lettre de Lemaitre, lieutenant à la 2ème demi-brigade, à la Commission militaire" (10 Frimaire VII).
42 A.N. AF III 144ª, Pflieger, "Aperçu sur l'état actuel de la cavalerie de la République, et le moyen le plus probable de la rétablir" (IV).
43 A.N. AF II 210, "Lettre de Lecomte, adjudant-major au 1er bataillon des Côtes-du-Nord, aux citoyens composant le Comité de salut public, section militaire" (16 Prairial III).
44 A.N. AF III 158, Simon, "Idées rapides."

measured by total years of service. Writing to Jacques Ferrand, one of their former *officiers de fortune* who had just been elected to the Conseil des cinq-cents (the lower of the two Directorial legislative chambers), the non-commissioned officers of the 97th *demi-brigade* (which they tellingly referred to by its Old Regime name, the "Brie regiment") warned of dire consequences if seniority of service was not respected.[45] Despite their vast experience and all their years of service, they would have to cede their places to volunteer officers who had been elected to their ranks "with farm tools still in their hands." When these rank amateurs had joined up, the veterans wrote, they had "worn themselves out" trying to teach them the rudiments of the military art. "Was it fair," they asked, that men "who had just left the plow" and "to whom we had taught [military] exercises" take their places? Although they had been split between two different *demi-brigades* by the first *amalgame*, the non-commissioned officers of the "former La Marck regiment" issued a collective petition in which they voiced similar concerns.[46] If the reductions were not carried out according to the principle of seniority of service, they wrote, then the unproven newcomers would displace "men of experience, ... those of the old corps [who had been] promoted at the end of 1792 and in the course of 1793 and 1794." For these veterans, *concours* did not provide an accurate measure of merit. In their view, only time of overall service could guarantee the essential military qualities of professional commitment and practical experience.

Barraged with these conflicting demands, the Directory ultimately opted for an entirely different method of reduction, seniority in the grade. Inflexible, objective, and neutral, it ensured simplicity of execution and seemed to promise that neither confusion nor recrimination would attend the reductions.[47] But these hopes for a harmonious process were soon dashed. Although it seemed the fairest, least contentious, and simplest way of downsizing the officer corps, seniority in the grade pleased no one. Although it seemed to eliminate the possibility of arbitrariness, this method encountered widespread opposition on the grounds that it was completely arbitrary. Officers of all professional origins condemned it as fatally imprecise and necessarily unjust. A misguided application of the principle of equality, seniority in the grade only "consecrate[d] the blind movements of chance by placing all officers in a common class, without distinction of merit and

---

45 A.N. AF III 182, "Pétition des sous-officiers de la 97ème demi-brigade d'infanterie, ci-devant 24ème régiment, à Ferrand" (6 Thermidor V).
46 A.N. AF III 145^b, "Lettre des officiers du cy-devant 77ème régiment, actuellement 141ème et 142ème demi-brigades, aux citoyens directeurs" (27 Fructidor IV).
47 According to the instructions sent by the Directory to the generals charged with carrying out the downsizing, the operation was not to be "an individual purge," nor "carry with it any character of preference." A.G. B^{1}69, "Lettre du général de brigade, chef de l'état-major Desbruly, au général de division Souham" (16 Pluviôse IV).

service." If all officers "had enrolled the same day, had the same capacity, [and] had served the *patrie* equally," then seniority in the grade would have been a valid way of proceeding with the reduction of cadres.[48] But this was not the case. The officer corps had been recruited over a long period, from different sources, by different means, and with varying attention to the aspirants' qualifications. Successive changes in the laws of advancement, moreover, had reinforced its heterogeneity. Making no distinction between "merit and ineptitude, *mœurs* and immorality, bravery and cowardice," seniority of service left "everything to chance."[49] What meritocracy demanded in this instance and what the army needed so desperately, all officers felt, was not an illusory equality that gave "inept men and anarchists" places that were the rightful due of "merit and bravery," but rather careful scrutiny and deliberate selections.[50] In the absence of discerning choices, they felt, the opportunity for a purge would be lost and the second *amalgame* would be nothing more than a random reduction of cadres, one which would leave the army in the hands of an officer corps smaller than – but little different in composition from – that bequeathed to the Directory by the Convention.

"Disgusted and discontent" by the adoption of seniority in the grade, the officers tried to circumvent its application and turn the reductions to their own advantage.[51] In some *demi-brigades*, commanders took advantage of the downsizing to remove officers who had recently been attached to their corps and were thus perceived as strangers. One example of this occurred in the Army of the Rhine, whose *demi-brigades* had just been forced to absorb hundreds of officers who had been serving with volunteer battalions in the Vendée. Examining the records of the reduction operations for that Army, its inspector-general, General Schauenbourg, was surprised to find that almost all the Vendée officers had tendered their resignations. Rightfully suspicious, he asked for an explanation, but the units ignored his query or responded evasively. The matter was never resolved.[52] Even in units which were relatively homogenous, the reductions were not always carried out according to the letter of the law. Some *demi-brigades*, in which veterans soldiers of the former royal army occupied key administrative positions, deliberately misconstrued the sense of the official directives and proceeded with the downsizing on the basis of seniority of total service.[53] In units

48 A.N. AF III 158, "Lettre de Lhoir."
49 A.N. AF III 158, Simon, "Idées rapides."
50 A.N. AF III 158, "Projet sur l'épuration du corps des officiers par le capitaine R.E., 27ème demi-brigade" (1 Messidor V).
51 A.G. $X^b 300$, "Rapport du commandant de la place de Cherbourg" (22 Germinal V).
52 Bibliothèque de l'Université de Strasbourg (henceforth B.U.S.), MS 451, "Lettre du général Schauenbourg au général Regnier" (15 Frimaire V).
53 The Directory was aware of this problem, but proved powerless to do anything about it. A.N. AF III 147, "Rapport au Directoire exécutif par le ministre de la guerre, sur la formation du contrôle des officiers réformés, ordonné par l'arrêté du 18 Nivôse IV" (18 Prairial IV).

which observed this criterion of retention, the proportion of line officers kept on active service could be more than twice as great as in *demi-brigades* which adhered to seniority in the grade.[54]

Another problem was the general hostility of the officers retained on active duty – whatever their professional origins – to the reinstatement of the supernumeraries, a process sure to paralyze advancement. The Directory had originally planned to form a global list of supernumeraries, ranked by seniority in the grade, in order to spread the burden of reabsorption evenly across the entire army. But the resistance of the officers thwarted this initiative. Some *demi-brigades* refused to provide the required information, and others submitted lists which were unusable because they were ranked by seniority of total service.[55] Stymied, the Directory abandoned this equitable – if overly ambitious – procedure, and instead made it the responsibility of each *demi-brigade* to recall its own supernumeraries to active service when vacancies occurred. But many units deliberately neglected to inform them when their opportunity for reinstatement arrived because "their recall hindered the advancement of the officers in place." When the innocently unaware supernumeraries failed to report for duty, they were discharged for illegal absence.[56] Subverted in practice by the self-interested manipulations of the officers, the second *amalgame* revealed a military profession increasingly willing to resist what it perceived as inappropriate political interference.

Sensing the general discontent with the reduction procedure it had adopted, the Directory began to retreat from its initial position. In order to permit generals a measure of flexibility in determining which officers to keep on active service, it authorized them to encourage the resignation and retirement of incapable officers. By pushing "subjects of inferior merit" to leave the service, the generals were instructed, the military profession could be recomposed of "the most distinguished officers, those most valuable for their principles, instruction, love of discipline, and courage."[57] One officer who made full use of this tacit authorization to purge the officer corps was General Reynier. He defended his decision to remove "a large part" of the cadres of the 5th *chasseur* regiment on the grounds that, if he had proceeded according to seniority in the grade, many "bad officers would have occupied places while the good ones would have

---

54 In the 44th demi-brigade, which carried out its reductions according to the principle of seniority of total service, 58 percent of the royal army veterans were retained. In contrast, units like the 39th and 75th demi-brigades, which observed seniority in the grade, retained only 34 percent and 26 percent, respectively.

55 A.N. AF III 147, "Rapport au Directoire exécutif par le ministre de la guerre sur la formation du contrôle des officiers réformés, ordonné par l'arrêté du 18 Nivôse IV" (18 Prairial IV).

56 A.N. 138 AP 15, Daru, "Mémoire sur l'infanterie" (VIII), and "Officiers et sous-officiers d'infanterie et de troupes à cheval" (n.d.).

57 A.G. B^{13}*31, "Lettre du Directoire exécutif au ministre de la guerre" (18 Messidor IV).

become auxiliaries."⁵⁸ Other officers were pushed out of the service for political reasons. For example, Adjutant-Major Monguyon of the 86th *demi-brigade* was removed from the service because of his "Jacobin conduct and dress, by which he seeks to foment anarchy and discord."⁵⁹ The Directory usually endorsed decisions by general officers to dismiss personnel for professional or political reasons, a sign that the army was successfully beginning to assert a measure of independent control over its composition.⁶⁰

The second *amalgame* was a traumatic experience which had a profound impact on the officer corps. The internecine divisions inflamed by the reduction of cadres, the insecurity of careers, and the virtual evaporation of advancement engendered what one contemporary described as "general discontent" among the officers.⁶¹ But the downsizing had other, more positive consequences which helped lay the foundations of what would become the imperial military establishment. The painful, but necessary, consolidation of under-strength *demi-brigades* proved so effective that Napoleon retained the units created by the second *amalgame* as the core of his army. The only change he made was to rename them regiments and restore the Old Regime nomenclature of officer rank. The reduction of cadres had another unexpected effect. The dramatic slowing of advancement after the second *amalgame* helped establish Napoleon's reputation as the Revolution's greatest practitioner of meritocracy. Just as Napoleon was establishing his power in the year VIII (1799–1800), the backlog of supernumeraries created by the reductions was finally being fully absorbed, allowing advancement to resume. Many officers must have associated the revival of promotions with the accession of Napoleon. Finally, the massive layoffs of the second *amalgame* strongly reinforced the professionalism of the officer corps. To lighten the burden of reabsorption, officers who were so inclined were encouraged to tender their resignations. For those not fully committed to the military profession, the second *amalgame* offered an opportunity to withdraw with honor and a small pension. Others, tired of waiting for reinstatement as supernumeraries, gave up their hopes of resuming their military careers and reentered civilian life. Only those men completely dedicated to the profession of arms, or who believed that they had no other career options, remained.⁶² Whether they had begun their military service as sons of active citizens, National Guard volunteers, or soldiers in the former royal army, the officers who remained after the second *amalgame* were all committed professionals.

58 A.G. B¹*177, "Lettre du général de brigade Reynier au général Salu" (22 Pluviôse IV).
59 A.G. Xᵇ300, "Rapport du commandant de la place de Cherbourg" (22 Germinal V).
60 A.G. B¹³*31, "Lettre du Directoire exécutif au ministre de la guerre" (9 Brumaire V).
61 A.N. AF III 145ᵃ, "Lettre anonyme qui annonce le mécontentement général qu'occasionne dans l'armée la réforme de plusieurs officiers qu'elle livre à l'indigence" (30 Ventôse IV).
62 A.G. B²49, "Lettre de Lafitte, soldat à la 65ème demi-brigade au Directoire exécutif" (18 Germinal IV).

The Military Commission and the *coup d'état* of 18 Fructidor V (4 September 1797)

Although it would eventually engender a new professionalism, at the time of its execution the second *amalgame* was perceived by officers as yet another example of the instability to which military careers had been subjected since 1789. The first troubles had of course arisen with the insubordination of the troops and emigration of the nobles officers in 1790–92. But in the eyes of many officers, it was under the Convention that the greatest disruption had occurred. Flawed laws on advancement, the meddling of representatives-on-mission, and the rise of demagoguery within the army itself had degraded the composition of the officers, subjected military careers to politicized favoritism, and thrown the administration into disorder. The root problem, as many officers saw it, was that "men foreign to the *métier* of war" had taken control of military policy and "subverted the army by introducing democratic forms." In their attempt to restructure the army along republican lines, they had passed "a multitude of decrees" which had only succeeded in "exacerbating the chaos of military laws" and rendering the structure of the military career exceedingly unstable.[63] The only remedy, the officers felt, was to put the army back in charge of its own affairs by forming a "commission composed primarily of military men" to conduct the "revision of all military laws." Assembled in a definitive military code, their work would shelter the army from the fickle winds of political change and provide officers with the career stability they sought.[64] The formation of a military commission charged with drafting a comprehensive set of legislation for their profession would have been unthinkable during the Convention because it smacked of corporatism. But with the "destruction of the former government" and the removal of the "perverse men who dominated it," such an undertaking was now feasible.[65] Responding to this strain of opinion, the notoriously right-wing Conseil des cinq-cents elected in Germinal V seized the opportunity to establish such a commission, creating it on 4 Prairial V (24 May 1797), only three days after its convocation. According to its principal sponsor and future member, François Aubry, the "Commission for the Revision of All Military Laws" would "eliminate the chaos which currently reigns" in the army by drafting a "complete military code."[66]

Although a professionalizing agenda shaped the work of the Commission, the darkening climate of political strife also influenced its reforms. Having

---

63 A.N. AF IV 1115, "Sur l'armée française" (n.d.).
64 A.N. 138 AP 4, Daru, "Mémoire sur le département de la guerre."
65 A.G. MR 2018, Joincheval, "Vues sur les changements à faire dans les corps militaires et des nouveaux établissements susceptibles d'en faire le bien" (1796).
66 A.N. AD XVIII^c 444, François Aubry, *Motion d'ordre fait par F. Aubry, pour la formation d'une commission chargée de présenter au corps législatif un code militaire complet* (4 Prairial V).

returned a conservative, if not royalist, majority openly hostile to the Executive Directory, the elections of Germinal V initiated a period of destabilizing conflict between the legislative and executive branches of government. Led by the Conseil des cinq-cents, the legislature sought to disempower the executive. From its inception, the Military Commission played a critical role in this endeavor – to strip the Directory of its control over the state's coercive institutions. The formation of the Commission thus plunged the legislature into a contest with the executive over a fundamental constitutional issue with immediate power-political ramifications: control of the state's monopoly of force. Aubry made this explicit in his original appeal for the formation of the Commission.

> The creation and organization of the armed forces, do they fall within the purview of the Legislative Body or that of the Executive Directory? ... This is the important question I am submitting for discussion, a question which would not even be a question if the Directory, since its installation, had not usurped [these powers]. In effect, what are the functions of the Directory with regard to the armed forces?[67]

By approving Aubry's motion and voting to establish the Commission, the Conseil des cinq-cents challenged the Directory's power over the armed forces and announced its intention to redefine the relationship between the legislature and executive.

The composition of the Commission – Pichegru, Willot, Aubry, Gau, Ferrand, Normand, and Jourdan – reflected its dual professional and political aims. The most prominent members of the Commission, Pichegru and Willot were both serving generals, as well as leaders of the anti-Directorial forces in the Conseil des cinq-cents. The Director Barras reportedly regarded their election as president and secretary of the Conseil des cinq-cents, respectively, as an "act of war."[68] Pichegru had been a non-commissioned officer in the artillery for twelve years before being elected to lead a volunteer battalion in 1792. From this elevated position, he advanced rapidly to army command, winning national renown for his conquest of Holland. Unbeknown to his compatriots, however, he had become a royalist agent in the year IV. His colleague Willot was a noble who had begun serving as an officer in 1771. He rose steadily during the early Revolution, but was suspended in 1793. Reinstated by the Thermidorean Convention, he was given command of the 8th military division, centered in Marseille, where he used his authority to persecute former Jacobins and terrorists. Willot deliberately cultivated his image as a muscular opponent of radicalism, sometimes arriving at sessions of the legislature on horseback,

---

67 Ibid.
68 Jean-Pierre Fabre de l'Aude, *Histoire secrète du Directoire* (Paris, 1832), vol. 3, 26.

brandishing pistols. He, like his colleague Pichegru, had secretly offered his services to Louis XVIII.[69]

Three other members of the Commission – Aubry, Gau, and Ferrand – displayed a similar mixture of military experience and political antipathy toward the Directorial regime. All had been implicated in the royalist-led Vendémiaire uprising in the year IV. We have already met Aubry, the former Old Regime artillery officer and member of the Convention who was imprisoned in 1793 for protesting the expulsion of his Girondin colleagues. Upon his reinstatement in the Convention after Thermidor, he directed a purge of reputed terrorists from the general staff and designed the 14 Germinal III law on advancement which signaled a marked retreat from the egalitarian promotion procedures of 21 February 1793.[70] Gau was the son of a wealthy Old Regime military administrator and himself became a *commissaire des guerres* in 1777. Attached to the War Council, where he worked closely with Guibert, he rose to the position of Director-General of Funds in the constitutional monarchy's war ministry after 1789. Although dismissed after 10 August 1792 as a result of the republican reorganization of the ministry, he was rehabilitated by his patron, Aubry, and named director of the Committee of Public Safety's war section in the year III (1794–95).[71] Ferrand was an Old Regime *officier de fortune* who became a general in 1793. Little is known of Normand, the least experienced member of the Commission, except that he was serving as a superior officer at the time of his election. The final member of the Commission, Jourdan, resembled Pichegru in that he was a general and a war hero, but differed from his colleague in that he was a staunch republican. Of all the Commission's members, he alone would escape proscription as a result of the Directory's purge of its political opponents in the legislature, the coup of 18 Fructidor V.

The Commission's first reforms concerned the Gendarmerie and National Guard. Taking as a model the decentralized organization adopted by the Constituent Assembly in 1791, the Commission sought to transfer power over these paramilitary institutions from the Directory to local administrations. With its authority over these forces fragmented, the Directory would be disarmed, unable to order them against the Conseil des cinq-cents and its other political

---

[69] Jonathan B. Devlin, "The Directory and the Politics of Military Command: The Army of the Interior in South-East France," *French History*, 4 (1990), 209–15; and Vaublanc, *Mémoires sur la Révolution*, vol. 2, 414. Information on Willot's career as a royalist agent comes from conversations with Stephen Clay, who is currently working on Willot's role in the bitter factional politics of Directorial Provence.

[70] On Aubry's role in the Thermidorean purge of generals, see Howard G. Brown, "Politics, Professionalism, and the Fate of Army Generals after Thermidor," *French Historical Studies*, 19 (1995), 133–52.

[71] A.N. 138 AP 17, "Lettre de Gau à Daru" (28 Ventôse XII); and Brown, *War, Revolution, and the Bureaucratic State*, 307.

enemies. When the newly elected deputies convened in Prairial V (May–June 1797), the Directory had already been authorized by the previous legislature to conduct a purge of the Gendarmerie. Precipitously expanded from 4,700 in 1789 to 21,000 in the year II, many believed that it, like the officer corps, had been recruited carelessly during the Convention. Lacuée, an Old Regime officer in the Conseil des anciens (the upper chamber of the Directorial legislature), believed it was composed of "apostles of anarchy, friends of the levelers, and partisans of terrorism." He called for a purge to enhance the quality and reputation of the corps, a measure which would allow it to enforce the laws more effectively, even with a smaller staff and budget.[72] "By augmenting the consideration of the individuals" who composed it, echoed the Directorial war minister Petiet, "we will be able to reduce their number, their service will be better coordinated, and the state will reap considerable savings."[73]

The Directory had already begun to carry out these reductions when the conservative legislature elected in Germinal V convened. On 27 Prairial V (15 June 1797), Delarue, a leader of the legislative opposition to the Executive Directory, called for a halt to these operations. Afraid that the Directory would use its purge authority to remove conservatives and retain former supporters of the Terrorist regime, he invited the newly formed Military Commission to propose a more politically acceptable method of downsizing.[74] Willot presented the Commission's recommendation to limit the Directory's role in the reorganization on 18 Messidor V (6 July 1797).[75] The Directory would be left the nomination of the superior officers of the corps, but its choice would be severely constrained. It would only be allowed to appoint them from the ranks of superior officers currently on active service, as well as from those who had been unjustly suspended during the Terror by the "twelve-man tyranny [the Committee of Public Safety] and the proconsuls sent into the departments." To be eligible for nomination, moreover, they had to have already been captains in the Gendarmerie in 1791. This restriction, effectively limiting the Directory's choice to former officers of the Old Regime *maréchaussée*, was intended to ensure that the reconstituted Gendarmerie was commanded by politically moderate professionals who owed their places to long service rather than revolutionary patronage. These superior officers would then collaborate with departmental juries dominated by locally

---

72   A.N. AD VI 66, Lacuée, *Rapport fait au nom d'une commission spéciale, par J. G. Lacuée, séance du 12 Pluviôse an V de la République, sur l'organisation et la composition de la Gendarmerie nationale* (12 Pluviôse V).
73   A.N. AF III 148[a], Petiet, "Mémoire sur l'administration du département de la guerre" (n.d.).
74   A.N. AD VI 66, Delarue, *Motion d'ordre de Delarue, sur l'organisation de la Gendarmerie nationale* (27 Prairial V).
75   A.N. AD VI 66, Willot, *Rapport par Willot, au nom de la Commission chargée de la révision des lois militaires, composée des représentants Pichegru, Ferrand, Willot, Jourdan, Aubry, Normand, et Gau, sur l'organisation de la Gendarmerie* (18 Messidor V).

elected officials in carrying out the purge of lower-ranking officers. Those retained in active service would thus owe their places to their immediate military and civil superiors, not the Executive Directory.

Grasping the intent of Willot's plan, the Directory urged the Conseil des cinq-cents to let stand the reduction operations it had already carried out. It had already expedited letters of nomination. Moreover, it argued, as the proposed departmental juries included no representatives of executive, they could not have the "same knowledge of the ensemble of subjects as the Directory" and would "necessarily limit their choices to [their] local acquaintances." "Anarchy" would be the inevitable "result of this independence."[76] The Directory's supporters in the legislature joined in the counterattack, pointing out that the conditions of eligibility for superior officers advanced by Willot limited the pool of potential nominees to "old *maréchaussée* officers."[77] The former member of the Convention, Savary, expressed doubt that "there is a single officer among those who began the war of liberty who can make the proof" of long service demanded by Willot.[78] Officers of the Gendarmerie also added their voices to the chorus of dissent. One officer, Leroux, claimed that candidates would have "to be noble in order to be admitted." Those who had served the Republic loyally would thus be excluded, and the "fruit of their labors ... would go to their former privileged officers," men who had "taken no risks during the Revolution."[79] Others condemned Willot's plan as a "scheme tending to reestablish the old *maréchaussée*."[80] Swayed by these arguments, a majority of deputies agreed that the plan was too reactionary and rejected it on 30 Thermidor V (17 August 1797).

The Commission also sought to strip the Directory of its power over the National Guard. The decrepit state of this institution provided an ideal pretext for reform. In the few places where it still functioned, according to the minister of general police Cochon, the National Guard served with "indifference" and "apathy."

> The different posts confided to [it] are poorly guarded ... Even the most important – such as prisons, houses of detention, and public buildings – are abandoned ... There are no night patrols, [and] force is lacking when it is a question of arresting brigands, assassins, deported priests, [and] émigrés ... With the exception of Paris,

---

76 A.N. AD VI 66, *Message du Directoire exécutif au Conseil des cinq-cents* (29 Messidor V).
77 A.N. AD VI 66, Dugué-d'Assé, *Opinion de Dugué-d'Assé à la tribune des Anciens, séance du 28 Thermidor V, contre les résolutions du Conseil des cinq-cents, des 10 et 25 du même mois, relatives à l'organisation de la Gendarmerie nationale* (28 Thermidor V).
78 A.N. AD VI 66, Savary, *Opinion de Savary sur le projet de résolution relatif à l'organisation de la Gendarmerie présenté le 18 Messidor par Willot au nom de la Commission militaire,* (10 Thermidor V).
79 A.N. AF III 158, "Lettre de Leroux, chef de brigade adjoint à la première inspection de la Gendarmerie nationale à Willot" (6 Thermidor V).
80 A.N. AD VI 66, Marbot, *Rapport fait par Marbot, sur la résolution du 11 Vendémiaire relative à la formation d'un jury de révision pour l'organisation de la Gendarmerie* (18 Vendémiaire VI).

Bordeaux, Lyon, Strasbourg, Marseille, and several other communes ... the service of the National Guard is almost everywhere null.

Cochon hoped to revive the "generous ardor which animated all citizens during the first years of the Revolution," but he was not optimistic. If public enthusiasm was not forthcoming, he suggested, the government should consider imposing punitive taxes to force compliance.[81]

Like Cochon, the Commission took the National Guard of the early Revolution as its model, but not because of its revolutionary energy. Rather, the Commission believed that the Guard's original, decentralized structure, designed in part as a counterweight to monarchical power, could serve equally well against the Executive Directory. On 2 Thermidor V (20 July 1797), Pichegru presented the Commission's plan to transfer control of the National Guard from the Directory to the departments.[82] As Mathieu Dumas, one of the plan's supporters in the legislature pointed out, it "textually recalled the formation decreed by the Constituent Assembly."[83] Its principal provision revived the law of 10 August 1789, which gave municipalities the sole power to requisition the National Guard. Although this alone was enough to wrest control of the Guard from the Directory, the Commission also permitted the reestablishment of departmental armies of National Guards, suppressed by the Convention as instruments of federalism and civil war. The plan, moreover, would have allowed multiple departmental administrations to unify under a supreme commander all the Guard units within their jurisdictions. To ensure that local elites would control the reformed institution, Pichegru proposed the reestablishment of grenadier and *chasseur* companies, elite units whose costly equipment limited their recruitment to the well-to-do. In sum, Pichegru's proposal was intended to transfer control of the National Guard from the Directory to the localities, give departments the authority to raise their own armies, and guarantee that local elites would be in charge. Impressed with the revolutionary pedigree of the plan, the Conseil des cinq-cents approved these measures on 25 Thermidor V (12 August 1797) and sent the resolution on to the Conseil des anciens for final approval.

According to the Constitution of the year III, the Conseil des anciens was supposed to act as a brake on the impetuousness of the lower chamber. When

---

81 A.N. AF III 158, "Rapport sur la Garde nationale" (V).
82 A.N. AD VI 50, Pichegru, *Rapport fait par Pichegru au nom de la Commission de la revision des lois militaires, sur l'organisation de la Garde nationale* (2 Thermidor V). This idea was possibly suggested to Pichegru by his English spymaster, William Wickham, and his principal French collaborator, the former *constituant* d'Andrè. Harvey Mitchell, *The Underground War against Revolutionary France: The Missions of William Wickham, 1794–1800* (Oxford, 1965), 182 and 193.
83 A.N. AD VI 50, Mathieu Dumas, *Rapport fait par Mathieu Dumas, au nom de la Commission chargée de l'examen de la résolution sur la réorganisation définitive de la Garde nationale* (Thermidor V).

presented with the Commission's proposal to decentralize the National Guard, it very nearly succeeded. Directorial deputies in the Conseil des anciens attacked the plan as unconstitutional. Rabaut le jeune, the youngest brother of the famous member of the National Assembly, Rabaut-Saint-Etienne, denounced it for what it was, a deliberate attempt to paralyze the Directory. He warned that restricting the right of activating the National Guard to local authorities "deprived the Executive Directory of the constitutional right of convoking and requisitioning the National Guards." "According to the Constitution," he continued, the Directory "disposes of the armed forces, ... yet [by this resolution] it cannot convoke, cannot requisition the National Guard."[84] Other deputies spoke against the reestablishment of the elite companies. Rossée, an outspoken supporter of the Directory, branded the grenadier and *chasseur* companies a "corporation" and an "order." He claimed that they would "establish privileges, distinctions, [and] form a particular caste of rich citizens."[85] Despite these objections, however, the Conseil des anciens approved the Commission's plan on 13 Fructidor V (30 August 1797). But coming only five days before the Directory's coup, this law came too late to help the parliamentary opposition. By conjuring up the specter of elite-led departmental armies marching on Paris, it may have even provoked the Directory to strike when it did.

The Commission also took steps to detach the regular army from the Executive Directory. Unlike the locally rooted National Guard, the army had been a highly centralized institution since the Old Regime. For all their grumbling, the officers remained loyal to the central government. Indeed, the insecurity of careers produced by the reductions of the second *amalgame* may have even increased their dependence on the Executive Directory. In the months before 18 Fructidor, the armies of the Republic – notably Hoche's Army of the Sambre-et-Meuse and Bonaparte's Army of Italy – had sent the Directory resounding declarations of fidelity which implied that they stood ready to march on Paris to crush the royalist conspirators in the legislature. Indeed, detachments from both armies had been sent toward Paris in the weeks preceding 18 Fructidor. Of all the institutions of the Republic, the army offered the strongest support to the executive and the greatest obstacle to the commission's project of disempowering the Directory.

The Commission believed that the Directory's unrestrained power to cashier officers – a surviving legacy of the Convention – was largely responsible for reducing the army to this dangerous state of blind obedience. To reduce the officers' excessive dependence on the executive, as well as restore stability and security to

---

84 A.N. AD VI 50, Rabaut le jeune, *Opinion de Rabaut le jeune, sur le service de la Garde nationale* (13 Fructidor V).

85 A.N. AD VI 50, Rossée, *Rapport de Rossée, député du Haut-Rhin, sur la résolution du Conseil des cinq-cents relative à l'organisation de la Garde nationale sédentaire* (25 Thermidor V).

their careers, the Commission drafted a law forbidding the Directory to remove officers without a formal legal hearing. Presented by Aubry on 1 Thermidor V (19 July 1797), it deplored that the Directory's arrogation of arbitrary authority over military careers had placed the officers' "*état*" and "honor" at the mercy of the government.[86] The officers's honor, according to Aubry, was his personal property and an invaluable military resource which had to be "maintained in all its purity" against the incursions of Directorial "despotism." To strip an officer of his grade was to cast aspersions on his capacity, sully his reputation, and compromise his honor. Cashiering an officer was thus a grave matter which had to follow a strict and impartial legal procedure. If officers could be arbitrarily stripped of their hard-won ranks by unilateral government action, moreover, *émulation* would decline. What was the point of striving if the fruit of one's labors could be taken away without warning or recourse? It had long been recognized as well that the Directory's power to remove arbitrarily officers not only "undermined the solidity of the formation of the cadres," but also posed a serious threat to political liberty by placing the officers "in an almost servile dependence upon the executive power."[87] With their professional existence guaranteed by nothing but the continued goodwill of the government, the officers "would become, sooner or later, the passive instrument of the first usurper" to impose his "despotism over the troops." It was necessary to protect the military profession from this outside political influence because only a free officer corps would dare to stand up against tyranny. Without an end to arbitrary dismissals, Aubry concluded, both military professionalism and the Constitution would be in jeopardy.

Supporters of the Directory responded by arguing that the Directory's power to remove officers was not merely compatible with liberty, but even necessary to preserve the Republic. They claimed that the Commission's plan to assimilate military grades to personal property was incompatible with republicanism. The Constitution, they pointed out, implicitly authorized the Directory to fire officers. Article 196 allowed the Directory to "suspend or dismiss immediately, whenever it thinks necessary, either departmental or cantonal administrators." If the Directory could remove democratically elected administrators, they concluded, surely it could also remove military personnel who did not owe their positions to so respectable a mandate.[88] Moreover, the Commission's proposal

---

86 Unless otherwise indicated, all citations in this paragraph are from A.N. AD XVIII^{c}444, Aubry, *Rapport fait par Aubry au nom de la Commission chargée de la révision des lois militaires, composée des représentants Pichegru, Gau, Ferrand, Willot, Jourdan, Normand, et Aubry, sur les destitutions militaires* (1 Thermidor V).
87 A.N. AD VI 66, Mathieu Dumas, *Opinion de Mathieu Dumas sur la résolution relative à l'avancement, la solde, l'administration, et la police de la Gendarmerie nationale* (12 Ventôse V).
88 A.N. AD XVIII^{c}444, Guillemardet, *Opinion de Guillemardet sur le rapport d'Aubry sur les destitutions* (21 Thermidor V).

was based on maxims "entirely contrary to the nature of republican government and to the principles of [the] Constitution." Honor, the "soul" of Aubry's report, was a "feudal" notion which implied the existence of a "monarchy and hereditary nobility." If reinstituted as a form of military tenure, it would ineluctably transform the officer corps into a "privileged and permanent class." Assimilating public military functions to private property would turn the army into a "Republic in the midst of another Republic," encourage the military to see itself as independent of civil authority, and destroy the "action of the executive power over the armed forces."[89] If the Commission's plan were approved, warned the Directory's legislative supporters, France could soon expect military despotism and the reimposition of monarchical government. After a month of heated debate, these arguments carried the day, and the plan was rejected.

At the same time as it strove to free the officer corps from the power of the Directory, the Commission also sought to augment the officers' authority within the army itself. On 13 Messidor V (1 July 1797), Gau presented its plan for the reorganization of the units' administrative councils.[90] He began by noting that the Convention had replaced the streamlined councils of the constitutional monarchy, composed exclusively of officers, with unwieldy bodies dominated by the rank-and-file. This change had produced only "confusion, the total ruin of finances, anarchy, and all the evils which accompany it." Although certain military men in the legislature – like Mathieu Dumas who claimed that "military principles" demanded the total exclusion of soldiers and Lacuée who asserted that their inclusion by the Convention had been "dictated by politics" – wanted to eliminate soldiers entirely from the councils, Gau's plan at least paid lip service to democratic principle.[91] The new councils were to be composed of one soldier, one non-commissioned officer, and five officers. Outnumbering their inferiors five to two, the officers would thus control the internal affairs of their units. The Commission's plan to give the officers greater administrative control, coupled with its abortive proposal to protect their careers from arbitrary executive action, would have restored to the military profession an important measure of autonomy. The Commission considered this freedom from outside interference and the pressure of inferiors essential not only to reestablish the officer corps on a proper footing, but also to break the Directory's hold over the army.

---

89 A.N. AD XVIII^{c}444, Boulay de la Meurthe, *Opinion de Boulay de la Meurthe sur le rapport fait par Aubry sur les destitutions militaires* (21 Thermidor V).

90 Unless otherwise noted, all citations in this paragraph are from A.N. AD VI 69, Gau, *Rapport fait par Gau, au nom de la Commission chargée de la révision des lois militaires, sur l'organisation des conseils d'administration* (13 Messidor V).

91 A.N. AD VI 69, Mathieu Dumas, *Opinion de Mathieu Dumas sur la résolution concernant l'organisation des conseils d'administration des troupes de la République* (8 Germinal V); and Lacuée, *Opinion de J. G. Lacuée, sur la nouvelle composition des conseils d'administration* (8 Germinal V).

The Directory recognized the danger posed to it by the Commission's reforms, but was powerless to thwart its efforts through legislative action. Fearing for its survival, the Directory responded in an extra-parliamentary fashion, by moving troops from the armies fighting on the frontiers to the Paris region. As tensions mounted, the Commission reacted against these threatening deployments. A set of laws passed between 10 and 12 Thermidor V (28 and 30 July 1797) established stiff penalties against violations of the so-called "constitutional belt," a perimeter around Paris within which troops were forbidden without legislative approval. Although article 69 of the Constitution explicitly forbade the unauthorized entry of military forces within this zone, it did not establish punitive measures to be taken against transgressors. To give the article teeth, the Commission proposed placing warning signs around the constitutional belt, punishing officers who led troops toward the capitol, and taking action against civil authorities (including the Directors, if need be) who ordered such movements. These laws were to be publicized within the armies and read to the troops.[92] The Commission complemented these measures with a law forbidding generals to detach troops from their armies without formal authorization.[93]

At the same time, the Commission also tried to even the balance of forces in Paris itself. It sought to remove the thousands of supernumerary officers, laid off by the second *amalgame*, who had descended on the capitol hoping to obtain reinstatement from the war minister.[94] For all their professional frustrations, they remained loyal to the government, demonstrating their willingness to fight for the Directory by repeatedly clashing with gangs of anti-Directorial toughs. To get them out of Paris, where they might be used to support a Directorial coup, the Commission proposed that the supernumeraries only be allowed to collect their half-pay in their home towns.[95] The Commission also sought to build up the strength of the Legislative Guard and ensure its loyalty. In Thermidor V (July–August 1797), it proposed adding two mounted squadrons and an artillery company, steps which would have given the legislature a well-rounded, combat-ready pocket army. Commanding this force, and answerable only to the legislature, was Jean-Pierre Ramel, a career officer who described himself as one of the

---

92 *Loi contenant de nouvelles dispositions pour s'opposer à tout passage des troupes au delà des limites constitutionnelles ...* (10 Thermidor V); and *Loi ordonnant que la loi du 10 de ce mois et relative aux limites constitutionnelles sera lue à la tête des troupes* (11 Thermidor V).

93 *Loi portant que dans l'intérieur aucun mouvement de troupes ou changement de troupes ne peut être effectué que d'après un ordre écrit du ministre de la guerre relatant l'ordre du Directoire exécutif et que tout général ou chef absent de son poste ne peut adresser aucun ordre aux troupes faisant parti de son commandement* (12 Thermidor V).

94 Patrice Mahon, *Etudes sur les armées du Directoire: première partie, Joubert à l'armée d'Italie: Championnet à l'armée de Rome (octobre 1798–janvier 1799)* (Paris, 1905), 46. See also, A.N. AF III 182, "Lettre de Richard aux citoyens législateurs" (19 Thermidor V).

95 A.N. AD XVIII^{c}444, Aubry, *Motion d'ordre*.

"*honnêtes* men who wanted to restore order and end the iniquity of the revolutionary laws."[96] With the help of one of the Commission's sympathizers in Conseil des anciens, the career officer Mathieu Dumas, Ramel purged the army of radical guardsmen, replacing them with soldiers drawn from General Moreau's reputedly more moderate army. Although these steps might have helped the legislature meet a show of force, they were not yet complete when the Directory struck. On 18 Fructidor V, troops led by General Augereau, Napoleon's trusted lieutenant, invaded the legislature. Over fifty opposition deputies, including nearly all the members of the Commission, were expelled. The army had become the last resort of a shaky government seeking to perpetuate itself in power.

Civil–military relations: professionalism and politics

While historians have generally agreed that the *coup d'état* of 18 Fructidor marked a crucial turning point in French civil–military relations, they have offered differing assessments of its significance. Some scholars – notably Jean-Paul Bertaud and Albert Mathiez – have argued that 18 Fructidor was the moment when the army broke free of civilian political control. Jealous of its professional autonomy, contemptuous of a weak government which had compromised its legitimacy by corruption and political fraud, and disdainful of a society which seemed to have abandoned the revolutionary ideals for which the troops were still fighting, the army came to believe that it alone possessed the moral authority to shape France's political destiny. Indeed, according to this interpretation, the multiple political, social, and economic crises which plagued the Directory virtually demanded that the military act to restore order and vigor to the national life. Gradually after Thermidor, concluded Bertaud, the army became a "parallel power, a counter-power," convinced that a "regeneration of civil by military society was necessary."[97] The importance of the Fructidor *coup* – in addition to demonstrating yet again the extent to which the bitter political legacy of the Revolution had divided the French and the inability of democratic institutions to cope with these hatreds – was to reveal to the army its own power. The Directory's recourse to military intervention taught generals who had once "trembled before the great Committee of Public Safety" that the government now "depended almost solely on their swords."[98] From this perspective, Napoleon's *coup* of 18 Brumaire was the inevitable outcome of the growing politicization of the army.

---

96 Jean-Pierre Ramel, *Journal de l'adjudant-général Ramel* (London, 1799), iv.
97 Bertaud, *La Révolution armée*, 340–1.
98 Albert Mathiez, "Le Coup d'état du 18 Fructidor an V," *Annales historiques de la Révolution française*, 6 (1929), 550. For a similar assessment, see Marcel Reinhard, "L'Armée et Bonaparte en 1801," *Annales historiques de la Révolution française*, 133 (1953), 292.

Although it has been widely accepted and integrated into many textbook accounts, this interpretation has been challenged by several important scholars of the French Revolution. The most influential skeptics – Jean Jaurès and Georges Lefebvre – have argued that, far from becoming increasingly involved in politics, the growing professionalism of the army during the Directorial years led it to embrace political neutrality and unquestioning subordination to civilian political authority. Despite developing into a professional army, asserted Georges Lefebvre, the military "never became praetorian." "The Republic never experienced a *pronunciamento*: soldiers and generals carried out the *coup d'état* of 18 Brumaire, like that of 18 Fructidor, only at the behest of the bourgeoisie."[99] While Lefebvre's insistence on the class character of the *coups* may be questioned, his contention that its increasingly distinct professional identity in no way induced the army to usurp an autonomous political role cannot be dismissed lightly. The *coup d'état* of 18 Brumaire began, after all, as a plot woven by Sieyès and allied legislators, not an independent bid for power by General Bonaparte. Indeed, only a small clique of officers and a handful of soldiers actually took part in the *coup*; the army, as an institution, was not involved. Even in his famous plea to replace the professional army with the nation-in-arms, *l'Armée nouvelle*, Jean Jaurès acknowledged the political neutrality of the revolutionary military. The army, he began, was "only an instrument."

> It does not have its own force, autonomous will, or politics. It is, at least in France, the servant of the civil power. Even when it commits odious excesses, even when it violates the Constitution, menaces or crushes liberty, fires on the people, it is not on the initiative of its leaders that it acts ... The grenadiers of Brumaire were not operating on behalf of a caste ... Bonaparte himself affected to be outside and above the army.[100]

For Lefebvre and Jaurès, military professionalism, even though detestable because it separated the army from the nation, did not lead the officers to question their subordination to civil authority. Although the *coup* of 18 Fructidor undoubtedly encouraged a few generals' political ambitions, most officers learned a different lesson from their encounters with the treacherous world of revolutionary politics.

The turbulent events of the revolutionary decade left their mark on the officer corps, instilling in unanticipated ways a new sense of professionalism in its members. The hardships of war, coupled with the dramatic reductions of the second *amalgame* had weeded out all those who did not really want to make the military profession their lifetime career. Those disgusted with the instability the

---

99 Georges Lefebvre, *Le Directoire* (Paris, 1946), 77.
100 Jaurès, *L'Armée nouvelle*, vol. 2, 380–1 and 391.

Revolution had brought to the military profession, those dissatisfied with the rewards offered by the military career, and those who had only joined the army out of patriotic motives during a period of national emergency were free to leave and, indeed, were encouraged to do so. Far from drawing those who remained into a praetorian role, the chronic political instability of the revolutionary years reinforced their single-minded dedication to their military duties. Recognizing that those who attached themselves too closely to a particular ideology were apt to find themselves out of a job if the winds of political fortune shifted, the officers sought refuge in political neutrality. If it had weakened military professionalism in other ways, political turbulence had at least taught the officers that activism and partisanship were poor strategies of career advancement and professional survival. This is not to say that the officer corps was happy with the government of France or that it actually managed to insulate itself from politics. On the contrary, officers at all levels – from the lieutenant leading a squadron in pursuit of draft evaders to generals trying to sort through the bloody chaos of factional score-settling in their military districts – were forced (to their great frustration) to confront politics as part of their routine activities. Some – like Pichegru, Willot, and Bonaparte – even sought to take an active part in the political struggles of the day. But the military profession as a whole did not relish, and generally sought to avoid, the political role into which it had been thrust by the Revolution. Traumatized by the intense and unpredictable scrutiny to which it had been subjected during the Reign of Terror and Thermidorean reaction, the officer corps had already adopted a new credo – attention to duty and impersonal obedience to central authority, rather than outspoken adherence to the political orthodoxy of the day – by the time the Directory came to power. A good republican officer did not waste his time shouting slogans, cultivating politicians, and coddling soldiers, but, rather, was a stranger to all but his military occupations. Requesting an active posting, General Turreau succinctly expressed this new ideal of apolitical military professionalism when he proudly claimed that he had always shunned "intrigues, factions, and all the parties that have emerged during the Revolution."[101] Professionalism had become the officer corps's defensive response to revolutionary politicization.

Although a refuge from the partisan divisions of the Revolution, the new spirit of professionalism engendered attitudes that, in the context of Directorial rule, came perilously close to political stances. Committed to the good of their profession, officers could not help but feel disgust at the government's inability to solve its problems. Political instability in Paris and perceived civilian opposition to the war effort (expressed through draft evasion and resistance to requisition) fed the army's feeling that it was fighting and dying on behalf of

---

101 A.N. AA 52, "Lettre du général Turreau" (8 Fructidor III).

an egotistical society.[102] Fiscal and logistical breakdown, the multiplication of paperwork, and the perceived spread of corruption discredited the government further. Controversial personnel policies, such as those implemented as part of the second *amalgame*, fueled the discontent, as did the virtual halt of advancement. But frustration with the inability of the Directorial regime to meet the army's needs and desires did not necessarily translate into a determination to see the army itself seize the reins of government. Although some officers may have hoped to see the Directory overthrown, few believed that this task should fall to the military. Although some were disgusted by government inefficiency and hoped for a regime that could mobilize national energies more effectively, they remained subordinate to the central authority of the state.

Perhaps the best illustration of this new spirit of politically passive professionalism can be found in the army's attitude toward the *coup* of 18 Brumaire, a *coup* which paradoxically brought a general to power. Although the *coup* is often imagined as the revenge of an increasingly insular army against a morally bankrupt government and an ungrateful society, it was nothing of the sort. Rather than revealing the politicization of the army, the events of 18 Brumaire demonstrate its political docility and willingness to obey whoever was currently occupying the seat of government in Paris. Although the army may have desired a more forceful government, particularly one headed by a general of proven skill, such diffuse sentiments were not what ensured the success of the *coup d'état*. Rather, it was the army's passivity, its determination not to become involved, that allowed the plot to succeed as totally and bloodlessly as it did. Had the army moved to defend the regime, the country might have been plunged into civil war. But this did not happen. Instead, it remained inactive, biding its time and, by its neutrality, insuring itself against the unpredictable outcome of what appeared at the time to be just the latest in the series of *coups* which had punctuated the political life of the Directory. The mentality of the *grande muette* (literally the "big mute," a term for the politically silent army of the nineteenth century) was already well-established by the end of the Directory and contributed substantially to its demise.[103]

---

102 Bertaud, *La Révolution armée*, 322–33.
103 On the *grande muette*, see Raoul Girardet, *La Société militaire et la France contemporaine* (Paris, 1953).

6 Napoleon's improbable synthesis: monarchy and meritocracy in the reconstruction of the officer corps, 1799–1815

Did Napoleon secure the "triumph of the Revolution," as Thiers put it, or, on the contrary, "were the principles of the Revolution ... perfectly forgotten during his reign," as Michelet claimed?[1] Historians who have attempted to make sense of the Napoleonic legacy are confronted with a regime whose actions often seem contradictory. Napoleon boasted of having ended the Revolution in France, even as he endeavored to spread it abroad. His rule was monarchical in all but name, but, master of the plebiscite, he invoked the national will as the source of his legitimacy. Through his famous Code, he consolidated the basic legal framework of the Revolution, even as he routinely violated the fundamental civil liberties proclaimed in 1789 – freedom from arbitrary detention, freedom of the press, and others. Given this ambiguous legacy, it is understandable that recent scholars of the regime have resorted to ambiguous formulations in attempting to characterize it. According to Jean Tulard, Napoleonic society was a fragile compromise, wavering between "a return to the past, a continuation of the present, or a preparation for the future."[2] For Martyn Lyons, the regime embodied a "contradictory mixture of the ancient and the modern."[3] And Louis Bergeron concluded that, "paradoxically, Napoleon was both behind and ahead of his time, the last of the enlightened despots and a prophet of the modern state."[4]

Nowhere were the apparent contradictions of the regime more salient than in its approach to meritocracy in the army. On the one hand, Napoleon respected the ideal of careers open to talent. His marshals represented the entire social spectrum, uniting scions of the Old Regime nobility – like Davout and Grouchy – with men from undistinguished *roturier* backgrounds – like Augereau, son of a domestic servant, and Lannes, son of a Gascon peasant. At the regimental level, plebeian soldiers continued to rise from the ranks, and that most controversial of all republican military practices, advancement by election, was maintained by the regime.[5] The Napoleonic slogan, "a marshal's baton in every soldier's backpack," suggests

---

1 Adolphe Thiers, *History of the Consulate and Empire*, trans. D. Forbes Campbell and H. W. Herbert (Philadelphia, 1853), vol. 1, 33; and citation from Stephen A. Kippur, *Jules Michelet: A Study of Mind and Sensibility* (Albany, 1981), 185.
2 Jean Tulard, *Napoleon: The Myth of the Saviour*, trans. Theresa Waugh (London, 1977), 4.
3 Martyn Lyons, *Napoleon Bonaparte and the Legacy of the French Revolution* (New York, 1994), 176.
4 Louis Bergeron, *France under Napoleon*, trans. R. R. Palmer (Princeton, 1981), xiv.
5 See my article, "Démocratie et professionalisme," 624–5.

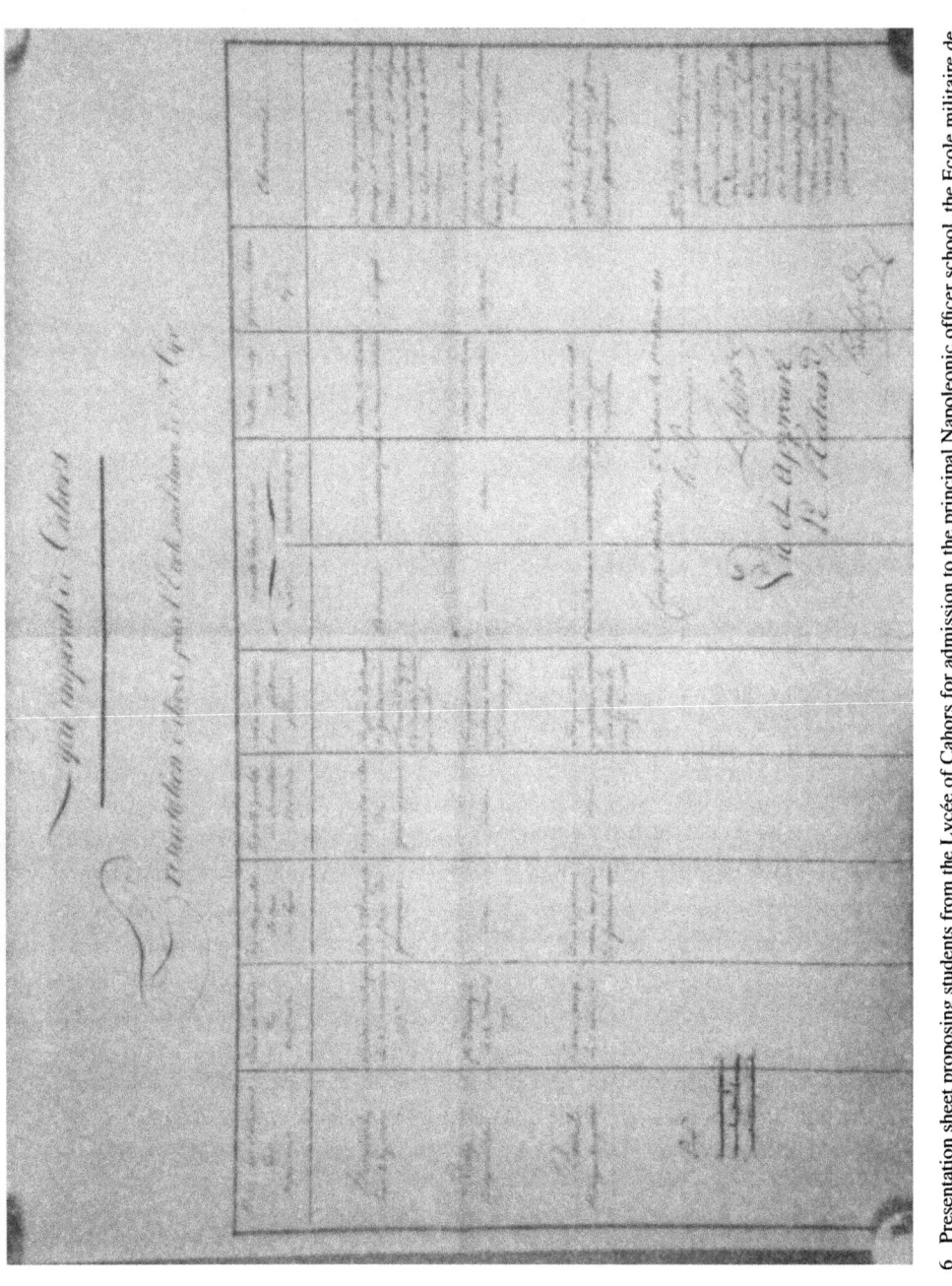

6 Presentation sheet proposing students from the Lycée of Cahors for admission to the principal Napoleonic officer school, the Ecole militaire de Saint-Cyr, May 1811.

the extent to which the military, more than any other institution, symbolized the regime's commitment to the principle of careers open to talent. Yet, other evidence reveals a progressive retreat from the Revolution's meritocratic legacy. Early in the Consulate, Napoleon reestablished direct officer recruitment and formal military schooling, practices which had been abolished in 1793 as inherently aristocratic. He also made special efforts to grant commissions and accelerated advancement to Old Regime nobles. And, in an open affront to republican egalitarianism, he restored honorific personal and, eventually, hereditary distinctions. The creation of the Legion of Honor in 1802 – denounced as "putting equality into question" and heralding "the return of the absurd feudal regime" – was followed in 1808 by the reestablishment of hereditary nobility.[6] What do these apparent contradictions reveal about the Napoleonic polity?

Napoleonic purges of the officer corps

Proclaiming the Revolution restored to "the principles which began it," the Brumairians moved to revive meritocracy in France.[7] Authorizing the government to grant decorations to military heroes and encouragements to the arts and sciences, the Consular Constitution signaled the new regime's intention to honor public service and superior talents.[8] In the military, the new spirit initially took the form of a reaction against the poor composition of the officer corps, allegedly compromised by the influx of men of little capacity, dubious character, and lowly social origin during the disorders of the Revolution. Within months of the Brumaire *coup*, Pierre-Antoine-Noel-Brune Daru, an Old Regime *commissaire des guerres* who had risen to prominence in the Directorial war ministry, informed the government that the only way to restore a "degree of perfection" to the army was to remove those officers "who corrupt it by their immorality and compromise it by their ignorance."[9] Baraguey d'Hilliers, an inspector-general and former noble who had begun his career as an officer before 1789, was only one of many high-ranking officers who supported the idea of a purge. In a scathing report, he urged the First Consul that he "could not move too quickly" to cashier "those officers that the Revolution, error, or luck" had placed in the army.[10] Such appeals did not fall on deaf ears. Troubled himself by the lack of "well-educated young

---

6 Chauvelin speaking before the Tribunate (28 Floréal X), *A.P.*, series 2, vol. 3, 721.
7 "Napoleon's Presentation of the Constitution of the Year VIII to the French People" (15 December 1799), in *A Documentary Survey of Napoleonic France*, ed. Eric A. Arnold, Jr., (Lanham, 1994), 35.
8 It was the revival of meritocracy, claimed Roederer, "that made the French so accommodating with their liberty under Napoleon." Pierre-Louis Roederer, *Œuvres* (Paris, 1858), vol. 3, 10.
9 A.N. 138 AP 15, Daru, "Mémoire sur l'infanterie" (VIII).
10 A.N. AF IV 1116, Baraguey d'Hilliers, "Mémoire au premier consul: rapport de l'inspection de l'an XI dans les 9ème, 10ème, 11ème, et 20ème divisions militaires" (1 Floréal XI).

men" in the military, the First Consul was already well disposed toward a thoroughgoing renewal of the officer corps.[11] By ending the conflict with Austria, France's last continental enemy, the Treaty of Luneville (9 February 1801) provided him with the opportunity he had been waiting for.

It was perhaps inevitable that a systematic attempt to rejuvenate the officer corps would follow the first general peace after a decade of warfare. The years of hard campaigning had taken their toll, especially on those officers who had begun serving before 1789. Already in the second *amalgame* carried out in the years IV and V (1796–97), the Directory had begun to remove aged, infirm, and war-weary veterans from active service. In the year VI, these efforts were supplemented with the creation of permanent depot companies where worn-out officers could finish their careers instructing new recruits and carrying out administrative tasks.[12] But the military emergency of the following year, in which the forces of the Coalition threatened to invade France itself, had forced the postponement of this measure. Only with the end of the continental struggle in 1801 was the effort to revitalize the officer corps renewed. In army-wide reviews, officers whose advanced age and debilitated physical condition prevented them from continuing their service were proposed for retirement, often with generous pensions. The postwar winnowing of the aging and infirm tended to fall disproportionately on those officers, generally of modest social background, who had begun their military careers as soldiers during the Old Regime.[13] These reductions confirmed and accelerated the generational shift in the army, already apparent during the Directory, as men who had begun their military service before 1789 increasingly gave way to a new cohort of officers which had gained its experience in the wars of the Revolution.

In addition to identifying worn-out officers for retirement, the inspectors also attended to the army's level of formal technical instruction, which had been neglected during the incessant campaigning of the past decade. Although, as officers of the Revolution, the inspectors had won memorable victories leading citizen-soldiers, as military professionals, they dreamed of a more regular military establishment, honed by study, drill, and spit-and-polish regulations. In unit after unit, they ordered officers to hold classes on tactical doctrine and practice what they had learned by maneuvering special demonstration squadrons.[14] Theoretical instruction, generally meaning the study of military legislation, was

---

11 Quoted in *Napoléon: pensées politiques et sociales*, ed. Adrien Dansette (Paris, 1969), 288.
12 On these operations, see A.G. $X^b 129$ and GD 58.
13 In the 32nd *demi-brigade*, for example, ten of the thirteen officers awarded retirement at this time were veterans of the royal army. They were all middle-aged men, 45 to 55, who had joined the army as teenagers as much as three decades earlier. A.G. $X^b 253$, "Etat nominatif des officiers de la 32ème demi-brigade qui se sont trouvés sans emploi" (24 Pluviôse XI).
14 A.G. $X^c 253$, General d'Hautpoul, "Revue d'inspection, 8ème hussards" (1 Germinal X); and $X^c 135$, General Laboissière, "Livret de revue, 2ème dragons" (10 Floréal X).

also targeted for special remediation. Officers were ordered to study the regulations on maneuvers, service in garrison and on campaign, discipline, advancement, military justice, pay, military hospitals, and accounting.[15] The inspectors also examined each officer individually and noted his level of instruction. Those who "understood maneuvers and fulfilled their duties with zeal," "possessed knowledge of mathematics," or simply "knew their *métier*" received good marks. Those who lacked these qualities, however, were singled out for reprimands or worse.[16] Yet, if counterbalanced by seriousness, application, and a will to succeed, ignorance alone was not fatal to a military career in the Napoleonic army. Although Captain Pradez of the 39th *demi-brigade* did not have "much knowledge," he "made up for it by his great zeal," eventually winning the Legion of Honor.[17] Despite his "feeble" instruction, Lieutenant Luau of the 75th was nonetheless noted as a "good officer" and was ultimately promoted to superior rank.[18] While knowledge of the military art was encouraged and rewarded, what Napoleon's inspectors esteemed most highly in the officers was not technical mastery.

What interested the inspectors most were "social qualities," those attributes that lent bearing, signaled morality, and inspired respect.[19] Officers who displayed "morality," "*mœurs*," "probity," or even a "fine appearance and bearing" were recommended for advancement.[20] Where these qualities were conspicuously absent, however, the inspectors showed little mercy. Officers found to lack "the dignity of their *état*" or "the appropriate sentiments" were dismissed.[21] Of particular concern to the inspectors were officers given over to what was referred to as "crapulous" behavior. Defined as the "habitual debauchery of women or wine," the term additionally denoted anything *vilain*. Signifying anything which was "dirty, dishonorable, impure, miserable, [or] infamous," the word *vilain* had originally carried a social meaning, denoting peasants, lowly *roturiers*, and all other "men of nothing."[22] These unflattering social connotations suggest why the inspectors took a dim view of drinking, gambling, and sex, activities which were, after all, an accepted part of the military lifestyle. In their eyes, the problem with the crapulous officer was not his pursuit of vice, but rather that he pursued it in

---

15 For an example, taken from the 8th Hussars, see A.G. $X^c 253$, General d'Hautpoul, "Ordre du clôture" (12 Germinal X).
16 A.G. $X^b 431$, General Schauenbourg, "Revue, 43ème demi-brigade," (30 Vendémiaire XIII)
17 A.G. $X^b 425$, Général Vilatte, "Etat nominatif des officiers" (13 Vendémiaire XIII).
18 A.G. $X^b 293$, General Suchet, "Etat nominatif des officiers de ce corps" (5 Prairial X).
19 A.G. $X^b 134$, "Rapport de la 3ème division au ministère de la guerre" (25 Thermidor X).
20 A.G. $X^c 100$, General Oudinot, "Etat nominatif des officiers du 4ème cuirassiers" (13 Messidor XI).
21 A.G. $X^b 425$, General Suchet, "Rapport au ministre," (1 Frimaire XII).
22 *Encyclopédie*, vol. 4, 435; and *Dictionnaire de l'Académie française*, 4th ed. (Paris, 1762), vol. 1, 236, and vol. 2, 938–9.

ways which compromised his dignity, blurred hierarchical relations, and engendered dishonorable social promiscuity.

The purge of crapulous officers from the 2nd dragoons brings out this nuance.[23] Second Lieutenant Bazin, who had begun his career as a soldier in the royal army in 1785, was dismissed not only because he "got drunk every day," but, more importantly, because he compromised his authority by tippling "indistinctly with his subordinates and the most degenerate civilians, provided that they paid." Lieutenant Nicot, also an Old Regime veteran, was drummed out of the army for "borrowing indiscriminately from his subordinates and the bourgeoisie." Lieutenant Colliquet, raised in the regiment from the age of six and son of a simple soldier, was sent away for consorting with a prostitute, "a crapulous girl from the gutter with whom he has often had scandalous scenes in the middle of the street." Lieutenant Villette, yet another veteran of the Old Regime, was purged for contracting a "marriage unworthy of an officer." By taking a prostitute as his wife, he had lost the "esteem of his comrades who tried everything to dissuade him from entering into this dishonorable union." As these examples suggest, it was less the vice itself than the open (and, hence, demeaning) manner in which it was pursued that warranted sanction.

The inspectors' efforts to remove officers whose public behavior undermined the dignity of the military profession were part of a broader push to raise the social standing of the officer corps. Although plebeian soldiers were considered capable of eventually overcoming their "old non-commissioned officer habits," the regime believed it a better investment of limited resources to recruit officers from higher social strata.[24] As Major Blancheville, named directly to the officer corps in 1792 as the son of an active citizen, put it, young men from good families were "capable of learning," while crusty old veterans were incorrigible, set in their coarse and ignorant ways. Efforts to improve them, he asserted, were doomed to failure, as pointless as trying to "scrub the color from the face of a negro."[25] Napoleon shared this assumption. A pragmatist who had long ago shed his youthful revolutionary idealism, he had little confidence in the ability of the government to engineer dramatic social changes. Rather than attempt to raise up a new military elite from the common mass of Frenchmen, he believed that the state would be better served by "taking existing fortunes and employing them in its service."[26] Although he

---

23 The citations in this paragraph are taken from two letters written by the regiment's commander, Colonel Pryvé. A.G. X^{c}134, "Lettre au ministre de la guerre" (15 Frimaire XII), and "Lettre au ministre de la guerre" (10 Prairial XII).
24 A.G. X^{b}431, General Schauenbourg, "Revue d'inspection du 43ème régiment" (30 Vendémiaire XIII).
25 Jean-Baptiste-Antoine-Marcelin Marbot, *Mémoires du général baron de Marbot* (Paris, 1983), vol. 1, 134.
26 Quoted in Dansette, *Napoléon*, 187.

never abandoned the ideal of the career open to talent, Napoleon's preference for officers from more elevated backgrounds reflected his assumption that seeking out recruits in the lower echelons of society could only yield meager returns.[27]

This social bias was reflected in the growing importance of general education as a criterion of officer recruitment and advancement. Officers with a "distinguished education" or "a spirit cultivated by education" were praised by the inspectors and noted as likely subjects for promotion to superior rank.[28] Since no French citizen was legally prevented from obtaining an education, this new emphasis remained formally consistent with revolutionary meritocracy. In practice, however, access to secondary schooling was restricted to the minority of families which could afford it. Napoleon's elitist educational reforms, in conjunction with the failure of revolutionary attempts to institute a system of free public schooling, ensured that education would remain a privilege of the relatively well-to-do. While model institutions of secondary education (notably the militarized *lycées* created by Napoleon to replace the *collèges* of the Old Regime) were created, free public primary schooling was neglected.[29] Unable to mount the first step on the pedagogical hierarchy, the lower echelons of society were effectively excluded from the Napoleonic educational system. Some scholarships were available, but the government's policy of reserving them for the children of military officers, magistrates, and other public servants – men who generally possessed more wealth than their fellow citizens – tended to reinforce existing inequalities. Several schools, known collectively as the Prytanée français, were established to provide a free education to orphans, the sons of soldiers, and other children of the "inferior classes," but only sought to give them "an education suited to their existence." The Prytanée would furnish France with skilled artisans, the *lycées* with lawyers, doctors, and military officers.[30] In the Napoleonic conception, education was not supposed to foster social mobility, but rather offered a politically acceptable way of making class-based social selections.[31]

In part, the regime's desire to improve the social composition of the officer corps was intended to reinforce hierarchical subordination. Although they had made their reputations commanding the troops of the Republic, Napoleon and his inspectors regretted the passing of the precise gradations of the royal army where

---

27 Jean-Paul Bertaud, "Napoleon's Officers," *Past and Present*, 112 (1986), 94.
28 A.G. X^{c}253, "Bataillon complémentaire, 32ème demi-brigade d'infanterie de ligne" (IX).
29 Isser Woloch, *The New Regime: Transformations of the French Civic Order, 1789–1820s* (New York, 1994), 190–236. Information in this paragraph on Napoleonic educational reforms is from Frederick B. Artz, *The Development of Technical Education in France, 1500–1800* (Cambridge, MA, 1966), 112–81.
30 Cited in Dansette, *Napoléon*, 238.
31 On the use of education as a social filter, see Pierre Bourdieu and Jean-Claude Passeron, *Reproduction in Education, Society, and Culture*, trans. Richard Nice (London, 1977); and Bourdieu, *La Noblesse d'état: grandes écoles et esprit de corps* (Paris, 1989).

a clear-cut "line of demarcation" separated the officers from the lower ranks.[32] The Revolution, in their view, had eroded this line. In their postwar reviews, the inspectors found that, although the soldiers generally obeyed their officers, subordination was too loose and relations between the ranks too democratic. Baraguey d'Hilliers described discipline in the 83rd *demi-brigade* as "very lax, very unhierarchic," and expressed shock at the "great familiarity" which existed between officers and their men.[33] General Suchet found such a lack of subordination in the 75th *demi-brigade* that he felt compelled to remind its officers "that the interest and existence of the army is linked to discipline, that passive obedience ought to link the inferior to the superior."[34] Perhaps the relaxation of hierarchy was inevitable in an army issued from a democratic revolution, but Napoleon was determined to change this state of affairs. To sharpen distinctions between the ranks in an army still imbued with the principle of civil equality, it was necessary that officers possess a superior education, the "sole legitimate basis of inequality."[35] Marshal Marmont, Napoleon's former military school classmate, went even further. To strengthen "the structure of obedience," he wrote, the officer's authority should be bolstered by "instruction," "illustrious birth" and "elevated social position."[36]

The effort to raise the social level of the officer corps also served a political function. Destined to occupy a prominent place in the regime, the officers needed what Napoleon termed "civil qualities" to fulfill their new public obligations.[37] The "military character" of the Consular (and later Imperial) Court was particularly pronounced, with the upper ranks of the officer corps furnishing many of its highest dignitaries, like General Duroc (*grand maréchal du palais*), Marshal Berthier (*grand veneur*), and General Caulaincourt (*grand écuyer*).[38] Other officers of high rank, like Colonel Colbert, a descendant of Louis XIV's famous minister, were called upon to undertake diplomatic missions for the regime.[39] Although only the most prominent and best-connected officers were nominated to these illustrious positions, military professionals of more modest

---

32 A.N. AF IV 1115, "Réflexions sur l'avancement" (n.d.).
33 A.G. $X^b 298$, Baraguey d'Hilliers, "Revue d'inspection" (15 Prairial XI).
34 A.G. $X^b 260$, Suchet, "Revue d'inspection" (13 Thermidor XI), and A.G. $X^b 293$, Suchet, "Revue d'inspection" (5 Prairial X).
35 Quoted in Dansette, *Napoléon*, 288.
36 Auguste-Frédéric-Louis Viesse de Marmont, *The Spirit of Military Institutions*, trans. Frank Schaller (Westport, CT, 1974), 228.
37 Antoine-Claire Thibaudeau, *Bonaparte and the Consulate*, trans. G. K. Fortescue (New York, 1908), 140.
38 Philip Mansel, *The Court of France, 1789–1830* (Cambridge, 1988), 57. Mansel places particular emphasis on the sharp contrast between the military tone of Napoleon's Court and the distinctly civilian ethos of Versailles before the Revolution.
39 *Correspondance de Napoléon Ier, publiée par ordre de l'empéreur Napoléon III* (Paris, 1858), vol. 8, 298–9.

rank were also expected to play roles in the civil administration, providing a "reservoir on which state and society drew to exercise private as well as administrative activities."[40] The prefectoral corps drew particularly heavily on the army, recruiting 31 percent of its personnel from the military, and nearly sixty officers served as mayors of major French cities.[41] And 2,000 other military men were included in the general Napoleonic elite, the *notabilité*.[42] To mark the status of the military within the elite, the regime elaborated precedence regulations which tended to place officers ahead of their civilian counterparts in official ceremonies.[43] And to ensure that officers' "private conduct" reflected the public dignity of their *état*, the government moved to reimpose restrictions on military marriages, directing commanders to gather information on the "persons, fortune, and family" of prospective brides.[44] Napoleon's efforts to raise the standing of the officers and assign them a prominent place within the social hierarchy signaled his intention to base the regime not merely on a foundation of wealth, but also on one of service.

Direct officer recruitment and patterns of advancement

To make military careers attractive to young men of good family, Napoleon did more than just purge the officer corps of socially undesirable officers. He also reinstituted the practice, abolished by the Convention, of granting direct officer commissions. He believed that as long as republican egalitarianism continued to dictate officer recruitment policy – requiring those who aspired to commissions to begin their service as simple soldiers – the right kind of people would shun the military profession. Only the prospect of immediate officer rank – offering distinction from the common soldiery, the promise of more rapid advancement, and social status – would induce elite families to send their sons into the military profession. This is the policy Napoleon adopted. To place well-bred young men directly in the officer corps, he reestablished a variety of institutions, from a new military school to special guard units, that had been abolished during the Republic. By reviving direct officer recruitment, Napoleon sought to join the

---

40 Louis Bergeron, Guy Chaussinand-Nogaret, and Robert Forster, "Les Notables du 'Grand empire' en 1810," *Annales, E.S.C.*, 26 (1971), 1066.
41 Bertaud, "Napoleon's Officers," 109–10. Bergeron, Chaussinand-Nogaret, and Forster note that the military officers represented the second largest professional category (after *agriculteurs* and *fermiers*) from which the mayors were recruited.
42 Louis Bergeron and Guy Chaussinand-Nogaret, *Les 'masses de granit': cent mille notables du Premier empire* (Paris, 1979), 42–3.
43 Jean-Paul Bertaud, "La 'petite guerre' des honneurs sous Napoléon," *L'Histoire*, 66 (1984), 64–70.
44 A.G. X^c98, General Ney, "Revue, 4ème cavalerie," (14 Ventôse X); and A.G. X^b260, General Suchet, "Inspection, 39ème demi-brigade," (13 Thermidor XI). See also, A.N. 138 AP 17, Daru, "Observations sur les marriages des militaires" (n.d.).

scion of the "ancient military family," the "nephew of the mayor," and the son of the "rich landowner" in a new service elite.⁴⁵

The revival of direct officer recruitment was also significant for helping to redefine the relationship between state and society. A sharp departure from republican ideals of equality and virtue, it announced the regime's intention to restructure the polity along hierarchical and monarchical lines. Although the regime respected the principles of 1789, reviving neither privilege nor exclusion in its mechanisms of selection, Napoleon rejected those meritocratic institutions which hampered the concentration of power in his own hands. Notably, he defeated a proposal by the Council of State to reinstitute a system of competitive examinations, formerly the keystone of the Constituent Assembly's stillborn system of officer selection, because it would strip him of the monarchical prerogative of nomination. In Napoleon's view, the advocates of examination had, in focusing on the problem of defining and measuring the qualities which constituted merit, "entirely misunderstood" the more important "political object" of a system of selection. The "essential consideration," he insisted, was that "the government should have the means of recompensing the family of a deceased soldier or civil servant who has done good service, or of rewarding a deserving servant of the state during his lifetime." "Do you not think," he jabbed, "that this object altogether outweighs the advantage of rewarding boys who are able to satisfy the examiners that they know a little Latin and the four rules of arithmetic?"⁴⁶ If the power of nomination were entrusted to him alone, social elites would grow accustomed to "seeing only [himself] as remunerator," and a monarchical ethos of reciprocity based on the exchange of service for social distinction would once again bind the upper echelons of French society to their sovereign.⁴⁷ During his reign, Napoleon would use the power to award places and honors not to revive exclusive privileges, but rather to reconstruct a monarchical political order in which the social ideals of 1789 would be formally upheld. Meritocracy would be preserved, but would henceforth serve the cause of monarchical centralization.⁴⁸

It was several years, however, before formal institutions of direct officer recruitment could be created. Until then, commissions were awarded to young

---

45 A.G. X°9, "Rapport présenté à l'Empereur: élèves pensionnaires, Fontainebleau" (7 Fructidor XIII).
46 Thibaudeau, *Bonaparte and the Consulate*, 104.
47 André-François, comte de Miot de Mélito, *Mémoires* (Paris, 1858), vol. 1, 309.
48 De Tocqueville noted the role played by meritocracy within the long-term process of state centralization. In notes for the projected sequel to *The Old Regime and the French Revolution*, he described how public offices, "rendered revocable, hierarchized, and locked into the grand system of centralization," served to place "all citizens under the hand of the central power and all those who possessed them in its strict and daily dependence." *Œuvres complètes*, ed. J. P. Mayer (Paris, 1953), vol. 2, *L'Ancien Régime et la Révolution: fragments et notes inédites sur la Révolution*, ed. André Jardin, 316.

men from good families on an *ad hoc* basis. In the year VIII (1800), for example, Mathieu Dumas was charged to form a special cavalry corps "composed of volunteers, chosen from the best families, who would clothe, mount, and equip themselves at their own cost." The "brilliant youth" who answered Dumas's summons included some of the great names of the old military nobility: Ségur, Lameth, Choisy, and others.[49] In the regular units, commanders quietly reinstituted the Old Regime practice of recruiting young men from well-connected military families as volunteers with the assurance that they would be proposed for the first available second lieutenancies. Jean-Baptiste-Antoine-Marcelin Marbot, the son of a general, was commissioned in this way after only one year of service. Although technically a soldier, Marbot was treated differently from his nominal peers. Even though regulations assigned two soldiers to a bed, he occupied a bed of his own in the non-commissioned officers' quarters. The false pigtail and greasepaint moustache he sported disguised neither his youth nor his favored status.[50] This was not an isolated case. Other young men from similar backgrounds also received favorable treatment. Jean-Augustin-Michel Rampon, the great-nephew of a serving general who later became a senator, was promoted rapidly to officer rank after promising – in words commonly used before 1789 – that he would "follow in the footsteps" of his relative.[51] Where an aspirant's family had no military credentials, its wealth, social standing, and connections were often enough to secure a commission. While from a civilian background, Marc Vaucour nonetheless received favorable treatment because he possessed "a certain level of material well-being which would enable him to maintain himself honorably."[52] In their social status, political connections to the regime, and military antecedents, the Napoleonic volunteers foreshadowed the kind of people that the regime would seek through formal institutions of direct officer recruitment. Although it declined with the rise of these institutions, the practice of volunteering eventually furnished 18 percent of all direct officer nominees between 1799 and 1812.

This somewhat anarchic expedient soon became the target of criticism. Some officers felt that it threatened to see the military profession "perpetually recompose itself through the favoritism of generals or family members."[53] Napoleon was also uncomfortable with the practice of volunteering, although for different reasons. He opposed it not only because it took the power of nomination out of his own hands, but also because he was afraid that such appointments, based purely on personal connections, would be perceived as "an injustice by the rank and file."[54] Experience

49 Mathieu Dumas, *Souvenirs*, vol. 3, 178.
50 Marbot, *Mémoires*, vol. 1, 54–88.
51 A.G. X^b411, "Lettre de Darricau au ministre de la guerre" (29 Ventôse XIII).
52 A.G. X^c134, "Rapport fait au ministre de la guerre" (XIII).
53 *Correspondance de deux généraux sur divers sujets, publiée par le citoyen T**** (Paris, 1801), 33–4.
54 Quoted in Dansette, *Napoléon*, 288.

had shown that soldiers would gladly follow an officer who had accomplished more or even as much as they had themselves. But was it "even conceivable," he asked, that veterans would obey a neophyte who "had not yet given any proof of his existence other than his own existence?"[55] Only a superior education and practical military instruction, he believed, could give an untested young man authority over seasoned troops.

Napoleon moved to put these views into practice on 11 Floréal X (30 April 1802) with the foundation of a new military school, the Ecole spéciale militaire. First housed in the Fontainebleau château, the school was moved to the former Old Regime girls' school at Saint-Cyr in 1808. By 1814, it had provided over 4,000 officers, 38 percent of all direct nominees, and would survive the regime, remaining France's premier institution of officer recruitment (albeit with modifications) to the present day.[56] Allowing Napoleon to place young men advantageously in military careers, the school gave him a powerful means of forming a service elite attached to his person. In contrast to the decentralized system of volunteering, the state-run system of military schooling would "attach fathers to the government through their sons."[57] Letters requesting admission to the school reflected the monarchical ideal of reciprocity – faithful service for honorific recompense – that Napoleon sought to foster. Asking for a place for his son, General Schauenbourg, who had begun his career as an officer during the Old Regime, promised that this favor would serve as a "new incentive for me to increase, if possible, my zeal for the service and my great devotion to the person of the Emperor."[58] The gift of a place at the military school could also bind to the regime families which had not yet served it. Writing on behalf of his son, a lawyer named Morlac assured Napoleon that, if the favor was granted, his entire family "would never forget that it was from your hand" that it had been bestowed.[59] Appreciating "how much influence a well-directed education gave to the government of Napoleon," the Restoration would maintain his policies, but use them to attach families to "the legitimate dynasty."[60]

Although instrumental in reviving an ethos of reciprocity binding social elites to their sovereign, Napoleonic military education differed in important ways from its Old Regime predecessor. Unlike the royal military school, which had been reserved for *gentilshommes* until 1790 and for the sons of officers thereafter, the

---

55 Pierre-Louis Roederer, *Mémoires sur la Révolution, le Consulat, et l'Empire*, ed. Octave Aubry (Paris, 1942), 142.
56 Gilbert Bodinier, "Du soldat républicain à l'officier impérial: convergences et divergences entre l'armée et la société," in *Histoire militaire de la France*, ed. André Corvisier, vol. 2, *De 1715 à 1871*, ed. Jean Delmas (Paris, 1992), 295.
57 Roederer speaking before the Legislative Body on 11 Floréal X, *A.P.*, vol. 3, series 2, 572.
58 A.N. AF IV 1148^b, "Lettre et mémoire du général de division Schauenbourg au ministre de la guerre" (12 February 1808).
59 A.N. F^{17}6756, "Lettre de Morlac, avocat" (2 August 1808).
60 A.G. X°254, "Lettre d'Albiganc au ministre de la guerre" (21 November 1815).

Ecole spéciale militaire respected the principle of careers open to talents. Neither birth nor profession constituted an obstacle to admission. If their families could afford the annual tuition of 1,200 francs, applicants from all walks of life could hope to obtain places. And as intended, the sons of *émigré* nobles and revolutionary officers, former magistrates in the *parlements* and lawyers of the revolutionary law courts, feudal lords and purchasers of nationalized property all mingled at the school, making it an important crucible in which the new Napoleonic elite was forged.[61] Fully one-third of the students were drawn from the families and clients of *grands notables*, an indication that an even greater percentage was linked to the lesser *notabilité* by blood or patronage.[62] While no one was formally barred, the school's formidable tuition effectively excluded all but the prominent and well-to-do. Families of land owners furnished 11 percent of the students, commercial and financial families another 11 percent, and the liberal professions 6 percent. There were no peasants, and the artisan classes were almost completely absent, represented by only a handful of the most prestigious trades (jewelry, clock-making, book-selling, etc.). Significantly, within the elite student body, service families were heavily over-represented in comparison with the general Napoleonic *notabilité*. Civil servants, 34 percent of the *notables*, accounted for nearly 47 percent of the students. And while only 2.35 percent of *notables* were military men, 23.4 percent of the students were the sons of Old Regime and revolutionary officers, making the military the largest socio-professional group represented at the school. In all, 70 percent of the students came from families occupying places in the administrative, judicial, or military institutions of the regime. Within the formally meritocratic (but elitist) framework of the school's admission policy, a pronounced preference for service was emerging, foreshadowing the evolution of Napoleon's social priorities.[63]

61 Figures on the social composition of Napoleonic military schooling given in this paragraph are based on the 1,184 students whose socio-professional backgrounds are indicated in A.G. 4 Y^b31–2, "Registre de contrôle: Ecole spéciale militaire." Comparative figures on the *notables* are from Bergeron and Chaussinand-Nogaret, *Les "masses de granit"*, 43.
62 Generally, the *grands notables* were those who figured on the lists of the thirty highest-taxed, sixty highest-taxed, and sixty "most distinguished by their fortune and their public and private virtues." For this calculation, I cross-referenced matriculation records for the military school with the series of works on the *grands notables* edited by Bergeron and Chaussinand-Nogaret, excluding students from departments not covered by the volumes published to date.
63 The government's bias in favor of public service, particularly of the military kind, was even more pronounced in its scholarship policy. Of those admitted to the Ecole spéciale militaire, nearly 50 percent of military families and 20 percent of judicial and administrative families were granted scholarships. Scholarships were also used to attach non-service families to the regime, although much less frequently. Only 10 percent of commercial and financial families and 5 percent of landowning families received such aid. Despite the small proportion of scholarships devoted to non-service families, the fact that they received any assistance at all indicates that Napoleon viewed military education not merely as a means of recompensing state service, but also as a way of bringing new groups into his service elite. A.G. 4 Y^b31–2.

Letters of application and recommendation – concerned more with the service traditions of families than the personal qualities of the applicants – suggest the revival of an ethos of hereditary service among Napoleonic elites. Applicants clearly recognized that, in the new regime, as in the old, a history of military service offered the strongest argument for preferment. The Courville boys, sons of a deceased naval officer, noted that they came "from a family which has consecrated itself to state service from time immemorial" and that they desired admission in order "to follow in the footsteps of their ancestors."[64] The family of the young applicant Ponsort was lauded for its "constant devotion to the profession of arms." In addition to "officers, *aides-de-camp*, [and] superior officers," it had furnished a "de Ponsort who, during the League, had been able to maintain the cities of Chalons and Soissons in obedience to Henri IV."[65] Writing on behalf of her four sons, "all destined for the career of arms," the widow Lafitte emphasized that "for many centuries, the authors of their days have distinguished themselves in this career" and promised that her "children will make themselves worthy of them."[66] Applicants also invoked their families' traditions of civil service. In addition to citing the services of his maternal grandfather, a former general officer, Cugnon d'Allincourt noted that his other grandfather had "rendered important services in the civil order."[67] Asking for a place for her youngest son, Madame Chaurand cited "the constant service" of her first-born, "who, during the recent events of Saint-Domingue, had been employed in the civil administration ... and had the honor of dying at his post."[68] After the brief hiatus of the Republican years, family service was once again seen as the strongest title to state recompense, as well as the surest guage of future aptitude and loyalty.

While highly prized, a hereditary tradition of service was not a necessary qualification for admission to the Napoleonic military school. The regime also sought to draw into the service "young men who received a careful education and whose parents are wealthy."[69] Numerous applicants successfully invoked their families' standing, connections, and fortune on behalf of their candidacies. The young Daubenton presented himself as the "nephew of the famous naturalist," and Boilly proudly noted that he was the son of the "distinguished painter and a close relative of M. Arnault, member of the Institute."[70] An applicant named Martinez described himself as specially "honored by the benevolence of Her

---

64 A.N. F^{17}7140, "Lettre de Millot de Fontaines, chef de bureau à la marine, tuteur des mineurs de Courville, à Fontanes" (14 July 1810).
65 A.N. F^{17}6756, "Note sur la profession et le service des parents du jeune de Ponsort" (10 June 1810).
66 A.N. F^{17}6761, "Lettre de Lafitte, née Coufitte, à Fontanes" (n.d.).
67 A.N. F^{17}6760, Presentation slip for Cugnon d'Allincourt.
68 A.N. F^{17}6756, "Lettre de Madame Chaurand à Fourcroy" (28 July 1808).
69 A.D. Bas-Rhin, 1 R 9, "Lettre du ministre de la guerre au préfet du Bas-Rhin" (18 Ventôse XIII).
70 A.N. F^{17}6757, Presentation slips for Daubenton and Boilly.

Majesty the Empress."[71] Finally, in the absence of a service tradition, celebrity, or powerful patronage, applicants could always cite their wealth as a title to consideration. The father of Bouire-Beauvallon, who boasted of an income of 400,000 francs, based his request for a place for his son squarely on wealth.[72] Although Napoleon used military education to reward and encourage hereditary service vocations where they already existed, he also used admission to the Ecole spéciale to initiate similar traditions in the elite more broadly.

Non-service families were under-represented at the military school not for any lack of interest on their part, nor for any neglect on the part of the regime. The capacity of the Ecole spéciale was nearly always strained to the breaking point, taking in more students, training them more rapidly, and producing more officers than initially foreseen. Even efforts to accommodate the demand, such as the adoption of a drastically truncated program of instruction (only three months!) and the creation of a second school at Saint-Germain-en-Laye, failed to keep pace with the requirements of war and the solicitations of parents. Applicants turned away from the crowded school were not, however, abandoned by the regime. They were invited to enter less selective institutions of direct officer recruitment, created specifically for them by Napoleon. Of these, the most important were the corps of *vélites*, special units attached to the Imperial Guard. Created in the winter of the year XII (1803–04), they gave more modest families and those without service traditions a way to place their sons directly as officers, thereby saving them from conscription while also proving their loyalty to the regime. Young men could become *vélites* if they were physically fit and could pay 200 francs per year. The modesty of this annual fee permitted recruitment from a broader social pool than found at the Ecole spéciale. Although the sons of a few generals, Old Regime nobles, administrators, and judges entered the corps, most *vélites* came from non-service backgrounds.[73] Less than 18 percent of the *vélites* came from civil service families: 12.3 percent from the judiciary, and 5.3 percent from the administration. More striking still, only 1.5 percent came from military backgrounds. The rest of the *vélites* came from families which cited no service credentials whatsoever, and many of these were of relatively humble condition. The majority were classified as property holders – 46 percent as land owners or *rentiers*, presumably well-off families that neither worked for a living nor exercised a public function, and a further 10 percent in various branches of agriculture like wine-growing. Another 25 percent came from commercial milieux

---

71 A.N. F^{17}6757, Presentation slip for Martinez.
72 A.N. F^{17}6757, Presentation slip for Bouire-Beauvallon.
73 Socio-professional data are taken from a sample of 1,237 foot-grenadier *vélites*. A.G. 20 Y^{c}12, "Grenadiers à pied: vélites." It is likely that the mounted *vélite* units recruited from more distinguished families than the foot unit analyzed here. Unfortunately, however, socio-professional information was not recorded for these units.

(13 percent), the liberal professions (5 percent), and artisan families (7 percent). In all 1,799 *vélites* were nominated to second lieutenancies in the line army, 27 percent of all directly commissioned officers, and another 274 were placed as non-commissioned officers.[74]

Napoleon also tried to rally Old Regime nobles to his regime by naming their sons to the officer corps. He directly commissioned a number of young men from illustrious families – including a Castellane, a Talleyrand-Périgord, a Latour d'Auvergne, and two Montesquieu-Fezensacs – as well as the sons of foreign sovereigns – including a Hesse-Darmstadt, a Radizwill, and a brace of Hohenzollerns.[75] He also raised two units, the quasi-proprietary La Tour-Maubourg and Issembourg regiments, to recruit as officers "those who had served against their country in the emigration," "officers whose service would bind influential families to the government," and young military nobles who "did not have any service."[76] But his most important attempt to attract young men distinguished by their "education, birth, and taste for the military" was the formation in 1806 of the Gendarmes d'ordonnance, a corps modeled after the Old Regime Gendarmerie.[77] To give it luster, Napoleon appointed Marshal Kellermann, an Old Regime military noble and hero of the Revolution, as its commander, and enlisted some of the most illustrious names of the Bourbon Court, including a Montmorency, a Monaco, and a Savoie-Carignan, to serve as officers.[78] To reinforce its exclusive social tone, aspirants were required to equip themselves at an estimated cost of 1,800 francs and pay an annual fee of 600 francs.[79]

Viewing the Gendarmerie d'ordonnance more as a political than a military institution, the regime made the recruitment of young men from prestigious families a high priority. Under the direction of the ministry of the interior, the prefects were instructed to encourage prominent families within their departments to send

---

74 These figures are derived from the following registers at the A.G.: 20 Y^c5bis–6, "1er régiment des grenadiers à pied, garde impériale;" 20 Y^c9, "2ème grenadiers à pied, garde impériale;" 20 Y^c12, "Grenadiers à pied vélites;" 20 Y^c15–16, "Fusil-grenadiers, garde impériale;" 20 Y^c38, "1er régiment des chasseurs à pied, garde impériale;" 20 Y^c48, "Chasseurs à pied, vélites;" 20 Y^c136, "1er régiment grenadiers à cheval, garde impériale;" 20 Y^c138, "Escadron des vélites, grenadiers à cheval;" 20 Y^c143, "Chasseurs à cheval, garde impériale;" 20 Y^c147, "Chasseurs à cheval vélites;" 20 Y^c149–50, "Dragons, garde impériale;" 20 Y^c174, "Bataillon de vélites de Turin;" and 20 Y^c175, "Bataillon de vélites de Florence."
75 On this practice, see Anatole de Montesquieu-Fezensac, *Souvenirs sur la Révolution, l'Empire, la Restauration, et le règne de Louis-Philippe* (Paris, 1961).
76 A.G. X^h8, "Rapport à l'Empereur" (19 March 1806). Information on the personnel in these units is found in A.G. X^h8 and 11, and 2 Y^b1115–17 and 1123–4.
77 A.N. $F^9$1033, "Lettre du conseil d'administration du corps de MM. les Gendarmes d'ordonnance à pied de sa majesté l'empereur et roi à M. le préfet du Lot et Garonne" (19 February 1807).
78 A.N. $F^9$1032, "Formation du corps de la Gendarmerie d'ordonnance à cheval" (n.d.)
79 A.N. $F^9$1032, "Lettre de Kellermann au ministre de l'intérieur" (10 November 1806); and "Lettre de Kellermann au ministre de l'intérieur" (7 April 1807).

their sons into the new corps. Some, particularly in impoverished regions, reported difficulty in finding enough suitable candidates. The prefect of the Creuse informed the Minister of the Interior that, although there were several families from the "agricultural class" who were interested in placing their sons, they were not "worthy by their education and fortune of the honor of serving in such a favored manner."[80] In most departments, however, "*rentiers,* merchants, land owners, and former nobles" flocked to the corps to show "their devotion to the service of His Majesty."[81] As intended, many Old Regime nobles enlisted. In addition to the officers already cited above, the unit's roster featured names like Vergennes, Albignac, Saint-Pern, Forbin, Salm-Salm, and many others.[82] The recommendations offered on behalf of applicants to the unit – such as the letter praising the young Montigny, son of an Old Regime colonel, for the "talents and sentiments of honor hereditary in his family" and his desire to "embrace the career of his ancestors" – offer further confirmation of its noble tenor and composition.[83]

Table 6.1 **Sources of recruitment of directly commissioned officers, year VIII–1812**

Institutional source of recruitment	Percentage of directly commissioned officers
Formal military schooling	38.2
Corps of vélites	26.6
Service as a regimental volunteer	17.9
National guard	4.7
Imperial guard	3
Gendarmes d'ordonnance	2.6
Auxiliary battalions and free companies	2
Imperial navy	2
Foreign military service	2
Staff assignment	1
Gardes d'honneur	Less than 1
Instruction battalion at Fontainebleau	Less than 1
Military engineers	Less than 1
Imperial pages	Less than 1
No information	Less than 1

Source: a nine-regiment sample composed of the 3rd infantry (A.G. 2 Y^b119–21 and 2 Y^b401, "Contrôles des officiers"), 32nd infantry (A.G. 2 Y^b221–5, "Contrôles des officiers"), 39th infantry (A.G. 2 Y^b252–6, "Contrôles des officiers"), 43rd infantry (A.G. 2 Y^b267–70, "Contrôles des officiers"), 4th cavalry ((A.G. 2 Y^b677–9, "Contrôles des officiers"), 2nd dragoons (A.G. 2 Y^b728–30, "Contrôles des officiers"), and 8th hussars (A.G. 2 Y^b974–6, "Contrôles des officiers")).

80 A.N. $F^9$1033, "Lettre du préfet de la Creuse au ministre de l'intérieur" (28 November 1806).
81 A.N. $F^9$1033, "Lettre du préfet de la Loire inférieure au ministre de l'intérieur" (1 June 1807).
82 A.G. 20 Y^c134, "Gendarmes d'ordonnance à pied et à cheval."
83 A.N. $F^9$1034, "Lettre du préfet de la Moselle au ministre de l'intérieur" (13 April 1807).

In all, about half of the approximately 400 *gendarmes* bore names with the *particule* (the "de" that often signaled nobility, or at least pretension to nobility). While not an accurate indicator of noble status, this conceit was a sure sign of the spirit which infused the corps.

Despite these attempts to refurbish the military profession by recruiting Old Regime nobles, the sons of service families, and even young men from respectable civilian backgrounds directly as officers, the regime was forced to rely heavily on the promotion of soldiers from the ranks to replenish the regimental cadres. Advancement of this sort, sometimes awarded on the battlefield by Napoleon himself, was largely responsible for perpetuating the myth that the regime's meritocratic commitment extended equally to all echelons of the social hierarchy.[84] But Napoleon was no enthusiast for this revolutionary practice. Rather, he believed that "soldiers ought to become officers only with great difficulty," never filling more than one-quarter of vacant positions.[85] Napoleon's trusted advisor, Daru, would have restricted such promotions even more severely, to only one in six.[86] In practice, however, the government never came close to attaining these proportions. Even at the peak of their performance, in 1809, the military school, *vélites*, and similar institutions fell far short of Napoleon's ideal, accounting for only 43 percent of newly commissioned officers.[87] In all, 77 percent of Napoloeon's second lieutenants began their military careers as simple soldiers.[88]

Although it failed to limit the number of soldiers promoted from the ranks, the regime succeeded in restricting their advancement, generally to the rank of captain or below. This "glass ceiling" existed more in practice than in law. With the exception of several decrees imposing service prerequisites on candidates for promotions – laws which highlighted the distinction between directly commissioned officers and those promoted from the ranks by giving the former a six-year lead in advancement – Napoleon was content to let the existing Thermidorean (14 Germinal III) and Directorial (18 Nivôse IV) advancement legislation subsist. But as these laws gave the executive full discretion over promotions above the rank of captain, they allowed Napoleon to impose a *de facto* social filter between the subaltern and superior ranks. An examination of the professional destinies of captains serving when Napoleon seized power reveals the extent to which the regime favored directly commissioned officers when making promotions to the

---

84 For a good description, see Philippe-Paul, comte de Ségur, *Napoleon's Russian Campaign*, trans. J. David Townsend (Alexandria,VA, 1965), 4.
85 Quoted in Dansette, *Napoléon*, 289.
86 138 AP 15, Daru, "Officiers et sous-officiers d'infanterie et de troupes à cheval" (n.d.).
87 This figure is based on the personnel records of the following regiments at the A.G.: 3rd infantry (X^b347–8), 43rd infantry (X^b431–2), 44th infantry (X^b433–4), 4th cuirassiers (X^c100), and 2nd dragoons (X^c135).
88 Bodinier, "Du soldat républicain à l'officier impérial," 292.

superior ranks (major and above). Of the 138 captains serving in a sample of six infantry *demi-brigades* in the year VIII, every fourth man who had been elected directly as an officer or non-commissioned officer in a National Guard volunteer battalion was eventually promoted to superior rank, as was every third "son of an active citizen."[89] In contrast, only one of the thirty-three captains who had entered the regular army as simple soldiers was promoted to a superior grade. The others were condemned to finish their long careers stalled at the rank of captain. While unable to restrict the promotion of soldiers from the ranks, Napoleon succeeded in imposing an unofficial cap on their advancement that would endure well into the nineteenth century.

Carefully selected by the regime, the superior officers constituted a social, as well as a professional, elite. Some were the sons of Old Regime nobles, promoted rapidly to high rank by a regime eager to rally illustrious names of the monarchy. In the six regiments sampled above, these included a Custine, a Faudoas, a Coetlosquet, a Carignan, and an Adobrandini-Borghese. Others, one-quarter of the total, were *grands notables*, the cream of the Napoleonic elite.[90] Whereas some – like Pierre-François-Jean-Gaston Bisson, the son of a lowly drum-major who had been raised in his father's regiment as an *enfant du corps* – were self-made men who had achieved social prominence through their military service, most of these superior officers came from well-established families.[91] Typical of these was Emmanuel Attanoux. Son of the bourgeois lord of Roquebrune in Provence, Attanoux had been able to parlay his father's standing into election as captain of a local National Guard volunteer battalion in 1791 and advanced from there.[92] Whether self-made or not, Napoleon made sure that, once promoted to superior rank, the officers' honored status in Imperial society was reinforced with titles of nobility. Of the 144 superior officers in my sample, 79 (55 percent) were ennobled. The superior officers, recruited disproportionately from men whose military careers had begun with a direct commission, figured prominently within the regime's elite.

Napoleon's tacit division of the officer corps into two classes set the pattern for the nineteenth-century French officer corps. Had his rule not ended in 1815, military school graduates, *vélites*, and other directly commissioned officers would very likely have furnished the next generation of military leaders after the direct

[89] This sample is based on the following sources at the A.G.: 3rd (2 Y^b119–21 and 2 Y^b401), 32nd (2 Y^b221–5), 39th (2 Y^b252–6), 43rd (2 Y^b267–70), 44th (2 Y^b271–5), and 75th (2 Y^b375–8).
[90] For this estimate, I cross-referenced the superior officers from the six-regiment sample detailed in footnote 89 with the series on the *grands notables* published by Bergeron and Chaussinand-Nogaret. Officers from departments not covered in the series were excluded from the calculation.
[91] Marcel Vitte, "Saône et Loire," *Grands notables*, ed. Bergeron and Chaussinand-Nogaret, vol. 16, 63.
[92] Frédéric d'Agay, "Var," *Grands notables*, ed. Bergeron and Chaussinand-Nogaret, vol. 18, 188–9.

nominees of 1791–93 had retired from the service. Even with the demise of the regime and the efforts of the Bourbons to replace them with its own supporters, Napoleon's directly commissioned officers were still strongly represented in the highest ranks of the army. An examination of the professional destinies of the first 500 graduates of the Ecole spéciale confirms their importance.[93] Of the 229 who survived the Napoleonic wars and were still serving in 1846, 161 (70 percent) rose above the rank of captain, with 43 becoming generals and 118 becoming superior officers. Far from doing away with the bifurcated career structure Napoleon had created, the Bourbons perpetuated it through their institutional reforms and personnel practices. Although only one-third of officers recruited between 1815 and 1870 were graduates of the military school, they dominated the upper ranks, accounting for three-quarters of all superior officers on the eve of the Franco-Prussian War. Their predominance was felt even more strongly at the rank of general and in staff positions.[94] Napoleon had succeeded in creating a professional structure capable of preserving social distinctions without openly violating the meritocratic principles of 1789.

The Legion of Honor

Napoleon took a major step toward realizing the fusion of monarchy and meritocracy in 1802 with the foundation of the Legion of Honor, an honorific distinction to illustrate merit in all fields.[95] With its 6,000 projected members to be nominated by the First Consul alone, the creation of the Legion represented the restoration of a monarchical prerogative unknown in France since the Old Regime. Anticipating opposition to an institution which so closely resembled a chivalric order, the government insisted on its meritocratic constitution. Far from planting the seeds of a new hereditary elite, it would be awarded only to "personal merit" without distinction of birth.[96] Rather than violating the principle of equality, the Legion would give it meaning by distinguishing the useful and worthy from the idle and selfish. And far from becoming the exclusive privilege of the military, membership in the Legion would also reward merit displayed in "legislative functions, diplomacy, administration, justice, and science." Above all, the Legion would combat the materialistic ethos which, since the revolutionary

---

93 A.G. X°9, "Ecole spéciale militaire de Fontainebleau: état nominatif des élèves du no. 1 au no. 500 et leur position au 1 janvier 1847."
94 Pierre Chalmin, *L'Officier français de 1815 à 1870* (Paris, 1957), 370.
95 The following sections on the creation of the Legion of Honor and the imperial nobility draw on my article, "The *Ancien Régime* Origins of Napoleonic Social Reconstruction," *French History*, 14 (2000), 408–23.
96 The citations in this paragraph are taken from the text of the law creating the Legion of Honor, Roederer's report of 25 Floréal X to the Legislative Body, and his 29 Floréal X speech to the Senate. *A.P.*, series 2, vol. 3, 684–5 and 738–40.

abolition of honorific incentives, had made wealth the only distinction "with the power to fix regards and attract respect." By restoring to the government a means of directing national energies toward useful ends, the Legion would pull the French from the morass of self-interest into which they had sunk.

The foundation of the Legion of Honor confirmed the shift in Napoleon's social priorities, away from wealth and toward service. Signaling the emergence of a new elite of service, the creation of the Legion announced the regime's intention to distance itself from the *notabilité*, the elite of wealth imposed on him just two years earlier by the Brumairians.[97] Born into the provincial nobility, a class which had been recasting its claims to social superiority in terms of service before 1789, Napoleon was suspicious of wealth.

> One cannot make wealth a title. A rich man is often lazy and without merit! Even a rich merchant often owes his wealth to the art of selling cheaply or stealing ... I do not see a title to consideration in riches, nor a political distinction ... Today wealth is the fruit of theft, of plunder. Who is the rich man? The buyer of national domains, a military supplier, a thief. How can we found a *notabilité* on wealth thus acquired?[98]

Far from considering wealth the essence of his elite, Napoleon suspected it of fostering an ethos of grasping individualism fundamentally at odds with the spirit of loyal, self-sacrificing service he considered essential for the stability of his regime and the prestige of its ruling classes. With their status deriving from entrepreneurship or, as was more often the case, inherited wealth, the *notables* were too independent from the regime and thus too little interested in its fate to secure Napoleon's dynastic ambitions. If financial self-interest ensured the *notables'* attachment to political stability in general, nothing guaranteed that they would continue to recognize Napoleon, and still less his descendants, as the necessary source of this stability. One day self-interest might lead them to betray their current protector. At the same time, the system of *notabilité* failed to provide a means of rewarding faithful servants who, in dedicating life, limb, and property to the regime, had voluntarily renounced their opportunities for personal gain. Yet, it was precisely these qualities of fidelity and sacrifice, rather than the venality and egotism of the wealthy, which Napoleon saw as the real strength of the regime. The Legion of Honor, a kind of *notabilité* that "emanated from him alone," gave Napoleon the means of recognizing these qualities and attaching them to his person.[99]

Despite its monarchical underpinnings, the creation of the Legion did not signal a return to the ways of the Old Regime. While similar to the Order of Saint-Louis, the Legion differed in that it was open to non-military merit. It

---

97 Roederer saw the creation of the Legion of Honor as tantamount to "the abolition of the *notabilité*." *Œuvres*, vol. 3, 417. On the original conception of the *notables*, as formulated by Sieyès, see Sewell, *A Rhetoric of Bourgeois Revolution*.
98 Cited in Roederer, *Œuvres*, vol. 3, 341.
99 Roederer, *Œuvres*, vol. 3, 439.

would be a mistake, however, to attribute its inclusivity entirely to revolutionary inspiration. The Legion also drew on a conception of social amelioration which had been much discussed, but little implemented, during the last decades of the Old Regime. "Enlightened" writers had suggested making the nation's selfish drives work for the common good through a system of honors.[100] The *Encyclopédie* seems to have gone farthest in its support of this idea. In an article on "Honor," it advocated using distinctions to stimulate productivity and innovation in every field of endeavor, including agriculture and the mechanical arts. Recognizing that there were "honors for every class," the wise legislator would not fail to mobilize the whole nation by the skillful deployment of honorific inducements.[101] Although advocated in the *cahiers* of all three orders, this approach to reform was left to languish by the National Assembly, for reasons that we have already discussed. Thus, in creating the Legion of Honor, Napoleon was belatedly realizing both an unrealized Enlightenment notion of reform and a stillborn aspiration of 1789.

Although formally open to civilian merit, in practice the Legion was dominated by the military, a tendency which grew increasingly pronounced. By 1814 only 5 percent of the legionnaires were civilians.[102] The rare "civvy" was made to feel like an outsider. Sentries routinely refused to present arms to civilian legionnaires, even to Lacépède, Grand Chancellor of the order.[103] As it became more military, the Legion also grew more plebeian. Although most high-ranking officers enjoyed membership, the regime used the decoration to reward veterans whose lack of education and social polish made them ill-suited for promotion. By 1810, nearly 45 percent of its members were simple soldiers or non-commissioned officers.[104] The Legion's increasingly undistinguished social composition, as well as the creation of more exclusive orders after 1808 (the Trois toissons d'or, Couronne de fer, and the Order of the Reunion), announced its eclipse.

Nor did the Legion fulfill the ambitious political role originally assigned to it. More than a decoration, the Legion had been envisioned as an institution capable of structuring the polity and shaping public opinion. Divided into fifteen regional cohorts, it was to extend the influence of the regime to the local level through its presence in the electoral colleges, extensive land holdings, and network of charitable institutions. In practice, however, severe financial problems made it impossible for the Legion to achieve a meaningful territorial

---

100 For the specific case of France, see Reinhard, "Elite et noblesse," 5–37. For a general discussion, see Albert O. Hirschman, *The Passions and the Interests: Political Arguments for Capitalism before its Triumph* (Princeton, 1977).
101 *Encyclopédie*, vol. 8, 289–90.
102 Reinhard, "Elite et noblesse," 33.
103 A.N. AF IV 1038, "Lettre de Lacépède à l'empereur" (11 Vendémiaire XII).
104 A.N. AF IV 1039, "Etat de situation de la Légion d'honneur" (1810).

implantation.[105] Although it received over 75,000,000 francs worth of nationalized lands, these holdings were so fragmented that administrative costs alone absorbed one-sixth of their revenue. The remaining income these properties generated went to pay the legionnaires' annual stipends (from 240 francs for a simple member to 5,000 francs for grand officers), leaving no money to meet the cohorts' other expenses. In addition, the Legion became embroiled in costly legal struggles with other powerful groups, particularly the senators who were seeking to establish their own land holdings and the returning *émigrés* who were trying to recover their domains. Its financial predicament was further exacerbated by the headlong growth of membership. The initial ceiling of 6,000 was quickly surpassed as Napoleon created thousands of new legionnaires after every campaign. By 1814 the Legion counted nearly 40,000 members, an inflation that, in conjunction with its increasingly plebeian recruitment, may have reduced its prestige.

Perhaps the main reason why Napoleon abandoned his plans to base his rule on the Legion of Honor is that the nature of his regime changed in 1804 with the establishment of the Empire. As a non-transmissible, individual distinction, the Legion of Honor was a perfectly adequate institution on which to anchor his lifetime Consulate. But with the transformation of his government into a hereditary monarchy, Napoleon came to believe that the Legion no longer provided a satisfactory social foundation for his regime. While its membership incarnated the values of loyalty, service, and self-sacrifice held in such great esteem by the Emperor, its unimpressive social makeup could add but little luster to the imperial court and was unlikely to bolster the legitimacy of the new dynasty in the eyes of the courtiers and diplomats of Old Europe. Above all, the Legion was ill-suited to the consolidation of the dynasty in France itself, being a purely personal distinction that lapsed with the death of its bearer. The Legion was too unstable to ensure the imperial succession. Only a hereditary elite bound to the fortunes of the dynasty by the desire to preserve its own status from generation to generation could offer a sufficient guarantee that imperial sovereignty would pass intact to Napoleon's descendants. Thus, while the Legion continued to grow under the Empire, remaining a coveted award despite the inflation of its numbers, its political function was transferred to a new institution better suited to Napoleon's dynastic ambitions, the imperial nobility.

The imperial nobility

A hereditary elite of wealth and service, qualities which had until then been divided between the *notables* and legionnaires, the imperial nobility was

---

105 Jean Tulard, *Napoléon et la noblesse d'empire* (Paris, 1986), 43–6.

established on 1 March 1808. In addition to providing a more potent stimulus of national energies than the lifetime distinction of membership in the Legion of Honor, the new nobility was intended to play an essential political role. First, it would ensure the transmission of sovereignty to Napoleon's descendants by surrounding the Throne with a phalanx of respectable families driven by self-interest to "maintain the great edifice" of imperial rule.[106] Unlike the *notables*, whose wealth gave them too much autonomy, and the *légionnaires*, who possessed only a fleeting distinction, a nobility created by the reigning dynasty could be counted on to support the Throne, if for no other reason than "to be supported by it" in turn.[107] Second, the creation of an imperial nobility would strengthen Napoleonic rule by rallying well-disposed nobles of the Old Regime. Even if they did not engage in counterrevolution, the old nobility still weakened the dynasty by diminishing the luster of its new elites. But, if integrated into the imperial hierarchy, the old nobles would lend prestige and legitimacy to the regime. Die-hards who refused to accept the new institution would fade from "public attention" and thus be "radically extinguished."[108] Finally, the imperial nobility would garner prestige and international legitimacy for the new dynasty by providing it with a polished elite capable of representing it in the established courts of Europe. Uniting men who had won brilliant reputations on the battlefields of the Revolution with some of the most distinguished scions of the Bourbon aristocracy, the new nobility would stand as a powerful symbol that France had laid to rest its revolutionary divisions and reentered the community of nations.

For all its potential benefits, however, the restoration of nobility also entailed serious risks. Even proponents of the measure were aware that this was a sensitive operation which, if improperly conceived, could undermine the regime. It was not, however, the prospect of contravening residual egalitarian sentiment that caused them the greatest concern. What gave them pause was the possibility that, in reviving nobility, they might reignite the kinds of internal conflicts which had fractured the elite and destabilized the monarchy during the last decades of the Old Regime. Although nobility had originally been based on sound meritocratic principles, they wrote, ill-conceived royal policies had denatured its "primitive constitution" with disastrous results.[109] Genealogy had been

---

106 A.N. AF IV 1310, "Réponse de Cambacérès, l'archi-chancellier, à la deuxième note de l'empereur" (30 June 1810).
107 A.N. AF IV 1311, Lévis, "Note pour sa majesté ... " On the resilience of the imperial nobility after the fall of the First Empire, see Natalie Petiteau, *Elites et mobilités: la noblesse d'empire au XIXème siècle (1808–1914)* (Paris, 1997).
108 A.N. AF IV 1310, "Réponse de Cambacérès ... "
109 A.N. AF IV 1038, Huguet de Semonville, "Mémoire sur les moyens de lier un système général d'hérédités en France avec les institutions existantes aujourd'hui, particulièrement avec celle de la Légion d'Honneur" (1807). Unless otherwise noted, the citations in this paragraph are from this *mémoire*.

elevated above public service, a shift which not only antagonized the Third Estate, but also split the nobility internally. At the same time, wealth had replaced merit as the key to social advancement, casting discredit upon the second order and turning poor military nobles into bitter enemies of Court and city. Setting service against lineage and poverty against wealth, these innovations had divided the "respective noble existences," shattered the unity of the elite, and, by turning its staunchest defenders into its most embittered opponents, sealed the fate of the monarchy. To avoid falling into the same errors, Napoleonic reformers carefully studied the lessons of the past. It was only by "proceeding from principles directly opposed to those followed under the last two reigns," one wrote, that the new nobility could be established on a solid footing.[110]

The reformers identified the displacement of service by lineage as one of the main causes of intra-elite conflict during the Old Regime. According to Huguet de Semonville, once a leader of the Paris Parlement's prerevolutionary resistance and now an imperial senator, nobility in France had not always been defined by bloodlines and parchment.[111] Until the eighteenth century, according to his fanciful view, it had been awarded to "services rendered to the state in all genres without distinction." As long as it had respected this principle, Semonville asserted, the nobility enjoyed "the approbation of the people." In 1760, however, this constitutional order was carelessly overturned by Louis XV's regulation on presentation to the Court. By excluding families whose nobility originated after 1400, this regulation made ennoblement, even if accorded for heroism, a "stain." "From the day that pedigree without service was recognized as an exclusive right and service with less ancestry a pretension," an "insurmountable barrier" was raised within the Second Estate. Encouraged by the regulation, "a multitude of obscure nobles" flocked to Versailles and "usurped all the highest places ... without ever having exercised civil or military functions." Service families which could not meet the new genealogical conditions were "secretly wounded in their *amour propre*" and forced "to take a seat on the benches of philosophy." The "chivalric mania" did not remain restricted to the upper nobility, but soon ramified downward, communicating its divisive influence to all French institutions. Genealogical proofs were demanded by the Maison militaire du roi, the chivalric orders of Saint-Esprit and Saint-Lazare, and the sovereign courts. Extended by the 1781 Ségur regulation to the military profession, which Semonville imagined to have been the traditional path to ennoblement, this trend finally aroused the anger of the Third Estate. "Attacking all classes of society," genealogical exclusivism was denounced by the entire

---

110 A.N. AF IV 1036, "Projet pour l'institution d'un livre d'or dans lequel seraient inscrits tous les membres de la Légion d'honneur" (n.d.).
111 A.N. AF IV 1038, Semonville, "Mémoire sur les moyens ... " Unless otherwise noted, the citations which follow in this paragraph are from this *mémoire*.

nation in 1789. But to Semonville's amazement, not a single *cahier* attacked nobility *per se*. Rather, the "unanimous wish of the nation" was to regenerate the nobility by making it the recompense of merit. Semonville urged Napoleon to fulfill this desire by creating a new "hereditary preeminence calculated on service."

The legislation creating the imperial nobility incorporated this recommendation. Titles were to be granted only to those "who have distinguished themselves by their services, by their devotion to the prince and the *patrie*." Although hereditary under certain conditions, the new distinction would confer neither privilege nor preference, thereby preserving a level playing field from which merit could emerge. Leaving careers open "to virtues and useful talents," the new nobility would encourage a "just and praiseworthy *émulation*" by providing state servants in all fields with an honorable distinction to strive for.[112] In an address to the Senate, Napoleon emphasized that the new institution was not intended for the military alone.

> If these rewards were accorded only to military service, it would cause notable damage to the civil services which prepare in silence ... the prosperity of the state and the triumph of our armies. Let [our subjects] contribute to the strength of this vast empire by professing the arts or sciences, by devoting themselves to agriculture or commerce, by serving the state in the tribunals, administrations, or armies; whether they are rich or poor, magistrates or simple citizens, they have an equal right to our affection.[113]

Imperial nobility could be acquired in two ways: automatically by the exercise of certain public functions or at the Emperor's discretion. Through the first mechanism, entire classes of public officials – Court dignitaries, ministers, senators, life members of the Council of State, presidents of the Legislative Body, archbishops, members of the electoral colleges, high magistrates in the imperial courts, bishops, mayors of the major cities, and members of the Legion of Honor – received noble titles. Through the second mechanism, the Emperor granted nobility to applicants whose superior merit was judged worthy. Even old nobles, especially encouraged to apply to facilitate social reconciliation, were held to the same rigorous standards as everyone else. The mere possession of noble status, no matter how ancient, was not enough to open the doors of the new elite. It was "proof of service," not "proof of nobility," that interested the imperial government.[114] Of the approximately 3,000 nobles created between 1808 and 1815, all exercised some sort of public function. Although military officers formed the majority of its membership, the imperial nobility was more professionally diverse than the

---

112   *A.P.*, series 2, vol. 10, 12.
113   A.N. AF IV 1040, Napoléon, "Adresse au Sénat" (n.d.).
114   See the exchange of letters between Cambacérès and Napoleon in A.N. AF IV 1310. The citation is from A.N. AF IV 1306, "Projet pour l'institution ... "

Legion of Honor or even the former Second Estate. If nearly 60 percent of imperial nobles were indeed officers, it is perhaps more significant that over 40 percent had earned their place through the exercise of civilian functions.[115]

Although awarded for individual accomplishment, open to all forms of service, and conferring no exclusive rights, imperial nobility risked departing from meritocratic principle in one respect: it could be passed from father to son. If not limited by serious safeguards, warned Napoleon's advisors, hereditary transmission threatened to adulterate the meritocratic basis of the imperial nobility and eventually transform it into a privileged caste. In principle, a young man born into nobility would feel an inescapable need to prove himself worthy by equaling or surpassing the achievements of his ancestors. But, as numerous examples from the Old Regime demonstrated, this was not always the case. Some nobles would inevitably fail to meet the promise and obligation of their birth. To maintain the service vocation of the imperial nobility from generation to generation, it was necessary to "present it with the fear of incurring derogation by repose."[116] The most effective way to do this, some reformers concluded, was to make the transmission of noble status "conditional" upon "the services that [the sons of nobles] would themselves render."[117] Semonville suggested one method of accomplishing this. He proposed ranking all imperial nobles within a three-tiered hierarchy according to the nature of their services. At birth, the son of a noble would enter the nobility one level below that of his father, rising to his full hereditary status (or beyond) only through his personal service. Each generation which failed to serve with distinction, however, would drop one step in the hierarchy until the family fell out of the nobility altogether. Thus, it was possible for a first-class noble to see his great-grandson revert to commoner status if the two intervening generations (his son and grandson) were idle. Although Napoleon rejected this scheme, preferring instead to augment his own power by requiring that nobles obtain imperial permission to transmit their titles, he agreed with the spirit of Semonville's proposal. Without careful attention to the personal qualities of those seeking to inherit nobility, warned Napoleon, "the multiplicity of titles and the inconsistence of the men who would bear them would eventually result in its degradation."[118] The body he established to review applications for the transmission of titles did not hesitate to deny requests when it found sufficient meritocratic credentials lacking. In such instances, it invariably found that the unsuccessful candidate exercised "no public function."[119]

---

115 Tulard, *Napoléon et la noblesse d'empire*, 94.
116 A.N. AF IV 1311, Lévis, "Note pour sa majesté ... "
117 A.N. AF IV 1038, Semonville, "Mémoire sur les moyens ... "
118 A.N. AF IV 909, "Note dictée par sa majesté" (12 February 1810).
119 This example is taken from the unsuccessful application of the former Old Regime noble Bethune-Hesdigneul. Other examples are found in Tulard, *Napoléon et la noblesse*, 84–5.

While committed to perpetuating the meritocratic basis of the nobility from generation to generation, Napoleonic reformers did not believe that merit alone gave it a sufficiently durable foundation. It was also necessary, they believed, to ensure that noble families also possessed enough wealth to uphold their status. The experience of the Old Regime had revealed the dangers of noble impoverishment. Believing that benefits it had earned through service were being usurped by plutocratic arrivistes and well-connected courtiers, the middling military nobility had grown embittered. Impelled by honor and tradition to sacrifice life and fortune in the king's service, but little rewarded for its pains, the provincial nobility had become rebellious. "Soon its fortune was no longer sufficient to show itself for what it should have been: worthy representatives of the majesty and bounty of the Throne. From this point, it had fallen into degradation, grown factious, and become a declared enemy [of the Court]."[120]

The monarchy's sale of ennobling office added to its resentment. Venality not only cheapened noble status, but also added to the ranks of the hated parvenus. "Under the last two reigns," noted the duc de Lévis, "finance, the least noble of the professions, became the sole means of acquiring nobility, ... a prize that monarchs had formerly accorded only to the most brilliant valor and the most striking services." The result of venal ennoblement had been to fill the military nobility with "envy" and split the Second Estate into hostile factions.[121] As a subaltern artillery officer, restricted in his advancement by the relative mediocrity of his birth and fortune, Napoleon himself had experienced these frustrations.[122] Years later as Emperor, he remembered the jealousy generated by social inequalities within the nobility. Heredity of nobility, without any mechanism for ensuring its material basis, would inevitably revive intra-noble tensions. "By giving titles in the air, without any idea of fact and reality," he observed, "children with a title but without fortune would [in turn] have children with titles while being even poorer."[123] To combat the reemergence of this tendency, Napoleon believed it necessary to make the transmission of titles contingent upon not only merit, but also the possession of a stable fortune.

Napoleon's advisors proposed numerous plans for ensuring the material basis of the imperial nobility. Although he insisted that noble status be granted only as a reward for state service, Emile Gaudin was no less insistent that it should not be accorded indiscriminately, without regard to the financial situation of

---

120 A.N. AF IV 1040, Gaudin, "Mémoire sur la necessité ... "
121 A.N. AF IV 1311, Lévis, "Note pour sa majesté ... "
122 For insight into the young Napoleon's attitudes toward the problem of intra-noble inequality within the royal officer corps, see the constitution he drafted for his regiment's *calotte* (a semi-secret brotherhood of junior officers). "Projet de constitution de calotte du régiment de la Fère," in *Napoléon: manuscrits inédits, 1786–1791*, ed. Frédéric Masson and Guido Biagi (Paris, 1914), 39.
123 A.N. AF IV 909, "Note dictée ... "

potential beneficiaries. To guarantee that imperial nobles possessed the means of upholding their rank, Gaudin suggested that they be required to make a substantial cash payment upon ennoblement and provide additional payments each time a family's title was passed to a new generation. He confidently predicted that these operations would not only allow the nobility to fund charitable, educational, and military institutions, but also provide the government with huge cash reserves.[124] Jouin de Saint-Charles hazarded an even more utopian forecast of the benefits such a scheme could bring. By requiring new nobles to pay up to 100,000 francs for their titles, the government could establish a comprehensive network of workhouses, hospitals, asylums, and old-age homes that would end misery in France.[125] The duc de Lévis proposed a more limited system for maintaining the nobility's financial health. Although it should be granted only as a reward for exemplary service, he wrote, nobility should be so inextricably "linked to landed property that, if the property is lost, the distinction would instantly cease."[126] His plan was ultimately adopted. The law creating imperial nobility stipulated that titles could only be transmitted if attached to an entailed landholding or permanently immobilized investment income. But Napoleon did not intend that these financial restrictions exclude meritorious state servants whose sacrifices prevented them from fulfilling these conditions. To help impecunious imperial nobles – usually military officers of plebeian origin, but also rallied Old Regime nobles who had lost their fortune in the Revolution – the Emperor made numerous land-gifts that could be used to constitute entailments. Nearly 60 percent of imperial nobles benefited from imperial largesse.[127] Although he saw poverty as incompatible with hereditary noble status, Napoleon did not intend to allow it to override the right of service to recompense. Far from setting up a conflict between wealth and service, the provision for making the transmission of nobility contingent upon possession of a stable fortune was intended to prevent inequalities of wealth from once again becoming the source of internecine strife.

Napoleon sought to realize what, at first glance, seems to be a most improbable synthesis: revival of the meritocratic social ideals of 1789 within a new monarchical framework of government. The pursuit of this project in the officer corps reveals, however, that these were not completely antithetical goals. The hierarchical nature of early revolutionary meritocracy, so energetically

---

[124] A.N. AF IV 1040, Gaudin, "Mémoire sur la necessité ... "
[125] A.N. AF IV 1310, Jouin de Saint-Charles, "Coup d'œil paternel du Grand Napoléon sur son peuple" (1806).
[126] A.N. AF IV 1311, Lévis, "Note pour sa majesté ... "
[127] Often formed from lands in the subjugated Eastern territories, these *dotations* had the added benefit of giving the new nobility a stake in preserving the Empire's conquests. Monika Senkowska-Gluck, "Les Donataires de Napoléon," *Revue d'histoire moderne et contemporaine*, 17 (1970), 680–93

denounced by egalitarian republicans, was not inherently incompatible with the social gradations of a monarchical polity. Indeed, Napoleon believed that restoring a system of meritocratic distinctions was necessary to build his monarchical power. Only by bestowing places, riches, and honors on exemplary public functionaries, he reasoned, could he constitute a loyal elite capable of serving and perpetuating his dynasty. The difficulty of fusing meritocracy and monarchy lay elsewhere, for both were predicated on inequality. The rock on which it foundered was the exclusivist tendency inherent in the monarchical notion of service that resurrected the hereditary ideal and subverted the principle of careers open to talent. Whereas meritocracy sought to discover and reward talent in the population as a whole, monarchy – rooted in an ideal of reciprocity binding the monarch and his elite – tended to narrow the government's bountiful gaze to a more circumscribed group, the families of those who had already served the regime. Although less pronounced in Napoleon's initial efforts to build a service elite, as the revolutionary *tabula rasa* had allowed him to recruit it broadly from the socially diverse group of "new men" who had served the Republic, this inclination toward autorecruitment grew stronger over time. As the founding generation of the Napoleonic service elite aged, the regime was obliged to look first to its children to take its place, thus leaving fewer and fewer opportunities for families which had not yet served the state. Gradually, Napoleon's reimposition of a monarchical political order led to the reassertion of a hereditary ethos of service that subverted his formal commitment to preserving the meritocratic ideal of 1789 and created lasting divisions in the officer corps.

Conclusion

The meritocratic legacy of the Old Regime, Revolution, and Empire is fraught with ambiguity. This is evident in a little-known controversy over military school recruitment which pitted the Chamber of Deputies against the monarchy during the first Bourbon Restoration of 1814. Only three months after Napoleon's first abdication, King Louis XVIII tried to reimpose a measure of formal noble privilege in the area of military education. His law of 30 July 1814 not only reopened the Paris military school founded by his ancestor in 1751, but also resurrected its original genealogical admissions requirement that all aspirants furnish proof of at least four generations of patrilineal noble descent. Reacting to petitions from outraged citizens, the Chamber of Deputies took up the matter. It found that the admissions policy violated the third article of the Constitutional Charter, guaranteeing that "the French are equally admissible to civil and military employments," and demanded that the Crown adopt a more acceptable procedure.[1] The Chamber's unanimous opposition to the revival of hereditary privilege forced the Crown to back down. But the revised admissions policy it issued did not institute a regime that can be described as meritocratic in the modern sense of the word. Although its preamble declared that all places at the school were open to applicants without distinction of birth, the body of the law formally granted preference to the sons of military officers, particularly those who had sacrificed life, limb, and fortune in the service of the state.[2] The Chamber accepted the new policy without dissent and even praised the King for favoring the "sons of those who had rendered services to the state."[3]

While the Crown's retreat marked the end of formal noble privilege in France, the episode suggests that neither the meaning nor even the ultimate triumph of the meritocratic order were assured. The fact that the Crown's ministers dared propose the reintroduction of genealogical proofs shows that at least some people believed that the principle of careers open to talent was not sacrosanct. Nonetheless, the overwhelming opposition to this initiative demonstrates that the Revolution had resulted in a real break with the past, one that would prove impossible to reverse. Never again would any French government attempt to

---

[1] *A.P.*, series 2, vol. 13, 25–7. For the text of the original, offending admissions policy, see A.G. X°1, "Loi du 30 juillet 1814."

[2] A.N. AF V 2, "Séance du Conseil des ministres" (19 September 1814). For the text of the revised policy, see A.G. X°1, "Loi du 23 September 1814."

[3] *A.P.*, series 2, vol. 13, 25–7 and 537–8.

revive the professional prerogatives the nobility had formerly enjoyed. And without this aid, the nobility would never recover its former preeminence in the officer corps. The formal link between the nobility and military profession had been severed for ever. Between 1848 and 1870, only 6 percent of officers came from the Old Regime nobility, while an additional 2 percent came from families ennobled during the nineteenth century.[4] While disproportionate to the percentage of nobles in the population as a whole, these figures do not begin to approach those of the Old Regime when as much as 95 percent of the officer corps was drawn from the Second Estate. No longer would the terms "officer" and "gentleman" serve as synonyms.

Yet, to focus only on this change risks overlooking long-term continuities in the meritocratic culture of the French military profession. The conception of merit that triumphed in 1814 cannot be described as wholly modern. Indeed, the revised military school admissions policy approved by the Chamber of Deputies gave off a distinctly archaic odor. Granting preferment to the sons of officers, it expressed a conception of merit whose assumption of hereditary vocational aptitude and deservedness has little in common with our current, individualistic understanding. This was neither accidental nor isolated. Throughout the nineteenth century the French military establishment continued to embrace traditional assumptions about the relationship between family background and suitability for the military profession. While it is not surprising to find a former Old Regime noble like the comte de Vogué touting in 1818 "the prodigious advantage that example ... gives to a son who embraces the same profession as his father," it is significant that even officers of *roturier* extraction and revolutionary credentials held similar views.[5] In a pamphlet of 1829, General Morand claimed that experience had shown that the ideal officer was one who had been "destined by his family for the profession of arms."[6] There is even evidence that notions of hereditary military professionalism survived into the twentieth-century French army. In their study of officer recruitment after the Second World War, Raoul Girardet and Jean-Pierre Thomas underlined the "growing importance ... of auto-recruitment" during the 1950s, 1960s, and 1970s. By 1972 more than 50 percent of the cadets attending Saint-Cyr were themselves the sons of officers.[7] The restoration

---

4 William Serman, *Les Origines des officiers français, 1848–1870* (Paris, 1979), 306.
5 A.P., series 2, vol. 20, 625.
6 Charles-Antoine-Louis-Alexis, comte de Morand, *De l'armée selon la Charte, et d'après l'expérience des dernières guerres* (Paris, 1829), 167. How Morand – who, as a young man, had abandoned a legal career to join a National Guard volunteer battalion in 1792 – would have applied this principle to himself is unclear.
7 Raoul Girardet and Jean-Pierre H. Thomas, "Problèmes de recrutement," in *La Crise militaire française (1945–1962): aspects sociologiques et idéologiques*, ed. Raoul Girardet (Paris, 1964), 39–46; and Serman, *Les Origines des officiers*, 236.

of formal noble privilege had been thwarted in 1814, but modern meritocracy had not replaced it. Between the poles of noble privilege and careers open to talent, another notion of merit, one based on the assumption that the family environment nurtured particular professional aptitudes, had emerged. First elaborated by military reformers during the Old Regime, it had weathered the transition of 1789 only to be suppressed four years later by the Convention. But, like a river running underground, it had emerged again with Napoleon's seizure of power and maintained its hold over the imagination of professional military men well into the twentieth century.

We cannot, however, judge the meritocratic legacy of the Old Regime, Revolution, and Empire by looking only at the question of officer recruitment. As we have seen throughout this book, meritocratic discourse always involved more far-reaching issues than that. Since the Old Regime, merit had always implied a certain conception of the place of the military profession in society, the relationship between the officer corps and the state (particularly when it came to making promotions), and the moral imperatives (reciprocity, equity, and justice) that were supposed to govern this relationship. This broader understanding of meritocracy – as a mutually-binding moral contract between the state and its military servitors – remained strong even after the officer corps ceased to be noble and kings ceased to be even theoretically absolute. But over the course of the nineteenth century, attempts made to prevent this relationship from being subverted by alien forces would unintentionally alter it beyond recognition.

Like their predecessors, the officers of the Restoration believed that the principal threat to the traditional ideal of service came from the infiltration of outsiders – parvenus who did not understand the military way, men whose excessive wealth and influence were misleading the judgement of the government, violating the rights of merit, and undermining the well-being of the military profession. Legitimist officers tended to blame the Revolution or the "usurper" Bonaparte for having introduced a new climate of arbitrariness and volatility into military society. According to General Préval, a prominent Restoration military reformer, the imperial regime had given "no real guarantee to either services or merit, wounded honorable rights, awarded premature advancement without measure, and ... rebuffed men whose only fault was [their refusal] to prostrate themselves before its power."[8] For officers who looked back nostalgically to the Revolution and Empire, in contrast, blame for their career frustrations fell entirely on the Restoration. Out of vengeance, wrote the Marshal Marmont, the government was unjustly dismissing Napoleon's most glorious veterans and replacing

---

8 Claude-Antoine-Hippolyte, vicomte de Préval, *De l'avancement militaire dans l'intérêt de la monarchie* (Paris, 1824), 38.

them with "old *émigrés* who had been military in name only," Vendée rebels, and Court favorites – all "ill-suited to inspiring the confidence of soldiers and officers."⁹ These injustices, according to the baron Pasquier, were "putting a large number of soldiers in a vengeful mood" and were even "resulting in a number of conspiracies."¹⁰

By 1817 the climate of dissension, recrimination, and division in the military profession had become so acute that observers could only compare it to the bitter struggles that had fractured the officer corps in the decades before 1789. As during the Old Regime, when the career privileges of the well-heeled Court nobility made a mockery of meritocratic advancement mechanisms and demoralized the provincial nobility, abuses of birth, wealth, and political connections during the Restoration were threatening to erode the composition of the officer corps and destroy military professionalism. Calvet-Madailhan, a former officer, described the plight of the officer corps by evoking "those abuses of long ago which often propelled a young man ignorant of the first elements of war from the boudoir of a woman in credit" to a position of command.¹¹ The comte de Roche-Aymon, an Old Regime officer of illustrious birth who was speaking from personal experience, drew a parallel between the present distress of the officer corps and its troubled state during "the last years of the reign of Louis XVI," years which had been marred by "intriguing, pretensions, and overly rapid advancement."¹² Another former officer, the Napoleonic general Brun de Villeret, shared this assessment. "By lavishing favors," he observed, "the King, like his illustrious ancestor, has only produced more discontented and ungrateful men."¹³ Despite their different social backgrounds and political leanings, officers during the early Restoration shared a common understanding of the threats facing their profession, an understanding that would have resonated with their predecessors.

The army pursued a time-honored approach to these problems: to insulate decisions about promotion from the corrosive influence of favoritism, wealth, and social status by establishing an inflexible system of advancement. Designed by the war minister and former Napoleonic marshal, Gouvion-Saint-Cyr, the new system of advancement that responded to these concerns would remain (albeit with minor modifications) the basis of the French military profession until 1870.¹⁴ Presented to the Chamber of Deputies on 29 November 1817, the minister's plan strongly resembled that designed by the Constituent Assembly's military committee and

---

9 Marmont, *Mémoires*, vol. 7, 270.
10 Cited in Douglas Porch, *Army and Revolution: France, 1815–1848* (London, 1974), 1.
11 A.P., series 2, vol. 20, 650.
12 A.P., series 2, vol. 21, 123.
13 A.P., series 2, vol. 20, 413.
14 Serman, *Les Origines des officiers*, 12.

approved in September 1790.[15] Like the committee (and, indeed, like military reformers before 1789), Gouvion-Saint-Cyr counted heavily on the principle of seniority to ensure that "favoritism or credit do not destroy healthy competitive striving."[16] But at the same time, he, like the earlier reformers, believed it necessary to leave the government a measure of discretion over promotions in order to stimulate effort and reward talent. The key, he felt, was to strike the right balance between seniority, which provided career stability but stifled innovation and effort, and government nomination, which spurred excellence but opened the door to abuses. As during the Old Regime, Revolution, and Empire, Restoration military reformers viewed the system of advancement as a delicately balanced motivational machine which could easily break down without precautions against favoritism and unmerited preferences.

However well designed, reform of the system of promotions was unable to satisfy everyone. Throughout the 1820s, frustrated officers continued to complain that the Bourbon government was using its discretionary power over advancement in ways antithetical to the army's professional interest. They believed that the Court was ignoring the rights of experienced officers in order to promote reinstated *émigrés* and "courtiers completely foreign to the service."[17] Even some of the beneficiaries, like an *émigré* named Puymaigre, felt guilt at "inserting [himself] into the ranks of those who had acquired their grades at the price of their blood."[18] Napoleonic officers particularly resented the reconstitution of the Maison militaire du roi and the creation of a new royal guard, units which, like their Old Regime counterparts, offered prestige, high pay, and elevated grades to favored officers. Alfred de Vigny, the noted military writer who began his career in the Maison militaire in 1814, recalled the "hateful prejudices [which] the luxury and grades of these bodies of officers gave the army."[19] Marshal Marmont believed that these corps were composed of individuals "who, never having served, [had not merited] the grades that were lavished on them."[20] He considered this and similar abuses, like the decision to give the infant duc de Bordeaux six *aides-de-camp* and the nomination to the ministry of the marquis de Clermont-Tonnerre, an "officer of the

---

15 According to one deputy, the comte de Bondy, the principles of the Constituent Assembly's law on advancement were "still the basis of the mode of advancement submitted to your deliberation." A.P., series 2, vol. 20, 248. Alexandre de Lameth also noted the similarity between Gouvion-Saint-Cyr's system of advancement and the one he had shepherded through the military committee in September 1790. In 1818 Lameth even had his 1790 report on advancement reprinted with a new commentary on the current debate. Alexandre de Lameth, *Rapport fait à l'assemblée constituante sur l'avancement militaire avec des observations préliminaires* (Paris, 1818).

16 A.P., series 2, vol. 19, 652.

17 Marmont, *Mémoires*, vol. 8, 338.

18 Edmond Bonnal de Ganges, *Les Royalistes contre l'armée* (Paris, 1906), 265.

19 Alfred de Vigny, *Servitude et grandeur militaires* (Paris, 1835), 43.

20 Marmont, *Mémoires*, vol. 7, 40.

parade ground and Court," as symptomatic of the infiltration of non-military values into the military sphere.[21] He denounced the Bourbon regime as one which, in "placing itself under the tutelage of lawyers," had diminished "the consideration owed to military men."[22] No defender of the imperial regime, General Préval nonetheless complained that the Restoration had allowed pseudo-military personnel to creep into the army. He condemned the newly created military administration service for usurping advancement and distinctions which should have been awarded for real military service. He also railed against the regimental almoners, "another class of functionaries who resemble the military administrators by both their antimilitary character and the excessive advantages they enjoy."[23] Military reformers during the Restoration felt that the Gouvion-Saint-Cyr law, while well conceived, did not offer the army enough protection against the encroachments of the Court and civilian society.

Resentment of outside intrusion into what were perceived as internal military affairs grew even sharper after the catastrophe of the Franco-Prussian War. Just as it had in the aftermath of the humiliating defeat of the Seven Years' War, the French officer corps of the 1870s placed the blame for its dismal performance squarely on the ignorance of politicians and complacent materialism of society. General Brincourt was one who spared no venom in denouncing the insidious effects on the army of petty politicians and self-satisfied civilians. In his opinion, responsibility for the defeat lay with "all these good bourgeois [who], accustomed for half a century to enjoying their property, their routines in peace, ... have refused to the *patrie* the means of defending itself." By placing the desire for "sordid economies" above military readiness, by "having lawyers discuss military affairs," France had brought disaster upon itself.[24] Brincourt's assertion – that the defeat of 1870–71 was merely a symptom of profound national malaise – echoed claims made by the officer corps a century earlier. Seeking to understand the reasons for the army's disastrous performance in the wars of the mid-eighteenth century, the influential military reformer Guibert had advanced a similar explanation in his widely read book, the *Essai général de tactique* where he had blamed the military crisis on the corrosive influence of general social trends. Although separated by a century, Guibert and Brincourt – like their brothers-in-arms generally – viewed French society itself as the source of military decline, as the reason why meritocracy was failing.

It followed from this assumption that military revival could only be achieved by insulating the army from the corruption of a self-indulgent society.

---

21 Ibid, vol. 8, 4 and 448.
22 Ibid, vol. 7, 69.
23 A.G. MR 1937, Préval, "Notes" (1829).
24 Henri-Augustin Brincourt, *Lettres du général Brincourt (1823–1909)* (Paris, 1923), 393 and 400.

Sharing the belief that "everything was rotten in France" except the army, which alone remained "clean and honorable," the postwar head of state, Thiers, sought to carry out this separation.[25] To shelter the army from the destabilizing influence of the broader society, Thiers adopted a traditional remedy: the creation of a Superior War Council to act as intermediary between military and civilian spheres. Although historians have viewed the establishment of this committee of general officers as an attempt to imitate the Prussian General Staff, which had proven its worth during the recently concluded conflict, this institution had deep roots in French military culture. Like the War Council formed by Guibert nearly a century earlier, it was just the most recent manifestation of the intermittent isolationist reflex that periodically seized the French military profession. Contemporary commentators were fully conscious of the links between the new body and its Old Regime model and namesake. As well as noting obvious structural continuities, they also perceived more unexpected similarities in the meritocratic thinking of the two bodies. The great contribution of Thiers's Superior War Council, recalled General Thoumas in 1888, was to have rediscovered key principles of advancement which had originally been posed by the original War Council before the Revolution.

> When one reads the ordinances of 1788, one is shocked to find dispositions which, after having been forgotten for many years, have been adopted in our days as the result of recent studies ... It is truly incredible that, having possessed in 1788 such wise and simple ideas, we had to wait more than eighty years to return to them in 1871, after having recognized their compelling truth in a disastrous experience![26]

A special commission formed in 1895 to refine the system of advancement echoed Thoumas's expressions of pleasant surprise, writing that Guibert's advancement law of 17 March 1788 "seemed to have been written yesterday."[27]

Although the attempt to erect institutional barriers between the army and society was intended to preserve the traditional conception of meritocratic state service by protecting the military from the extraneous forces that were subverting it, the isolationist impulse paradoxically ended up transforming the very notions of reciprocity which it had sought to defend. As control of advancement was gradually transferred from the sovereign to promotion boards drawn from the upper ranks of the military profession itself, the historic moral link between the officer corps and the state – the duty to serve and the obligation to reward – was weakened. Advancement ceased to be understood in terms of a solemn contract between the sovereign and his servitors, but rather came to be seen as something

25 Cited in Alistair Horne, *The French Army and Politics, 1870–1970* (New York, 1984), 14.
26 Charles-Antoine Thoumas, *Causeries militaires* (Paris, 1889–1913), 221–2.
27 A.G. MR 2164, "Apperçu historique sur l'avancement" in "Registre des procès-verbaux des séances de la commission d'études sur l'avancement du 1er mars 1895 au 10 avril 1895."

internal to the military itself. Although their brevets of rank continued to be issued in the name of the current government (whether a monarchy, empire, or republic), the officers knew that the real authority to make or break careers lay with the promotion boards and their supposedly "objective" criteria of promotion. Increasingly, the concept of merit narrowed in scope, to emphasize those personal qualities which would secure advancement, rather than the notions of deservedness, just recompense, and reciprocity it had previously evoked. By the late nineteenth century a new sense of bureaucratic professionalism was replacing the traditional notion of service that had previously informed the structure of the military profession and the officers' own sense of themselves.

Bibliography

Archival and manuscript sources

Archives nationales (A.N.)

Series AA (collections de lettres et pièces diverses) 51, 52, 54, 61.
Series AB XIX (documents isolés et papiers d'érudits) 702, 704, 3506, 3900, 3901.
Series AD I (textes administratifs – régime administratif et politique) 83.
Series AD VI (textes administratifs – armée) 9–10^a, 43, 49–52, 66–9, 76, 77.
Series AD XVIII^a (rapports, discours, et opinions des députés) 15.
Series AD XVIII^c (impressions des assemblées) 82, 83, 87, 88, 91–4, 183, 184, 188, 288, 294, 295, 297, 304, 307, 308, 383, 385, 442, 444, 471, 491, 519.
Series AD XIX G (documents administratifs – guerre) 1.
Series AF I (Régime royal constitutionnel) 3–5.
Series AF I* (Régime royal constitutionnel – registres) 18–20.
Series AF II (Conseil exécutif provisoire, Convention, Comité de salut public) 9, 14–16, 52, 198–213, 226–8, 232–41, 244, 290–3, 361, 362, 364–8, 391.
Series AF II* (Comité de défense générale) 45.
Series AF III (Directoire exécutif) 144^a–150, 152^a, 154^a–8, 178, 182, 184, 187.
Series AF III* (Directoire exécutif – registres) 202, 203, 274.
Series AF IV (Secrétaire d'état impériale) 909, 945, 964, 1013, 1035–40, 1100, 1115–20, 1148^b–53, 1297, 1298, 1300^b, 1306, 1310–13, 1322, 1323, 1591, 1592, 1599, 1604, 1654^b, 1660^a.
Series AF V (Régime royal) 2.
Series 4 AP (chartrier du comté de Brienne) 188–90.
Series 138 AP (archives Daru) 4, 6–13, 15, 17–28, 287.
Series 182 AP (papiers Clarke) 2.
Series B^a (élections aux états-généraux) 24.
Series C (assemblées nationales) 30, 75, 82, 86, 89, 98, 122, 123, 164, 167, 173, 184, 185, 187, 221, 224, 229, 308, 311, 358, 359.
Series C^8 (ordres de chevalerie) 18.
Series D§ 1 (missions des représentants du peuple) 4–38.
Series D IV (Comité de constitution) 10–16, 21, 36–8, 41–4, 47–53.
Series D XV (Comité militaire) 1–6.
Series D XVII (Comité de judicature) 4.
Series D XL (Comité des pétitions, dépêches, et correspondances) 28.
Series F^7 (police générale) 7819.
Series F^9 (affaires militaires) 39^{b-c}, 40, 41, 43, 53, 54, 1032–34.
Series F^{17} (instruction publique) 366, 367, 1139–44, 1369, 1370, 1740, 1741, 6748–64, 7140, 7141.
Series K (cartons des rois) 148, 149.

Series M (ordres militaires et hospitaliers, universités et collèges, titres nobiliaires, mélanges) 158–62, 253–5, 639, 1019.
Series MM (idem – registres) 656, 658–9.

Archives de la guerre (A.G.)

Series A^1 (archives anciennes) 3487, 3510, 3715, 3720, 3753, 3754, 3766, 3768, 3785.
Series A^2 (fonds 'de Suède') 80, 81.
Series A^3 (fonds divers) 103, 125.
Series A^4 (cartons) 35 bis, 46, 56, 60–72.
Series B^1 (armées de la subdivision nord) 69.
Series B^{1*} (armées de la subdivision nord – registres) 177.
Series B^2 (armées de la subdivision est) 48, 49.
Series B^{12*} (correspondance du gouvernement – registres) 24, 47.
Series B^{13} (correspondance militaire générale) 25, 41–3, 51, 60, 63.
Series B^{13*} (corespondance militaire générale – registres) 31.
Series 1 K (fonds privés) 19, 440, 477, 644, 656.
Series MR (mémoires et reconnaissances) 1160, 1161, 1706–18, 1723, 1725–8, 1765, 1768, 1781, 1787, 1790–92, 1907, 1937–39, 1944, 1947, 1949, 1955, 1963, 1984, 1997, 1998, 2002, 2008, 2009, 2015, 2017, 2018, 2051, 2164, 2189, 2190.
Series X^b (infanterie) 23, 29, 35, 48, 53, 57, 59, 73, 75, 78, 90, 91, 106, 125–139, 166, 168, 170, 174, 176, 178, 179, 183, 184, 186, 190, 197, 203–7, 209, 211, 213, 214, 216, 217, 219, 226, 253, 260, 264, 265, 293, 298, 300, 347, 348, 411, 412, 425, 426, 431–4, 489, 490, 784–800.
Series X^c (cavalerie) 1–7, 29 bis, 34, 60, 98, 100, 134, 135, 252, 253, 298.
Series X^h (bataillons et régiments étrangers) 8, 11.
Series X^k (troupes spéciales) 38, 39.
Series X^m (Garde nationale) 1, 2.
Series X^o (écoles militaires) 1, 9, 10, 25, 173, 174, 185, 218–34, 254–6, 271, 280, 283.
Series X^s (organisation générale de l'armée et administration centrale) 4, 5.
Series X^v (volontaires nationaux) 1–24, 31–3, 37.
Series X^w (volontaires nationaux – archives départementaux) 1, 4, 30, 31, 42, 43, 46, 47, 51–3, 65, 67, 69, 76, 89, 100–3.
Series Y^a (documents collectifs ou d'intérêt général) 36, 57, 74, 145–9, 157–64, 208, 224, 228, 229, 234, 235, 238, 242–8, 250, 251, 269, 286, 307, 309, 319, 349.
Series Y^b (contrôles des officiers) 25, 67, 75, 76, 374, 380, 386, 398, 404, 409, 411, 425, 426, 428, 429, 432, 433, 446, 447, 719, 722, 880, 888, 900, 909, 910, 927, 928, 934, 946, 948, 958.
Series 2 Y^b (contrôles des officiers) 119–21, 221–5, 252–6, 267–75, 375–8, 401, 677–9, 728–30, 974–6, 1100–4, 1115–17, 1123, 1124.
Series 4 Y^b (École spéciale militaire – Saint-Germain, La Flèche) 29–32, 193, 375.
Series 20 Y^c (contrôles des officiers – garde impériale) 5 bis, 6, 9, 11, 12, 15, 16, 38, 41, 42, 48, 134, 136, 138, 143, 147, 149, 150, 174, 175.
Classement général alphabétique – officiers, 1791–1841.
Dossiers personnels – généraux de division.
Dossiers personnels – généraux de brigade.

Ordonnances militaires.
Travail du roi.

Bibliothèque du Ministère de la guerre (B.M.G.)

A.i.b. 1273. "Projet d'un code militaire de France." 3 vols. n.p., n.d.
A.i.b. 1377. Grandpré, M. le baron de. "Mémoires sur les moyens qu'il seroit facile d'employer pour parvenir surement, promptement, sans boulversement, et sans commotion à toute la perfection dont le militaire de France est susceptible; et pour établir la stabilité si désirée dans sa constitution et dans les ordonnances qui le concernent." n.p., 1787.
A.i.c. 279. Langeron, M. le comte de. "Considérations sur l'enseignement et l'éducation des élèves de l'école royale militaire vers l'année 1771." n.p., 1777.
A.i.c. 288. Rocquancourt. "Extrait d'un mémoire sur les écoles militaires et sur les formes de l'existence de la force publique dans les gouvernements constitutionnels." n.p., n.d.
A.i.e. 205. "Constitution de la cavalerie." n.p., 1789.
A.i.m. 148. "Réflexions militaires." n.p., n.d.
A.i.m. 149. "Essay d'un jeune militaire." n.p., n.d.
A.i.m. 151. "De l'ancienne administration de la guerre." n.p., n.d.
Archives historiques supplémentaires. 173–6, "Procès-verbaux du code militaire." 4 vols., 1781–84.

Bibliothèque du génie (B.G.)

In-4 33. Thieffries-Beauvoir, M. le comte de, "Plan et principes élémentaires de constitution d'armée, d'institution militaire, et d'économie politique." n.p., 1787.
In-8 11. "Mémoire pour servir à l'instruction des chasseurs à cheval." n.p., 1777.
In-fol 225. Lomet, "Mémoires divers de Lomet." n.p., n.d.
In-fol 286. "Ecole de Mars."
In-fol 287. "Ecole de Mars: registre des objets relatifs à l'instruction des fortifications et auquel sont joints les dix cahiers de leçons, ainsi que le cours révolutionnaire d'administration militaire pour servir à l'Ecole de Mars."

Archives départementales des Bouches-du-Rhone (A.D. Bouches-du-Rhone)
Series C (intendance) 2844–50.

Archives départementales du Bas-Rhin (A.D. Bas-Rhin)
Series 1 R (instruction publique) 9.

Archives départementales du Cher (A.D. Cher)
Series J (documents entrés par voies extraordinaires) 2192. "Mémoires particuliers de M. de Bouthilier, maréchal de camp des armées du roy et depuis major-général de l'armée de Condé." n.p., 1810.

Archives municipales de Strasbourg (A.M.S.)
Fonds des Jacobins. 2–7, 9, 11, 12, 15.

Bibliothèque de l'Université de Strasbourg (B.U.S.)
Manuscrits. 448, 450–2, 486, 490, 505.

Published primary sources

L'Académie militaire, ou les héros subalternes (Amsterdam, 1749).
Adresse des bas-officiers et soldats du régiment de Provence à la nation et au roi (n.p., n.d.).
Adresse du régiment d'Auxonne artillerie à l'Assemblée nationale (Metz, 1790).
Adresse des sous-officiers et soldats du 1er régiment d'infanterie, ci-devant Colonel-Général en garnison à Dunkirk, à toute l'armée (Dunkirk, 1791).
Anthoine, François-Paul-Nicolas, *Discours sur le licenciement des officiers de l'armée de terre, prononcé devant la société des amis de la constitution, séante aux jacobins* (Paris, 1791).
——. *Nouveaux développemens sur le licenciement du corps des officiers de l'armée de terre, projet de décrêt, et réponse à M. Dubois de Crancé* (Paris, 1791).
Archives parlementaires de 1787 à 1860, ed. J. Madival and E. Laurent (Paris, 1867–1913, 1985).
Arcq, Philippe-Auguste de Sainte-Foix, chevalier de, *La Noblesse militaire, ou le patriote françois* (n.p., 1756).
Argenteuil, Edmé le Bascle, marquis de, *Protestation* (n.p., 1790).
L'Armée française au conseil de la guerre (n.p., 1789).
Audoin, Xavier, *Histoire de l'administration de la guerre* (Paris, 1811).
Aux militaires (n.p., n.d.).
Avis important à la veritable armée française, avec le tableau de son courage et de son dévouement (Paris, n.d.).

Barnave, Antoine, *Œuvres de Barnave*, 4 vols., ed. Alphonse-Marc-Marcellin-Thomas Bérénger de la Drôme (Paris, 1843).
——. *De la révolution et de la constitution* (Grenoble, 1988).
Barras, Paul-François-Jean-Nicolas, *Mémoires de Barras*, 4 vols. (Paris, 1895–96).
Barrès, Jean-Baptiste, *Memoirs of a French Napoleonic Officer*, trans. Bernard Miall (London, 1988).
Barthélemy, François, *Mémoires de Barthélelmy, 1768–1819* (Paris, 1914).
Beaulieu, Jacques de Mercoyrol de, *Campagnes*, ed. le marquis de Vogüé and Auguste le Sourd (Paris, 1915).
Belleval, Louis-René de, *Souvenirs d'un chevau-léger de la Garde du roi* (Paris, 1866).
Berriat, H., *Législation militaire, ou recueil méthodique et raisonné des lois, décrêts, arrêtés, règlemens, et instructions actuellement en vigueur sur toutes les branches de l'état militaire* (Alexandria, 1812).
Berthier, Louis-Alexandre, *Mémoires du maréchal Berthier, prince de Neuchâtel et de Wagram, major-général des armées françaises* (Paris, 1827).
Besenval, Pierre-Victor, baron de, *Mémoires*, ed. M. F. Barrière (Paris, 1846).
Bèze, marquis de, *Réflexions sur les préjugés militaires* (Turin, 1779).
Bohan, François-Philippe Loubat, baron de, *Examen critique du militaire françois, suivi des principes qui doivent déterminer sa constitution, sa discipline, et son instruction*, 3 vols. (Geneva, 1781).
Bombelles, Marc-Marie, marquis de, *Journal*, 3 vols. (Geneva, 1993).

Bonaparte, Napoléon, *Correspondance de Napoléon 1er, publiée par ordre de l'empereur Napoléon III* (Paris, 1858).
——. *Manuscrits inédits, 1786–1791,* ed. Frédéric Masson and Guido Biagi (Paris, 1910).
——. *Napoléon: pensées politiques et sociales,* ed. Adrien Dansette (Paris, 1969).
Boussanelle, *Aux soldats* (Paris, 1786).
Bouthillier, Charles-Léon, marquis de, *Plan de constitution militaire* (Paris, 1790).
Brincourt, Henri-Augustin, *Lettres du général Brincourt (1823–1909)* (Paris, 1923).
Burke, Edmond, *Reflections on the Revolution in France* (Oxford, 1993).

Cahiers de doléances: Eure-et-Loir, 2 vols., ed. Denis Jeanson (Tours, 1990).
Cahiers de doléances: Indre-et-Loire, 3 vols., ed. Denis Jeanson (Tours, 1991).
Cahiers de doléances: Loir-et-Cher, 2 vols., ed. Denis Jeanson (Tours, 1989).
Cahiers de doléances: Loiret, 3 vols., ed. Denis Jeanson (Tours, 1989).
Les Cahiers de doléances du tiers-état de la sénéchaussée de Nimes pour les états-généraux de 1789, ed. Alain Rouquette (Nimes, 1989).
Castelnau, *Lettres du baron de Castelnau, officier de carabiniers, 1728–1793,* ed. le baron de Blay de Gaïx (Paris, 1911).
Cerutti, J. A. J., *Correspondance abrégée entre Mme.*** et M. Cerutti sur la noblesse, sur le décrêt de l'assemblée nationale, et sur les observations de M. Necker concernant les titres, les noms, et les armoiries* (Paris, 1790).
Choiseul, duc de, *Mémoires,* ed. Fernand Calmettes (Paris, 1904).
Churchill, F. V. S., *Réimpression de l'état militaire de France pour l'année 1789 avec notes généalogiques et historiques* (Carnac, 1913).
Code militaire, ou recueil méthodique des décrêts relatifs aux troupes de ligne et à la gendarmerie nationale (Paris, 1793).
Considérations sur le décrêt de l'assemblée nationale, relatif à la noblesse héréditaire, aux noms, aux titres, et aux armoires (n.p., n.d.).
Correspondance de deux généraux sur divers sujets, publiée par le citoyen T*** (Paris, 1801).
Correspondance particulière du comte de Saint-Germain ... avec M. Paris du Verney, 2 vols., (London, 1789).

Dampmartin, Anne-Henri-Cabot, vicomte de, *Coup d'œil sur les campagnes des émigrés* (Paris, 1818).
——. *Idées sur quelques objets militaires adressées aux jeunes officiers* (Avignon, 1788).
——. *Mémoires sur divers événémens de la Révolution et de l'émigration,* 2 vols., (Paris, 1825).
Les Derniers soupirs de la noblesse (n.p., n.d.).
De la destruction de la noblesse en France (n.p., 1790).
Dictionnaire de l'Académie française, 4th ed., 2 vols., (Paris, 1762).
Discours de Maximilien Robespierre sur le licenciement des officiers de l'armée (Paris, 1791).
Dissertation sur la subordination, avec des réflexions sur l'art militaire (Avignon, 1754).
A Documentary Survey of Napoleonic France, ed. Eric A. Arnold, Jr. (Lanham, 1994).
Doléances du comité des chefs d'escadron, capitaines, lieutenants, sous-lieutenants de la brigade de cavalerie composée des régiments Royal et Artois (n.p., 1789).

Doléances militaires: régiment de Guyenne infanterie (Nîmes, 1789).
Dubois-Crancé, Edmond-Louis-Alexis, *Analyse de la Révolution française*, ed. Théodore Jung (Paris, 1884).
Dumas, Mathieu, comte, *Souvenirs du lieutenant-général le comte Mathieu Dumas de 1770 à 1836, publiés par son fils*, 3 vols. (Paris, 1839).

Ecole historique et morale du soldat et de l'officier, 3 vols. (Paris, 1788).
Encyclopédie, ou dictionnaire raisonné des sciences, des arts, et des métiers, ed. Denis Diderot, 17 vols. (Geneva, 1772–4).
Encyclopédie méthodique: art militaire, 4 vols. (Paris, 1784–98).
Encyclopédie militaire, par une société d'anciens officiers et de gens de lettres: ouvrage périodique (n.p., 1770).
Estourmel, L. M., marquis de, *Compte rendu par le marquis d'Estourmel, député de la noblesse du Cambrésis à ses comettans, le 20 juin 1790* (n.p., 1790).
Etrennes au militaire françois, ou analyse raisonné de l'ordonnance du roi du 25 mars 1776, portant règlement sur l'administration de tous les corps, tant d'infanterie que cavalerie, dragons et hussards, sur l'habillement, les recrues, les rengagemens, remonte, la discipline, etc. (London, n.d.).
Examen des règlemens des 9 et 23 octobre 1787 par rapport à l'ordonnance du roi du 6 mai 1814, portant établissement d'un conseil de la guerre (Paris, 1814).
Extrait d'une lettre écrite de Paris, en réponse à celle d'un lieutenant-colonel d'infanterie à son régiment (Paris, 1789).
Extrait du procès-verbal de l'assemblée générale des officiers, bas-officiers, et soldats du corps royal de l'artillerie présens à Strasbourg le 27 mai 1790 (n.p., 1790).
Faré, Charles A., *Lettres d'un jeune officier à sa mère, 1803–1814* (Paris, 1889).

Ferrières, Charles-Elie, marquis de, *Marquis de Ferrières, correspondance inédite (1789, 1790, 1791)*, ed. Henri Carré (Paris, 1932).
Fontette-Sommery, comte de, *Opinion d'un gentilhomme de Bourgogne sur ce qui s'est passée à l'assemblée de la noblesse de Berry, relativement à M. le comte de Guibert, en mars 1789* (n.p., 1789).

Gerbey, Joseph Servan de, *Adresse du ministre de la guerre à ses concitoyens* (Paris, 1792).
———. *Le Soldat-citoyen, ou vues patriotiques sur la manière la plus avantageuse de pourvoir à la défense du royaume* (Switzerland, 1780)
Gougon, *Lettre à M. le comte de Guibert* (n.p., 1789).
Gournay, B. C. *Journal militaire* (Paris, 1790–99).
———. *Supplément à la collection du Journal militaire* (Paris, VII–XIII).
Guibert, Jacques-Antoine-Hippolyte, comte de, *Ecrits militaires, 1772–1790*, ed. General Menard (Paris, 1977).
———. *Les Œuvres de Guibert, publiées par sa veuve*, 5 vols. (Paris, 1803).
———. *Précis de ce qui s'est passé à mon égard à l'Assemblée du Berry* (n.p., 1789).
———. *Projet de discours d'un citoyen aux trois ordres de l'Assemblée du Berry* (n.p., 1789).
———. *Stratégiques*, ed. Jean-Paul Charnay (Paris, n.d.).

Hasard, P. N. J., *Réclamations sur le collège de Nanterre* (n.p., 1789).
Hoche, Louis-Lazare, *Un mémoire de Hoche sur la réorganisation de nos armées en l'an V* (Paris, an V).

Jassaud, L. C. A de. *Invitation à la noblesse française* (Paris, 1790).
Journal militaire dédié à M. le frère du roi (Paris, 1784).

L. C. D. B., *Réflexions sur le décrêt qui ôte aux mains du roi la disposition des places de sous-lieutenant* (n.p., n.d.).
Lafayette, Marie-Paul-Joseph-Roch-Ives-Gilbert de Motier, marquis de, *Mémoires, correspondance, et manuscrits du général Lafayette, publiés par sa famille*, 6 vols. (Brussels, 1837–39).
La Gravière, marquis de, *Lettre d'un officier à M. D***, maréchal des camps et armées du roi, ci-devant commandant général des isles de France et de Bourbon* (n.p., 1790).
Lambert, *Abolition de la noblesse héréditaire en France, proposée à l'assemblée nationale par un philanthrope* (Paris, 1790).
Lameth, Alexandre-Théodore-Victor de, *Histoire de l'assemblée constituante*, 2 vols. (Paris, 1828).
——. *Rapport fait à l'assemblée constituante sur l'avancement militaire avec des observations préliminaires* (Paris, 1818).
Lameth, Théodore de, *Mémoires*, ed. Eugene Welvert (Paris, 1913).
——. *Notes et souvenirs de Théodore de Lameth, faisant suite à ses mémoires* (Paris, 1914).
La Tour-du-Pin, Henriette-Lucie Dillon, marquise de, *Recollections of the Revolution and Empire*, trans. Walter Geer (New York, 1920).
La Tour-du-Pin de la Charce, Charles-Humber-René, marquis de, *Feuillets de la vie militaire sous le second empire, 1855–1870* (Paris, 1910).
Leissac, M. de, *De l'esprit militaire* (London, 1783).
Lettre d'un citoyen à MM. du Conseil de la guerre (n.p., 1789).
Lettre d'un colonel aux officiers du régiment qu'il commande (Paris, 1791).
Lettre du régiment de Berwick à Monsieur et à Monseigneur le comte d'Artois, 23 juillet 1791 (n.p., 1791).
Lettres adressées au roi et au ministre de la guerre par le régiment d'Armagnac au sujet de l'opinion de M. Dubois de Crancé sur la constitution de l'armée (n.p., 1790).
Lettres militaires (Paris, 1779).
Lévis-Mirepoix, comte de, marquis de Beauharnais, and abbé Perrotin de Barmond, *Noblesse* (Paris, 1790).
Locke, John, *Some Thoughts Concerning Education* (Oxford, 1989).
Loisirs d'un officier d'infanterie, ou réflexions sur la discipline militaire conciliée avec l'esprit national (Brussels, 1784).

Malartic, vicomte de, *Protestation de M. le vicomte de Malartic, député de la noblesse de la sénéchaussée de la Rochelle* (n.p., 1790).
Malouet, Pierre-Victor, *Mémoires de Malouet*, 2 vols. (Paris, 1874).
Malzet, Jacques de, *Le Militaire citoyen, ou l'emploi des hommes* (Amsterdam, 1760).

Marbot, Jean-Baptiste-Antoine-Marcelin, *Mémoires du général baron de Marbot*, 3 vols. (Paris, 1983).
Marie-Antoinette et Barnave: correspondance secrète, ed. Alma Soderhjelm (Paris, 1934).
Marmont, Auguste-Frédéric-Louis Viesse de, *Mémoires du maréchal Marmont, duc de Ragusse, de 1792 à 1841*, 9 vols. (Paris, 1857).
———. *The Spirit of Military Institutions*, trans. Frank Schaller (Westport, CT, 1974).
Marmontel, Jean-François, *Poème héroique sur l'établissement de l'Ecole royale militaire* (n.p., n.d.).
Maubert, abbé, *L'esprit et l'excellence de la profession militaire selon les principes de vertu et de religion* (Paris, 1774).
Meilhan, Gabriel Senac de, *Des principes et des causes de la Révolution en France*, ed. Michel Delon (Paris, 1987).
Mémoire sur l'éducation et la discipline militaire (Villefranche, 1785).
Mémoire sur les troupes provinciales (Paris, 1790).
Mémoires historiques concernant l'ordre royal et militaire de Saint-Louis et l'institution du mérite militaire (Paris, 1785).
Miot de Mélito, André-François, comte de, *Mémoires*, 3 vols. (Paris, 1858).
Molé, Louis-Mathieu, *Souvenirs d'un témoin de la Révolution et de l'Empire (1791–1803)*, ed. le marquis de Noailles (Paris, 1943).
Moleville, Antoine-François de Bertrand de, *Mémoires particuliers pour servir à l'histoire de la fin du règne de Louis XVI* (Geneva, 1976).
Montbarey, Alexandre-Léonard de Saint-Mauris, prince de, *Mémoires*, 3 vols. (Paris, 1826–27).
Montboissier-Beaufort-Canillac, P. C., comte de, *Protestation* (Paris, 1790).
Montesquieu, Charles-Louis de Secondat, baron de, *De l'esprit des loix*, 2 vols. (Paris, 1748).
Montesquiou-Fezensac, Anatole, comte de, *Souvenirs sur la Révolution, l'Empire, la Restauration, et le règne de Louis-Philippe* (Paris, 1961).
Montlosier, François-Dominique de Reynaud, comte de, *Souvenirs d'un émigré (1791–1798)* (Paris, 1951).
Montverd, A. Guynet de, *Projet, ou nouveau système militaire, pour donner des moyens sûrs de tirer parti des gens de guerre dans les différents âges de la vie humaine* (n.p., 1771).
Morand, Charles-Antoine-Louis-Alexis, comte de, *De l'armée selon la Charte, et d'après l'expérience des dernières guerres* (Paris, 1829).

Napoléon: manuscrits inédits, 1786–1791, ed. Frédéric Masson and Guido Biagi (Paris, 1914).
Napoléon: pensées politiques et sociales, ed. Adrien Dansette (Paris, 1969).
Noblesse de France, elle doit incessamment aller au secours de l'état (n.p., n.d.).
Nouvelle maison d'éducation militaire pour la jeune noblesse, établie à Nanterre, par brevet du roi et sous la protection du gouvernement (n.p., 1789).

Observations sur l'administration des corps (Paris, 1815).
Observations sur le règlement du 22 mai 1782, concernant les preuves de noblesse exigées pour entrer au service (London, 1789).

Opinion de M. de Cazalès sur le serment exigé des officiers de l'armée (Paris, 1791).
Opinion de MM. de Cazalès et de Bouthillier, députés à l'assemblée nationale, sur l'engagement d'honneur exigé des troupes (Paris, 1791).
Opinion de Montlosier sur le nouveau serment demandé à l'armée (Paris, 1791).
Opinion de Stanislas Clermont-Tonnerre sur la question du serment individuel à exiger des officiers (Paris, 1791).

Plan général d'organisation de l'armée, arrêté par le roi le 7 juillet 1790 (Paris, 1790).
Porterie, M. de la, *Institutions militaires pour la cavalerie et les dragons* (Paris, 1754).
Préjugés militaires, par un officier autrichien (Kralovelhota, 1783).
Préval, Claude-Antoine-Hippolyte, vicomte de, *De l'avancement militaire dans l'intérêt de la monarchie* (Paris, 1824).
Projet d'éducation militaire nationale (Paris, 1789).
Projet de lettre à un citoyen, sur son discours projeté aux trois ordres de l'assemblée de Berry (n.p., 1789).
Protestation de M. de Grosbois, député de la noblesse du bailliage de Besançon, contre le décrêt rendu dans la séance du samedi 19 juin 1790 (n.p., 1790).
Protestation motivée de M. de Vauquelin, né marquis de Vrigny, député de la noblesse du bailliage d'Alençon (Paris, 1790).
Prudhomme, L. M., *Résumé général, ou extrait des cahiers des pouvoirs, instructions, demandes, et doléances*, 2 vols. (Paris, 1789).

Ramel, Jean-Pierre, *Journal de l'adjudant-général Ramel* (London, 1799).
Recueil de documents relatifs à la convocation des états-généraux de 1789, 4 vols., ed. Armand Brette (Paris, 1894–1915).
Recueil de listes des officiers des corps de cavalerie réformés de la maison du roi par ordre d'ancienneté pour servir au remplacement dans tous les autres corps (Paris, 1791).
Recueil de listes des officiers des corps de l'infanterie réformés de la maison du roi par ordre d'ancienneté pour servir au remplacement dans tous les autres corps (Paris, 1791).
Réclamation d'un vieux soldat à l'assemblée nationale (Paris, 1790).
Refutation de l'opinion de M. Necker relativement au décrêt de l'assemblée nationale concernant les titres, les noms, et les armoiries, par un citoyen du district de Cordeliers (Paris, I).
Réimpression de l'ancien Moniteur (Paris, 1858–70).
Réponse au numéro 69 de Marat, soi-disant l'ami du peuple, par les citoyens-soldats des bataillons nationaux casernés à Paris (Paris, 1792).
Le Reveil de la noblesse (n.p., n.d.).
Robespierre, Maximilien, *Discours sur le licenciement des officiers de l'armée* (Paris, 1791).
———. *Œuvres de Maximilien Robespierre, avec une notice historique, des notes, et des commentaires*, vol. 2, ed. Laponneraye (New York, reprint originally published 1840).
Roederer, Pierre-Louis, comte de, *Mémoires sur la Révolution, le Consulat, et l'Empire*, ed. Octave Aubry (Paris, 1942).
———. *Œuvres du comte P. L. Roederer*, 7 vols. (Paris, 1858).
Romain, Félix, comte de, *Souvenirs d'un officier royaliste*, 3 vols. (Paris, 1824–29).

Saint-Germain, Claude-Louis, comte de, *Mémoires* (Switzerland, 1779).
Salavile, *De l'organisation d'un état monarchique, ou considérations sur ... la monarchie française* (n.p., 1789).
Saxe, Maurice, comte de, *Les Rêveries, ou mémoires sur l'art de la guerre* (The Hague, 1756).
——. *Les Rêveries, ou notes et commentaires sur les parties sublimes de l'art de la guerre* (Paris, 1763).
Memoirs of Louis-Philippe, Comte de Ségur, ed. Eveline Cruickshanks (London, 1960).
Ségur, Philippe-Paul, comte de, *Napoleon's Russian Campaign*, trans. J. David Townsend (Alexandria, VA, 1965).
Ségur, Pierre-Marie-Maurice-Henri, marquis de, *Le Maréchal de Ségur (1724–1801), ministre de la guerre sous Louis XVI* (Paris, 1895).
Simon, Jean-Baptiste-Charles, *Vérités et idées d'un militaire* (Paris, V).
La Société des Jacobins: recueil de documents pour l'histoire du club des Jacobins de Paris, 6 vols., ed. F. A. Aulard (Paris, 1889–95).
Le Soldat aux états-généraux (Paris, 1789).
Les Soldats composant les troupes françaises à l'assemblée nationale (n.p., 1789).

Thibaudeau, Antoine-Claire, *Bonaparte and the Consulate*, trans. G. K. Fortescue (New York, 1908).
Thoumas, Charles-Antoine, *Causeries militaires* (Paris, 1889–1913).
Très-humbles représentations des officiers de fortune, à messieurs de l'Assemblée nationale (Paris, 1790).
Trochu, Louis-Jules, *L'Armée française en 1867* (Paris, 1870).

Vaissière, Pierre de, *Lettres d'aristocrates* (Paris, 1907).
Vaublanc, Vincent-Marie Viénot, comte de, *Mémoires sur la Révolution française et recherches sur les causes qui ont amené la Révolution de 1789 et celles qui l'ont suivie*, 4 vols. (Paris, 1883).
——. *Souvenirs*, 2 vols. (Paris, 1841).
Vigny, Alfred de, *Servitude et grandeur militaires* (Paris, 1835).
Vigo-Roussillon, François, *Journal de campagne (1793–1837)* (Paris, 1981).
Vœu militaire: régiment de Cambrésis, infanterie françoise (Bayonne, 1789).
Vœux d'un citoyen pour le militaire françois (n.p., n.d.).

Wimpfen, Félix-Louis, baron de, *Commentaires des mémoires de M. le comte de Saint-Germain* (London, 1780).

Secondary sources

Abbot, Andrew, *The System of Professions: An Essay on the Division of Expert Labor* (Chicago, 1988).
Actes du colloque Girondins et Montagnards (Sorbonne, 14 décembre 1975), ed. Albert Soboul (Paris, 1980).
Anderson, Perry, *Lineages of the Absolutist State* (London, 1974).
Artz, Frederick B., *The Development of Technical Education in France, 1500–1850* (Cambridge, MA, 1966).

L'Aude, Jean-Pierre Fabre de, *Histoire secrète du Directoire*, 4 vols. (Paris, 1832).
Aulard, F. V. A., *La Société des Jacobins: recueil de documents pour l'histoire du club des Jacobins de Paris* (Paris, 1889).

Bacquet, *L'Infanterie française au XVIIIème siècle* (Paris, 1907).
Baldwin, William Clinton, "The Beginnings of the Revolution and the Mutiny of the Royal Garrison in Nancy: *L'Affaire de Nancy*, 1790" (University of Michigan Ph.D. dissertation, Ann Arbor, 1973).
Barnard, H. C., *Education and the French Revolution* (London, 1969).
Béchu, Philippe, "Noblesse d'épée et tradition militaire au XVIIIème siècle," *Histoire, économie, et société*, 2 (1983), 507–48.
Beck, Thomas, "The French Revolution and the Nobility: A Reconsideration," *Journal of Social History* 15 (1981), 219–33.
Bécourt-Foch, C., "Destinées des condisciples de Napoléon à l'Ecole royale militaire de Paris," *Revue internationale d'histoire militaire* 37 (1977), 77–87.
Bell, David, *Lawyers and Citizens: The Making of a Political Elite in Old Regime France* (New York, 1994).
Bergeron, Louis, *France under Napoleon*, trans. R. R. Palmer (Princeton, 1981).
———. and Guy Chaussinand-Nogaret, *Les "masses de granit": cent mille notables du Premier empire* (Paris, 1979).
———. *Grands notables du Premier empire*, 23 vols. (Paris, 1978–95).
———. and Robert Forster, "Les Notables du 'grand empire' en 1810" *Annales E.S.C.*, 26 (1971), 1052–75.
Bergerot, Bernard, *Daru: intendant général de la grande armée* (Paris, 1991).
Bertaud, Jean-Paul, "Enquête sur les volontaires de 1792," *Annales historiques de la Révolution française*, 272 (1988), 151–70.
———. "Napoleon's Officers," *Past and Present*, 112 (1986), 91–112.
———. "La 'petite guerre' des honneurs sous Napoléon," *L'Histoire*, 66 (1984), 64–70.
———. "Le Recrutement et l'avancement des officiers de la Révolution," *Annales historiques de la Révolution française*, 210 (1972), 513–36.
———. *La Révolution armée: les soldats-citoyens et la Révolution française* (Paris, 1979).
———. "Tableau d'organisation des demi-brigades conformément au décrêt du 12 août 1793," (unpublished, Paris, 1975).
———. "The Volunteers of 1792," *Reshaping France: Town, Country, and Region during the French Revolution*, ed. Alan Forrest and Peter Jones (Manchester, 1991).
———. and Daniel Reichel, *Atlas de la Révolution française*, vol. 3, *L'Armée et la guerre* (Paris, 1989).
Best, Geoffrey, *Honour among Men and Nations: Transformations of an Idea* (Toronto, 1982).
———. *War and Society in Western Europe, 1770–1870* (Leicester, 1982).
Beyond the Terror: Essays in French Regional and Social History, 1794–1815, ed. Gwynne Lewis and Colin Lucas (Cambridge, 1983).
Bien, David D., "Aristocratie," in *Dictionnaire critique de la Révolution française*, ed. François Furet and Mona Ozouf (Paris, 1988), 639–51.
———. "The Army in the French Enlightenment: Reform, Reaction, and Revolution," *Past and Present*, 85 (1979), 68–98.

———. "Manufacturing Nobles: The Chancelleries in France to 1789," *Journal of Modern History*, 61 (1989), 445–86.

———. "Military Education in Eighteenth-Century France: Technical and Non-Technical Determinants," *Science, Technology, and Warfare: Proceedings of the Third Military History Symposium, U.S. Air Force Academy, 8–9 May 1969*, ed. Monte D. Wright and Lawrence J. Paszek (Washington, DC, 1971), 51–9.

———. "La Réaction aristocratique avant 1789: l'exemple de l'armée," *Annales E.S.C.*, 29 (1974), 23–48, 505–34.

Blanning, T. C. W., *The Origins of the French Revolutionary Wars* (London, 1986).

Blaufarb, Rafe, "The *Ancien Régime* Origins of Napoleonic Social Reconstruction," *French History*, 14 (2000), 408–23.

———. "Le Conseil de la guerre: aspects sociaux de la réforme militaire après l'édit de Ségur," *Revue d'histoire moderne et contemporaine*, 43 (1996), 446–63.

———. "Démocratie et professionalisme: l'avancement par l'élection dans l'armée française, 1760–1815," *Annales historiques de la Révolution française*, 310 (1997), 601–25.

———. "Noble Privilege and Absolutist State Building: French Military Administration after the Seven Years' War," *French Historical Studies*, 24 (2001), 223–46.

Bluche, François, *Les Honneurs de la cour* (Paris, 1958).

Bodinier, Gilbert, *Les Officiers de l'armée royale combattants de la Guerre d'indépendance des Etats-Unis* (Paris, 1983).

Boisnard, Luc, *La Noblesse dans la tourmente (1774–1802)* (Paris, 1992).

Bourdieu, Pierre, *La noblesse d'état: grandes écoles et esprit de corps* (Paris, 1989).

———. and Jean-Claude Passeron, *Reproduction in Education, Society, and Culture*, trans. Richard Nice (London, 1977).

Brancourt, Jean-Pierre, "Un théoricien de la société au XVIIIème siècle: le chevalier d'Arcq," *Revue historique*, 508 (1973), 337–62.

Briere, Annie, *Le Duc de Choiseul: la France sous Louis XV* (Paris, 1986).

Brown, Howard G., "A Discredited Regime: The Directory and Army Contracting," *French History*, 4 (1990), 48–76.

———. "Politics, Professionalism, and the Fate of Army Generals after Thermidor," *French Historical Studies*, 19 (1995), 133–52.

———. *War, Revolution, and the Bureaucratic State: Politics and Army Administration in France, 1791–1799* (Oxford, 1995).

Buttet, Henry-Joseph, "Le Comité de la brigade de cavalerie en garnison à Strasbourg (août 1789)," *Actes du 92ème congrès national des sociétés savantes, histoire moderne, Strasbourg–Colmar, 1967* (Paris, 1970), 363–94.

Camus, Michel, *Histoire des Saint-Cyriens* (Paris, 1980).

Caron, Pierre, *Les Papiers des comités militaires de la Constituante, de la Législative, et de la Convention (1789–an IV)* (Paris, 1912).

Carré, Henri, *La Noblesse de France et l'opinion publique au XVIIIème siècle* (Paris, 1920).

Censer, Jack, *Prelude to Power: The Parisian Radical Press, 1789–1791* (Baltimore, 1976).

Cerutti, Simona, *La Ville et les métiers: naissance d'un langage corporatif* (Paris, 1990).

Chagniot, Jean, "Une panique: les gardes françaises à Dettingen (27 juin 1743)," *Revue d'histoire moderne et contemporaine*, 20 (1972), 78–95.

———. *Paris et l'armée au XVIIIème siècle: étude politique et sociale* (Paris, 1985).

Chalmin, Pierre, *L'Officier français de 1815 à 1870* (Paris, 1957).

Chartier, Roger, *The Cultural Origins of the French Revolution*, trans. Lydia G. Cochrane (Durham, NC, 1991).

———. "Un recrutement scolaire au XVIIIème siècle: l'Ecole royale du génie de Mézières," *Revue d'histoire moderne et contemporaine*, 20 (1973), 353–75.

Chaussinand-Nogaret, Guy, *The French Nobility in the Eighteenth Century: From Feudalism to Enlightenment*, trans. William Doyle (New York, 1985).

Chill, Emanuel, *Power, Property, and History: Barnave's Introduction to the French Revolution and Other Writings* (New York, 1971).

Chilly, Lucien de, *Le Premier ministre constitutionnel de la guerre: La Tour-du-Pin: les origines de l'armée nouvelle sous la Constituante* (Paris, 1909).

Choppin, Henri, *Insurrections militaires en 1790* (Paris, 1903).

Chuquet, Arthur, *L'Ecole de Mars* (Paris, 1899).

———. *La Jeunesse de Napoléon*, 3 vols. (Paris, 1897–99).

Church, Clive H., *Revolution and Red Tape: The French Ministerial Bureaucracy 1770–1850* (Oxford, 1981).

Colin, Jean-Lambert-Alphonse, *The Transformations of War*, trans. L. H. R. Pope-Hennesy (London, 1912).

———. *L'Education militaire de Napoléon* (Paris, 1901).

Cormack, William S., *Revolution and Political Conflict in the French Navy, 1789–1794* (Cambridge, 1995).

Corvisier, André, *L'Armée française de la fin du XVIIème siècle au ministère de Choiseul*, 2 vols. (Paris, 1964).

———. *Armées et sociétés en Europe de 1494 à 1789* (Paris, 1976).

———. "Hiérarchie militaire et hiérarchie sociale à la veille de la Révolution," *Revue internationale d'histoire militaire*, 30 (1970), 77–91.

Decoufle, André, "L'Aristocratie française devant l'opinion publique à la veille de la Révolution (1787–1789)," *Etudes d'histoire économique et sociale du XVIIIème siècle*, ed. Robert Besnier and Robert Villers (Paris, 1966), 1–52.

Desan, Suzanne, *Reclaiming the Sacred: Lay Religion and Popular Politics in Revolutionary France* (Ithaca, 1990).

Deschard, Bernard, *L'Armée et la Révolution: du service du roi au service de la nation* (Paris, 1989).

Devlin, Jonathan D., "The Directory and the Politics of Military Command: The Army of the Interior in South-East France," *French History*, 4 (1990), 199–223.

Devos, Jean-Claude, and Pierre Waksman, "Les Compagnies d'ordonnance de la guerre de sept ans à leur dissolution (1788)," *Revue d'histoire moderne et contemporaine*, 20 (1973), 37–57.

Dictionnaire critique de la Révolution française, ed. François Furet and Mona Ozouf (Paris, 1988).

Doyle, William, "Was there an Aristocratic Reaction in Pre-Revolutionary France?," *Past and Present*, 57 (1972), 97–122.

———. *Origins of the French Revolution* (Oxford, 1980, 1999 (later ed.)).
Dufay, Pierre, *Les Sociétés populaires et l'armée (1791–1794): documents inédits* (Paris, 1913).
Duffy, Christopher, *The Military Experience in the Age of Reason* (London, 1987).
Dufraisse, Roger, "Les Notables de la rive gauche du Rhin à l'époque napoléonienne," *Revue d'histoire moderne et contemporaine*, 17 (1970), 758–76.
Dumont, Georges, *Les Bataillons de volontaires nationaux, 1791 (cadres et historiques)* (Paris, 1914).
Dupuy, Roger, *La Garde nationale et les débuts de la Révolution en Ile-et-Vilaine (1789–mars 1793)* (Rennes, 1972).
Durye, Pierre, "Les Chevaliers dans la noblesse impériale," *Revue d'histoire moderne et contemporaine*, 17 (1970), 671–9.

Egret, Jean, *La Pré-révolution française, 1787–1788* (Paris, 1962).
Elias, Norbert, *The Court Society*, trans. Edmund Jephcott (New York, 1983).
Ellis, Geoffrey, "The 'Marxist Interpretation' of the French Revolution," *English Historical Review*, 90 (1978), 353–76.
———. "Rhine et Loire: Napoleonic Elites and Social Order," *Beyond the Terror: Essays in French Regional and Social History, 1794–1815*, ed. Gwynne Lewis and Colin Lucas (Cambridge, 1983), 232–67.
Ellis, John, *Armies in Revolution* (London, 1973).

Fitzsimmons, Michael P., "Privilege and Polity in France, 1786–1791," *American Historical Review*, 92 (1987), 269–95.
Forrest, Alan, *Conscripts and Deserters: The Army and French Society during the Revolution and Empire* (New York, 1989).
———. *Society and Politics in Revolutionary Bordeaux* (Oxford, 1975).
———. *Soldiers of the French Revolution* (Durham, NC, 1990).
Forster, Robert, *The Nobility of Toulouse in the Eighteenth Century: A Social and Economic Study* (New York, 1971).
———. "The Survival of the Nobility during the French Revolution," *Past and Present*, 37 (1967), 71–86.
Foucault, Michel, *Discipline and Punish: The Birth of the Prison*, trans. Alan Sheridan (New York, 1979).
Fryer, W, *Republic or Restoration in France, 1794–7* (Manchester, 1965).
Furet, François, *Interpreting the French Revolution*, trans. Elborg Forster (Cambridge and Paris, 1977).
———. "The Monarchy and the Procedures for the Elections of 1789," *Journal of Modern History* 60 suppl. (1988), s58–s74.

Ganges, Edmond Bonnal de, *Les Royalistes contre l'armée* (Paris, 1906).
Girardet, Raoul, *La Société militaire et la France contemporaine* (Paris, 1953).
———. and Jean-Pierre H. Thomas, "Problèmes de recrutement," *La Crise militaire française (1945–1962): aspects sociologiques et idéologiques*, ed. Raoul Girardet (Paris, 1964).
La Gironde et les girondins, ed. François Furet and Mona Ozouf (Paris, 1991).

Godechot, Jacques, *Les Commissaires aux armées sous le directoire* (Paris, 1941).
———. "Les Insurrections militaires sous le directoire," *Annales historiques de la Révolution française*, 56–7 (1933), 129–52, 193–221.
Goodman, Dena, *The Republic of Letters: A Cultural History of the French Enlightenment* (Ithaca, 1994).
Goodwin, Alfred, "The French Executive Directory – A Revaluation," *History*, 22 (1937), 201–18.
Goujard, Philippe, "'Féodalité' et lumières au XVIIIème siècle: l'exemple de la noblesse," *Annales historiques de la Révolution française*, 227 (1977), 103–18.
Greer, Donald, *The Incidence of the Emigration during the French Revolution* (Gloucester, MA, 1966).
Gueniffey, Patrice, *Le Nombre et la raison: la Révolution française et les élections* (Paris, 1993).
Guibert, ou le soldat philosophe, ed. Jean-Paul Charnay (Vincennes, 1981).

Hahn, Roger, "L'Enseignement scièntifique aux écoles militaires et d'artillerie," *Enseignement et diffusion des sciences en France au dix-huitième siècle*, ed. René Taton (Paris, 1986), 523–7.
Hahn, Roger, and René Taton, *Ecoles techniques et militaires au XVIIIème siècle* (Paris, 1986).
Halkin, Léon H., "Pour une histoire de l'honneur," *Annales E.S.C.*, 4 (1949), 433–44.
Hampson, Norman, "The French Revolution and the Nationalisation of Honour," *War and Society: Historical Essays in Honour of J. R. Western, 1928–1971*, ed. M. R. D. Foot (New York, 1973), 199–211.
Hartmann, Louis, *Les Officiers de l'armée royale et la Révolution* (Paris, 1910).
Hennet, Léon, *Les Compagnies des cadets-gentilshommes et les écoles militaires* (Paris, 1889).
Herlaut, Auguste-Philippe, *Le Colonel Bouchotte, ministre de la guerre en l'an II*, 2 vols. (Paris, 1946).
———. "La Républicanisation des états-majors," *Annales historiques de la Révolution française*, 14 (1937), 385–409, 537–51.
Higonnet, Patrice, *Class, Ideology, and the Rights of Nobles During the French Revolution* (Oxford, 1981).
Hirsch, Jean-Pierre, *La Nuit du 4 août* (Paris, 1978).
Hirschman, Albert O., *The Passions and the Interests: Political Arguments for Capitalism before its Triumph* (Princeton, 1977).
Histoire militaire de la France de 1715 à 1871, vol. 2., ed. Jean Delmas (Paris, 1992).
Hood, James N., "Revival and Mutation of Old Rivalries in Revolutionary France," *Past and Present*, 82 (1979), 82–115.
Horne, Alistair, *The French Army and Politics, 1870–1970* (New York, 1984).
Humbert, Jean, *J. G. Lacuée, comte de Cessac, général de division, ministre de Napoléon 1er, 1752–1841* (Paris, 1939).
Hunt, Lynn A., "Committees and Communes: Local Politics and National Revolution in 1789," *Comparative Studies in Society and History*, 18 (1976), 321–46.
Huntington, Samuel D., *The Soldier and the State: The Theory and Politics of Civil-Military Relations* (Cambridge, MA, 1957).
Hyslop, Beatrice F., *A Guide to the General Cahiers of 1789* (New York, 1968).

Jaurès, Jean, *L'Armée nouvelle*, 2 vols. ed. Jean-Noël Jeanneney (Paris, 1992).
Jones, Colin, "Bourgeois Revolution Revivified: 1789 and Social Change," *Rewriting the French Revolution: The Andrew Browning Lectures, 1989*, ed. Colin Lucas (Oxford, 1991), 69–118.
———. "The Great Chain of Buying: Medical Advertisement, the Bourgeois Public Sphere, and the Origins of the French Revolution," *American Historical Review*, 101 (1996), 13–40.
Jones, P. M., *Reform and Revolution in France: The Politics of Transition, 1774–1791* (Cambridge, 1995).
Jouanna, Arlette, "Recherches sur la notion d'honneur au XVIème siècle," *Revue d'histoire moderne et contemporaine*, 15 (1968), 597–623.
Julia, Dominique, "La Formation des officiers de marine dans la seconde moitié du XVIIIème siècle: des gardes de la marine aux écoles d'Alès et de Vannes," *Vannes aux débuts de la Révolution* (Vannes, 1989), 57–124.
Jung, Théodore, *Dubois-Crancé (Edmond-Louis-Alexis): mousquetaire, constituant, conventionnel, général de division, ministre de la guerre* (Paris, 1884).

Kennedy, Michael, *The Jacobin Clubs in the French Revolution: The First Years* (Princeton, 1982).
———. *The Jacobin Clubs in the French Revolution: The Middle Years* (Princeton, 1988).
Kennett, Lee, *The French Armies in the Seven Years' War* (Durham, NC, 1967).
Kippur, Stephen A., *Jules Michelet: A Study of Mind and Sensibility* (Albany, 1981).
Kuscinski, Auguste, *Les Députés au corps législatif: conseil des cinq-cents, conseil des anciens de l'an IV à l'an VII* (Paris, 1905).
———. *Dictionnaire des conventionnels* (Paris, 1916).

Labatut, Jean-Pierre, *Les Noblesses européennes de la fin du XVème siècle à la fin du XVIIIème siècle* (Paris, 1978).
Labourdette, J. F., "La compagnie écossaise des gardes du corps du roi au XVIIIème siècle: recrutement et carrières," *Histoire, économie, et société*, 3 (1984), 95–122.
Larson, Magali Sarfatti, *The Rise of Professionalism: A Sociological Analysis* (Berkeley, 1977).
Latreille, Albert, *L'œuvre militaire de la Révolution: l'armée et la nation à la fin de l'ancien régime* (Paris, 1914).
Laulan, Robert, "Pourquoi et comment on entrait à l'Ecole royale militaire de Paris," *Revue d'histoire moderne et contemporaine*, 4 (1957), 141–50.
Lefebvre, Georges, *Le Directoire* (Paris, 1946).
———. and Jean Poperen, "Etudes sur le ministère de Narbonne," *Annales historiques de la Révolution française*, 105, 107, 108 (1947), 1–36, 193–217, 292–321.
Lemay, Edna Hindie, *Dictionnaire des constituants, 1789–1791*, 2 vols. (Paris, 1991).
Léon, Antoine, *La Révolution française et l'éducation technique* (Paris, 1968).
Léonard, Emile G., *L'Armée et ses problèmes au XVIIIème siècle* (Paris, 1958).
Loriga, Sabina, *Soldats: un laboratoire disciplinaire: l'armée piémontaise au XVIIIème siècle* (Paris, 1991).
Lucas, Colin, "Nobles, Bourgeois, and the Origins of the French Revolution," *Past and Present*, 60 (1973), 84–126.

———. "The Rules of the Game in Local Politics under the Directory," *French Historical Studies*, 2 (Fall 1987), 345–72.
———. *The Structure of the Terror: The Example of Javogues and the Loire* (Oxford, 1973).
Lynn, John A., *The Bayonets of the Republic: Motivation and Tactics in the Army of Revolutionary France* (Chicago and Urbana, 1984).
———. "Toward an Army of Honor: The Moral Evolution of the French Army, 1789–1815," *French Historical Studies*, 16 (1989), 152–82.
Lyons, Martyn, *Napoleon Bonaparte and the Legacy of the French Revolution* (New York, 1994).

Mahon, Patrice, *Etudes sur l'armée du directoire, 1ère partie: Joubert à l'armée d'Italie, Championnet à l'armée de Rome (octobre 1798–janvier 1799)* (Paris, 1905).
Mansel, Philip, *Court of France, 1789–1830* (Cambridge, 1988).
Markoff, John, *The Abolition of Feudalism: Peasants, Lords, and Legislators in the French Revolution* (University Park, PA, 1996).
Martin, Marc, "Journaux d'armées au temps de la Convention," *Annales historiques de la Révolution française*, 210 (1972), 567–605.
Massaguel, Jacques Fabre de, *L'Ecole de Sorèze de 1758 au 19 Fructidor an IV* (Issoudun, 1958).
Mathiez, Albert, "Le Coup d'état du 18 Fructidor an V," *Annales historiques de la Révolution française*, 6 (1929), 521–50.
———. "L'Intrigue de Lafayette et des généraux au début de la guerre de 1792," *Annales révolutionnaires*, 13 (1921), 89–105.
———. "Robespierre et l'armée," *Annales révolutionnaires*, 8 (1916), 131–42.
Maza, Sarah, *Private Lives and Public Affairs: The Causes Célèbres of Prerevolutionary France* (Berkeley, 1993).
Le Métier militaire en France aux époques des grandes transformations sociales, vol. 2, ed. André Corvisier and Jean Delmas (Vincennes, 1980).
Meyer, Jean, *Noblesses et pouvoirs dans l'Europe d'ancien régime* (Paris, 1973).
———. "Un problème mal posé: la noblesse pauvre, l'exemple breton, XVIIIème siècle," *Revue d'histoire moderne et contemporaine*, 18 (1971), 161–88.
Meynier, Albert, *Les Coups d'état du directoire: le dix-huit fructidor an V (4 septembre 1797)*, 3 vols. (Paris, 1927–8).
Michon, Georges, "Robespierre et la guerre (1791–1792)," *Annales révolutionnaires*, 12 (1920), 265–311.
———. "La Justice militaire sous la révolution," *Annales révolutionnaires*, 14 (1922), 1–26, 99–130, 197–222.
The Military Revolution and the State, 1500–1800, ed. Michael Duffy (Exeter, 1980).
Mitchell, C. J., *The French Legislative Assembly of 1791* (Leiden, 1988).
Mitchell, Harvey, *The Underground War against Revolutionary France: The Missions of William Wickham, 1794–1800* (Oxford, 1965).
Montzey, C. de, *Institutions d'éducation militaire jusqu'en 1789* (Paris, 1866).
———. *Institutions d'éducation militaire depuis 1789* (Paris, 1867).
Motley, Mark, *Becoming a French Aristocrat: The Education of the Court Nobility, 1580–1715* (Princeton, 1990).
Murphy, James, and Patrice Higonnet, "Les Députés de la noblesse aux états-généraux de 1789," *Revue d'histoire moderne et contemporaine*, 20 (1973), 230–43.

Nanteuil, Hugues de la Barre de, *Le Comte Daru ou l'administration militaire sous la Révolution et l'Empire* (Paris, 1966).

Ozouf, Mona, "War and Terror in French Revolutionary Discourse (1792–1794)," *Journal of Modern History,* 56 (1984), 579–97.

Palmer, R. R., "Frederick the Great, Guibert, Bülow: From Dynastic to National War," *Makers of Modern Strategy: From Machiavelli to the Nuclear Age,* ed. Peter Paret (Princeton, 1986), 91–119.

———. *Twelve Who Ruled: The Year of the Terror in the French Revolution* (Princeton, 1941).

Paret, Peter, "Napoleon and the Revolution in War," *Makers of Modern Strategy: From Machiavelli to the Nuclear Age,* ed. Peter Paret (Princeton, 1986), 123–42.

Parker, Geoffrey, *The Military Revolution: Military Innovation and the Rise of the West, 1500–1800* (Cambridge, 1988).

Patrick, Alison, *The Men of the First French Republic: Political Alignments in the National Convention of 1792* (Baltimore, 1972).

———. "The Second Estate in the Constituent Assembly, 1789–1791," *Journal of Modern History,* 62 (1990), 223–52.

Petiteau, Natalie, *Elites et mobilités: la noblesse d'empire aux XIXème siècle (1808–1914)* (Paris, 1997).

Petitfrère, Claude, *Les Bleus d'Anjou (1789–1792)* (Paris, 1985).

Poirier, Lucien, *Guibert (1743–1790)* (Paris, 1972).

Porch, Douglas, *Army and Revolution: France, 1815–1848* (London, 1974).

Prost, Antoine, *Histoire de l'enseignement en France, 1800–1967* (Paris, 1968).

Quoy-Bodin, Jean-Luc, *L'Armée et la franc-maçonnerie au déclin de la monarchie, sous la Révolution et l'Empire* (Paris, 1987).

Reichel, Daniel, *Davout et l'art de la guerre* (Neufchâtel, 1975).

Reinhard, Marcel, "L'Armée et Bonaparte en 1801," *Annales historiques de la Révolution française,* 133 (1953), 292–6.

———. *L'Armée et la Révolution pendant la Convention* (Paris, 1957).

———. "Elite et noblesse dans la seconde moitié du XVIIIème siècle," *Revue d'histoire moderne et contemporaine,* 3 (1956), 5–37.

———. "Observations sur le rôle révolutionnaire de l'armée dans la Révolution française," *Annales historiques de la Révolution française,* 168 (1962), 169–81.

Richet, Denis, "Autour des origines idéologiques lointaines de la Révolution française: élites et despotisme," *Annales E.S.C.,* 24 (1969), 1–23.

Riley, James, *The Seven Years War and the Old Regime in France: The Economic and Financial Toll* (Princeton, 1986).

Robert, Adolphe, Edgard Bouloton, and Gaston Cougny, *Dictionnaire des parlementaires français,* 5 vols. (Paris, 1889–91).

Roberts, Michael, *The Military Revolution, 1560–1660: An Inaugural Lecture Delivered before the Queen's University of Belfast* (Belfast, 1956).

Ross, Steven T., *Quest for Victory: French Military Strategy, 1792–1799* (New York, 1973).

Rothenberg, Gunther E., *The Art of Warfare in the Age of Napoleon* (London, 1977).
———. "Soldiers and the Revolution: The French Army, Society, and the State," *The Historical Journal*, 32 (1989), 981–95.
Rousset, Camile, *Les volontaires, 1791–1794* (Paris, 1870).

Schalk, Ellery, *From Valor to Pedigree: Ideas of Nobility in France in the Sixteenth and Seventeenth Centuries* (Princeton, 1986).
Scott, Samuel F., "Les officiers de l'infanterie de ligne à la veille de l'amalgame," *Annales historiques de la Révolution française*, 194 (1968), 455–71.
———. "Problems of Law and Order during 1790, the 'Peaceful' Year of the French Revolution," *American Historical Review*, 80 (1975), 859–88.
———. *The Response of the Royal Army to the French Revolution: The Role and Development of the Line Army, 1787–93* (Oxford, 1978).
———. "Les soldats de l'armée de ligne en 1793," *Annales historiques de la Révolution française*, 210 (1972), 493–512.
Senkowska-Gluck, Monika, "Les Donataires de Napoléon," *Revue d'histoire moderne et contemporaine*, 17 (1970), 680–93.
Serman, William, *Les Origines des officiers français, 1848–1870* (Paris, 1979).
———. *Les Officiers français dans la nation (1848–1914)* (Paris, 1982).
———. *La Vie professionnelle des officiers français au milieu du XIXème siècle* (Paris, 1994).
Sewell, William H., *A Rhetoric of Bourgeois Revolution: The Abbé Sieyès and What is the Third Estate?* (Durham, NC, 1994).
Shapin, Steven, and Simon Schaffer, *Leviathan and the Air-Pump: Hobbes, Boyle, and the Experimental Life* (Princeton, 1985).
Shapiro, Gilbert, and Philip Dawson, "Social Mobility and Political Radicalism: The Case of the French Revolution of 1789," *The Dimensions of Quantitative Research in History*, ed. William O Aydelotte, Allan G. Bogue, and Robert William Fogel (Princeton, 1972), 159–91.
———. and John Markoff, *Revolutionary Demands: A Content Analysis of the Cahiers de Doléances of 1789* (Stanford, 1998).
Shinn, Terry, *Savoir scièntifique et pouvoir social: l'Ecole polytechnique, 1794–1914* (Paris, 1980).
Shy, John, "Jomini," *Makers of Modern Strategy: From Machiavelli to the Nuclear Age*, ed. Peter Paret (Princeton, 1986), 143–85.
Six, Georges, *Dictionnaire biographique des généraux et amiraux français de la Révolution et de l'Empire (1792–1814)*, 2 vols. (Paris, 1934).
———. "Fallait-il quatre quartiers de noblesse pour être officier à la fin de l'Ancien Régime," *Revue d'histoire moderne*, 4 (1929), 46–55.
———. *Les Généraux de la Révolution et de l'Empire* (Paris, 1947).
Skocpol, Theda, *States and Social Revolutions: A Comparative Analysis of France, Russia, and China* (New York, 1979).
Smith, Jay Michael, *The Culture of Merit: Nobility, Royal Service, and the Making of Absolute Monarchy in France, 1600–1789* (Ann Arbor, 1996).
———. "Honour, Royal Service and the Cultural Origins of the French Revolution: Interpreting the Language of Army Reform, 1750–1788," *French History*, 9 (1995), 294–314.

Soboul, Albert, *Les Soldats de l'an II* (Paris, 1959).
Sydenham, M. J., *The Girondins* (London, 1961).

Tackett, Timothy, *Becoming a Revolutionary: The Deputies of the French National Assembly and the Emergence of a Revolutionary Culture (1789–1790)* (Princeton, 1996).
Thiers, Adolphe, *History of the Consulate and Empire*, vol. 1, trans. D. Forbes Campbell and H. W. Herbert (Philadelphia, 1853).
Thoumas, Charles Antoine, *Les Transformations de l'armée française: essais d'histoire et de critique sur l'état militaire de France*, 2 vols. (Paris, 1887).
Titeux, Eugène, *Saint-Cyr et l'Ecole spéciale militaire en France* (Paris, 1914–15).
Tocqueville, Alexis de, *Œuvres complètes,* ed. J. P. Mayer, vol. 2, *L'Ancien Régime et la Révolution: fragments et notes inédites sur la Révolution*, ed. André Jardin (Paris, 1953).
———. *The Old Regime and the French Revolution*, trans. Stuart Gilbert (New York, 1955).
Trollière, J. de la, and R. de Montmort, *Les Chevau-légers de la garde du roy* (Paris, 1953).
Tuetey, Louis, *Les Officiers sous l'Ancien Régime: nobles et roturiers* (Paris, 1908).
Tulard, Jean, *Napoleon: The Myth of the Saviour*, trans. Teresa Waugh (London, 1977).
———. *Napoléon et la noblesse d'empire* (Paris, 1986).

Van Crefeld, Martin, *Supplying War: Logistics from Wallenstein to Patton* (New York, 1977).
Vergé-Franceschi, Michel, "Un enseignement éclairé au XVIIIème siècle: l'enseignement maritime dispensé aux gardes," *Revue historique*, 559 (1986), 29–55.
Vidalenc, Jean, *Les Demi-solde: étude d'une catégorie sociale* (Paris, 1955).

Weiss, John Hubbel, *The Making of Technological Man: The Social Origins of French Engineering Education* (Cambridge, MA, 1982).
Wick, Daniel L., *A Conspiracy of Well-Intentioned Men: The Society of Thirty and the French Revolution* (New York, 1987).
Woloch, Isser, *The French Veteran from the Revolution to the Restoration* (Chapel Hill, 1979).
———. *The New Regime: Transformations of the French Civil Order, 1789–1820s* (New York, 1994).
———. "Napoleonic Conscription: State Power and Civil Society," *Past and Present*, 111 (1986), 101–29.
Wrong, Charles, "The *officiers de fortune* in the French Infantry," *French Historical Studies,* 9 (1976), 400–31.

Index

Page numbers in *italics* refer to illustrations

administration
    breakdown of 124–5, 127, 141–2
    of companies by captains 25–7
    regimental councils of 31, 56, 111, 158
advancement
    Constituent Assembly's system (1790) 60, 66–7, 106, 197–8
    Convention's systems (1793–year III) *107*, 115–24, 129–32, 136–40, 144
    Directory's system *see amalgame*
    electoral system discussed in Constituent Assembly (1789–90) 58–9, 69
    Guibert's system (1788) 40–5, 53–4, 49, 200
    Napoleonic system 181–3
    Restoration's system (1817) 197–9
    Saint-Germain's system (1776) 30–3
    Ségur's system (1782) 35–7
    two tracks of during Old Regime 18–19
    see also émulation; exam; honor; recruitment of soldiers; reform committee; service
amalgame
    first (21 February 1793) 115–24, 127
    second (18 Nivôse IV) 133, *134*, 140–50
    see also advancement; Dubois-Crancé; exam; National Guard volunteers
Arcq, P. A. de Sainte-Foix, chevalier de 17
Aubry, F. 139–40, 150–2, 156–8
Audouin, F. X. 128, 130
Augereau, C. P. F., General 160, 164

Baraguey d'Hilliers, L., General 166, 171
Barère, B. 113–14, 131–2
Barnave, A. 63, 75, 83

Beauharnais, A. F. M., vicomte de 54, 65, 82
Belle-Isle, C. L. A. Fouquet, duc de 24–5
Bonaparte, Napoleon *see* Napoleon
Bouchotte, J. B. N. 117, 128, 130
Bouthillier, C. L., marquis de 15, 58, 71–3, 85
Brissot, J. P., de Warville 61–2
Bureau de Pusy, C. D. 59, 84
Buzot, F. N. L. 116, 122

cadet gentilhomme 30–3, 40
cahiers de doléances see Estates-General
Caraman, V. M. de Riquet, comte de 16–17
Cherin, L. N. H. 1–2
    see also genealogy
Choiseul, E. F., duc de 24–7
citizen-soldiers 59, 111–13, 117
civil–military relations 156–8, 160–3
clubs 90, 112
    see also Feuillants; Jacobins
Cochon (de Lapparent), C. 154–5
commissaires see representatives-on-mission
Committee of Public Safety 126, 128–9, 136–7, 139, 142, 152–3, 160
concordat 24
concours 138, 140, 144–5
    see also advancement; *amalgame*; exam; officer recruitment, direct
constitution
    of 1791 (Constituent and Legislative Assemblies) 83–4, 91, 96
    of the year III (Directory) 155, 159
    of the year VIII (Consular Constitution) 166
    of 1814 (Constitutional Charter) 194

constitutional belt 159
coup d'état
   of 18 Fructidor V 150–61
   of 18 Brumaire VIII 160–3
Cross of Saint-Louis 31, 35, 41, 110–11, 184–5

Dampmartin, A. H. C., vicomte de 78, 99
Daru, D. A. N. B. 166, 181
Davout, L. N., Marshal 20, 164
Declaration of Rights 57, 61, 64
demi-brigade 115–24, 127, 142–3, 146–8
   see also amalgame
departmental guard 122–4
   see also National Guard; National Guard volunteers
depot companies 167
discipline 32–3, 40, 60, 79, 86, 111, 117–18
Dubois-Crancé (or Dubois de Crancé), E. L. A. 58–9, 69, 71–2, 92, 123–4, 133, 135, 143
   see also advancement; *amalgame*; reform committees
Dumas, Mathieu 40, 56–7, 91, 93, 155, 158, 160, 174
Dumouriez, C. F. (dit du Perrier), General 1, 99, 123, 125

election, advancement by *see* advancement; *amalgame*; Dubois-Crancé; National Guard volunteers; officer recruitment, direct; service
emigration of officers 61, 85–92, 123
   see also insubordination; National Guard volunteers; nobility; sons of active citizens
Emmery, J. L. C. 71, 79–80, 92
émulation
   justification for noble monopoly of officer commissions 15
   Napoleon's return to Old Regime notions of 177, 189
   republican attempts to revive 110, 130–2
   threats to 18–19, 28, 36–7, 157

   see also advancement; environmental conditioning; honor; officer recruitment, direct; service
environmental conditioning
   noble monopoly of officer commissions (pre-1789) 5–8, *13*, 14–15, 34–5, 40–4
   preference for officers' sons (1789 and after) 54–6, 69, 71–2, 93–4, 97–8, 174, 177–8, 195–6
   see also cadet gentilhomme; Cross of Saint-Louis; genealogy; military education; officer recruitment, direct; Ségur regulation; sons of active citizens
Estates-General
   cahiers de doléances 44–6, 48–52, 59, 64, 66
   calls for ennoblement of merit 188–9
   noble assemblies 44–6, 48–52
exam
   advancement by 131, 138, 140
   purge of officers by 144–6
   recruitment of officers by 70–2, 95, 109, 173
   see also concours

factionalism
   during the constitutional monarchy 81–5, 96–7
   during the Convention 9, 106, 115–24, 127–30, 133, 135–6
   at Court during the Old Regime 8, 27–8, 32–3
   during the Directory 10, 150–60
favoritism, denunciations of
   during the constitutional monarchy 66–7, 73–4
   under Napoleon 174–5
   in the nobility's *cahiers de doléances* 49–52
   in the officers' regimental *cahiers* 53–4
   during the Old Regime 8, 16–20, 29–33, 40–1
   during the Republic 108
   during the Restoration 10, 196–9

after Thermidor 135
see also nobility; patronage; presentation; venality
Ferrand, J. 146, 151–2
Feuillants 75, 81–91 *passim*

Gau, J. F. (des Voves) 151–2, 158
Gaudin, C. E. 191–2
Gendarmerie (of the Maison du roi) *see* Maison du roi
Gendarmerie (rural mounted police) 41, 90, 92, 152–4
Gendarmerie d'ordonnance 179–81
genealogy
    abolition of proofs 54–6
    abuses of during Old Regime 187–9
    admission to Ecole royale militaire *13*, 21–2, 194–5
    proofs 1–2, 5–7, 12, 31, 34–5, 40–2
    see also military education; nobility; officer recruitment, direct; presentation; Ségur regulation
Gerbey, J. Servan de 68, 70, 92
Girondins 106–24 *passim*
Gouvion-Saint-Cyr, L., Marshal 147–8
grande muette 160–3
grands notables see notabilité
Grégoire, H., abbé 95, 129, 137
Guibert, J. A. H., comte de 16–17, 37–45, 51, 56, 69, 152, 199–200

Hébertistes 106, 126, 128–9, 135–6
    see also ministry of war
honor 6, 56, 72, 109–11, 156–8, 166, 180
    see also émulation; Legion of Honor; service
Huguet de Semonville, J. A. 188–90

insubordination 126, 138–9, 144
    and repression 75–93, 96
    see also discipline; subordination

Jacobins 8, 62, 78, 81–91 *passim*, 96–7, 123, 126, 151
Jourdan, J. B., Marshal 151–2

King's flight 85–91, 100, 125
    see also emigration of officers; insubordination

Lacuée de Cessac, J. G. 70, 91, 153, 158
Lafayette, M. P. J. R. I. G. de Motier, marquis de 1, 63, 95–7, 123
Lameth, A. T. V. de 57, 60, 62, 66–73, 81–2, 86–8, 95
La Tour-du-Pin, J. F. Gouvernet, comte de 78–9
Legion of Honor 183–6
Legislative Guard 159–60
licenciement 81–5
loi martiale 89–90
    see also insubordination
lycée 165, 170
    see also military education

Maison du roi
    defended 33
    denounced 24–5, 198
    reduced in size 29–30, 38–9
    transfer of its personnel into the regular army 41, 43, 72–3, 92–3
    see also advancement; favoritism, denunciations of; nobility; supernumeraries; venality
Marat, J. P. 121–2
maréchaussée see Gendarmerie (rural mounted police)
Marmont, A. F. L. Viesse, Marshal 196–8
marriages of military personnel 112, 172
military constitution
    as an aspiration of Old Regime military reformers 34, 37, 43
    of Constituent Assembly 57–60, 66–74, 75, 77, 80
    military code of Conseil des cinq cents 150–60
    officers in 1789 demand creation of 53
    see also reform committees
military education
    Ecole de Mars 114–15

INDEX

Ecole royale militaire *13*, 20–4, 55, 69, 73, 93–4, 113–14, 194–5
Ecole spéciale militaire 175–8
see also *cadet gentilhomme*; environmental conditioning; genealogy; *lycée*; officer recruitment, direct; Prytanée franHais
ministry of war
  constitutional monarchy 58, 78–80, 92–4, 96, 99, 108, 152
  Convention 108–10, 115–19, 121, 125–30
  Directorial 141, 153, 159
  Old Regime 12–45 *passim*, 53–4, 56
  Restoration 197–8
  Thermidorean 135–6
  see also administration; *individual names*; reform committees
Montagnards 106–38 *passim*

Nancy, revolt of soldiers at (1790) 80–1, 91, 96
Napoleon
  denunciations of his arbitrariness 196
  and Directorial factionalism 156
  and legacy of Revolution 164, 166
  as military school student 20, 22
  and purge of officer corps 166–72
  see also *coup d'état*; Gendarmerie d'ordonnance; Legion of Honor; military education; nobility; service; *vélites*
National Guard 78, 86–7, 90, 93–4, 110, 152, 154–6
National Guard volunteers 100–5, 126, 136–7, 143–5
  see also advancement; *amalgame*; recruitment of soldiers
Night of 4 August (1789) 52, 54, 60–1, 63–4, 98
Noailles, L. M. d'Ayen, vicomte de 57–9, 63, 70–1, 82, 95
nobility
  abolition of 1, 60–6, 88

  calls for it to be awarded for merit 50–1, 61, 65, 189–91
  of the Court, its privileges denounced 17–20, 49–54, 61–2, 66–7, 196–9
  of the Court, official attempts to restrain its privileges 29–30, 35–7, 41–5, 73–4
  imperial 186–93
  liberalism of 4–5, 46, 48
  monopoly of officer commissions 1–2, 5–8, 12–45 *passim*, 66–8, 83, 95
  purged from officer corps 125–6
  rallied to Napoleonic regime 174, 179–91
  see also environmental conditioning; Estates-General; genealogy; Maison du roi; presentation; Ségur regulation; venality
noblesse militaire 20
nomination, advancement by see advancement; officer recruitment, direct; patronage; service
non-commissioned officers 146
  conflict with officers 89, 126
  dangers of promoting too many to officer rank 70–2, 84, 181
  granted preferences in advancement by Convention 119–20
  replacement of noble officers by 92, 98–9, 104–5
  see also advancement; Cross of Saint-Louis; officer recruitment, through the ranks; *officiers de fortune*
notabilité 171–2, 176, 182, 184

oath of loyalty 84–8, 91
officer recruitment, direct
  Old Regime 1–2, 5–8, 12–45 *passim*
  constitutional monarchy 8–9, 46, 54–5, 66–72, 91–105 *passim*
  Convention 9, 106, 108–9, 112–15
  Directory 113
  Napoleon 10, 166, 172–83
  Restoration 194–6

see also advancement; Gendarmerie d'ordonnance; genealogy; military education; National Guard volunteers; nobility; sons of active citizens; *vélites*
officer recruitment, through the ranks
constitutional monarchy 55–6, 66–7, 70, 72, 89, 92, 98–100, 129–32
Convention 115–24 *passim*
Napoleon 181–3
see also advancement; non-commissioned officers; *officiers de fortune*
officiers de fortune 31, 35, 41, 55–6, 72
see also advancement; Cross of Saint-Louis; *noblesse militaire*; non-commissioned officers

pages 40, 73, 180
patronage
of generals 86, 99–100, 117, 140
ministerial 53–4, 56, 73, 102, 108, 117, 128, 130
in nomination of sons of active citizens (1791–93) 76, 91–8
of Old Regime colonels 22, 31, 40–1, 55
of Paris sectional movement 135
in recruitment of Napoleonic regimental volunteers 174–5
in recruitment to Ecole spéciale militaire 177–8
royal 22–3, 40, 66–70, 108–10, 131
see also favoritism; military education; officer recruitment, direct; sons of active citizens
Pichegru, J. C., General 151–2, 155
political neutrality of officer corps see *grande muette*
political surveillance 93, 99–100, 110–12
see also Jacobins; *licenciement*; representatives-on-mission
presentation (or *présentés*) 18–19, 42–4, 49–52, 187–9
see also advancement; genealogy; nobility

Préval, C. A. H., vicomte de 196, 199
Prytanée franHais 170
purge of officers see *amalgame*; Gendarmerie; Napoleon; political surveillance; representatives-on-mission

Ramel, J. P. 159–60
reciprocity see service
recompense see advancement; Legion of Honor; nobility; service
recruitment of soldiers 58–9, 78–9, 100, 116, 124–5, 140–1
reform committees
calls for in officers' regimental *cahiers* (1789) 56
during the constitutional monarchy (1789–92) 57–60, 66–74, 79–85, 88–93, 197–8
of the Convention 115
of the Directory 150–60
of the nineteenth century 197–8, 200–1
of the Old Regime 34–45, 58, 67, 152, 200
see also military constitution; ministry of war
regimental officers' *cahiers* (1789) 47, 53–8
representatives-on-mission 86–9, 122, 124–32, 135–6, 153
Robespierre, M. 83, 109, 121, 133, 135, 144

Saint-Germain, C. L. comte de 17, 19, 24, 28–35, 37, 41, 58, 66–7
Saint-Just, L. A. 108, 112, 115–18
sans-culottes 126, 128, 130, 133, 135, 144
Saxe, M., comte de 17–18, 68
Schauenbourg, A. B. H. A., General 147, 175
Ségur, P. H., comte de 33–8, 40, 58
Ségur regulation 1–2, 5–6, 34–5
see also environmental conditioning; military education; nobility; officer recruitment, direct; reform committees

seniority, advancement by *see* advancement; *amalgame*; officer recruitment, through the ranks
service 200–1
   monarchical conceptions of (honor-based) 6, 8, 10, 12–17, 20–2, 50–1, 68–9, 200–1
   Napoleonic conceptions of (honor-based) 166, 172–8 *passim*, 194–6
   republican conceptions of (virtue-based) 106–13, 116–17, 130–2, 139–40, 156–8
   see also émulation; environmental conditioning, honor, Legion of Honor; nobility
Seven Years' War 12, 16–17, 24, 27–9, 37, 109
soldiers' committees 77–80, 89
sons of active citizens 76, 92–100, 104–5, 119–20, 137–8, 143–5, 149, 182–3
   see also emigration of officers; environmental conditioning; insubordination; officer recruitment, direct; patronage
subordination 68–71, 90, 111–13, 117, 140, 158, 170–1
supernumeraries 43, 72–3, 92–3, 159
   see also amalgame, Maison du roi

Thermidorean reaction in the army 133–40, 162

vélites 178–80
venality
   and abolition of nobility 65–6
   and Constituent Assembly's military constitution 67, 72–4
   denounced during Old Regime 8, 16–20, 24–32, 41
   denounced during Restoration 196–9
   denounced in *cahiers* (1789) 49–52, 53–4
   ennoblement by 1, 5–6, 34–5, 50–1, 65–6, 191–2
   of military office 24, 28–30, 54, 57
   see also Maison du roi; nobility; Ségur regulation
virtue *see* service
volunteers, regimental 93–4, 174–5

War of American Independence 39
War of Austrian Succession 16, 20, 25–6, 33
Willot, A., General 151–4
Wimpfen, F. L., baron de 33, 57–9, 71, 90–1

EU authorised representative for GPSR:
Easy Access System Europe, Mustamäe tee 50,
10621 Tallinn, Estonia
gpsr.requests@easproject.com

www.ingramcontent.com/pod-product-compliance
Ingram Content Group UK Ltd.
Pitfield, Milton Keynes, MK11 3LW, UK
UKHW041920140426
5217IPUK00013B/239